A Ladybird Bible Book

Moses the Prince

Text by Jenny Robertson
Illustrations by Alan Parry

Scripture Union/Ladybird

The Hebrew people were in despair! Hundreds of years before, their great-great-great-grandparents had gone to live in the land of Egypt. At first the Egyptians welcomed them because their leader, Joseph, was a friend of the king, but when the king died, the rulers that followed him began to treat the Hebrews badly. They made them their slaves, and finally one king gave a cruel order, 'Throw all the baby Hebrew boys into the River Nile in case they grow up and fight us!'

One brave mother decided to hide her baby. When he was too big to hide in the house, she covered a basket with tar to make it waterproof and put her son in it. Then she took the basket to the Nile and left it bobbing along the water. The baby's older sister, Miriam, stayed close by to see what would happen.

Before long one of the royal princesses came to bathe and noticed the basket. When she found the baby inside she was delighted; she had always wanted a baby of her own.

Miriam came up and curtseyed to the princess, 'Shall I find someone to look after him for you?' she asked, and she ran and fetched her mother.

'I am adopting this baby as my son,' said the princess to the slave woman. 'If you look after him for me until he's bigger I will pay you well.'

So the baby's mother took him home safely to look after him for the princess.

So the child grew up in his own family. His mother looked after him and taught him to worship the God of the Hebrew people. Then, when he was bigger, he went to live in the palace with the princess, who gave him the name Moses.

One day, after he was quite grown up, Moses went to see where the Hebrew slaves were working. He found them making bricks. As he watched, he saw an Egyptian overseer beating a slave. Moses grew angry. When he thought that no one was looking he killed the Egyptian and hid the body in the sand. The next day he went out again and met two Hebrews who were fighting. He tried to stop them.

'You shouldn't hit your fellow Hebrew,' he said.

'Who gave you the right to order us about?' snarled the slaves. 'Do you think you can kill us like you killed that Egyptian yesterday?' Moses was frightened to think that someone knew what he had done. If the king heard, Moses would be killed. He went back to the palace, but soon the king did hear, and Moses had to run away.

He made his way to the desert where no one would follow him. Only the shepherds and their families lived there, wandering with their flocks wherever they could find water.

One day Moses was resting beside a well when seven girls, all sisters, came along to fill their water jars. A crowd of shepherds came up and pushed the girls out of the way so that they could get to the water first. Moses leapt to his feet and drove the shepherds away. Then he helped the girls fill their jars and give water to their flocks. When the girls' father heard what he had done for them he was very pleased. He invited Moses to come and live with them in their tent. So Moses became a wandering shepherd.

Meanwhile the other Hebrews were still slaves in Egypt. In their misery they called out to God to help them. God heard their prayers. It was time for his special people, the Hebrews, to be freed, and Moses was going to be part of God's rescue plan!

One day, as Moses led his flock across the desert, he noticed that a bush had caught fire. Flames crackled along the branches, but the bush wasn't burnt up. Moses went closer to see why.

A voice spoke to him, 'Moses!' It seemed to be coming out of the fire.

'Here I am,' he answered.

'Don't come any closer! Take off your sandals! This is holy ground. I am God!'

Moses hid his head, afraid. He was even more frightened when he heard God say, 'I am sending you to the King of Egypt to rescue the Hebrew people from slavery.' He began to make excuses.

'No one will believe me. I'm just a nobody. I can't even speak properly!'

'I will go with you,' God promised. 'When the Egyptian priests try their magic out on you, I'll help you do even more wonderful things. I'll tell you what to say.'

'Please choose someone else,' Moses begged.
God grew angry. 'I have chosen you,' he said,
'but I will send your brother Aaron to meet you.
He will speak for you, and I will help you both.'
So Moses set off for Egypt.

His brother Aaron met him in the desert, just as God had promised. The two brothers were delighted to be together again. Quickly they made their way to Egypt. At once Moses and Aaron gathered the Hebrew leaders together. Aaron told them how God had spoken to Moses from the burning bush.

When the Hebrews understood that God had sent Moses to rescue them, they knelt down full of happiness and worshipped God. Then Moses and Aaron went to the king.

'Our God says, "Let my people go away to the desert to pray to me there," ' they said.

'What nonsense!' exclaimed the king, furiously. 'It's just an excuse to stop working.' He called his overseers. 'The Hebrew slaves must be made to work even harder! You give them straw to make their bricks, don't you? Well from now on they must find their own straw, and still make the same number of bricks!'

The slaves complained bitterly to Moses when they heard: 'See what you've done with your talk of freedom!'

Moses prayed to God and went back to the king with Aaron.

'You must prove that your God is real if you want me to listen to you,' said the king. Aaron threw his stick to the ground, and it turned into a snake.

'That's an old trick,' jeered the king. He ordered his magicians to do the same. The floor was covered with snakes – until Aaron's ate up the others! Still the king wasn't convinced, and he refused to let the slaves go.

So God told Moses he would show the king of Egypt even more of his power. Moses and Aaron went to meet the king by the River Nile.

'God sent me to tell you to let his people go, but you wouldn't listen. Now, look at the water, Your Majesty.'

The king looked. The water had turned red, like blood. It smelt bad. Dead fish swirled in the scum on the surface. All over Egypt the water in jugs and jars turned into blood, too. Desperately people began to dig along the river banks to find fresh water, but the king went back to the palace and paid no attention to Moses.

Then millions of frogs swarmed over Egypt. They hopped out of the Nile; and out of every pool and canal. They went everywhere. They found their way into the king's bedroom and hopped over his bed.

'Pray to your God for us!' the king begged Moses. 'Ask him to get rid of these frogs!' Moses prayed, and God answered his prayer. The frogs died. There were large piles of dead frogs everywhere, and the whole country stank of them.

In spite of this the king still refused to let the Hebrews go. Now God sent swarms of mosquitoes which tormented everyone. Still the king took no notice. Flies attacked the crops. Cattle and camels died of disease, but the king would not let the slaves go.

After the flies had gone, everyone in Egypt was covered with painful boils because the king would not listen to God. It made no difference; he still refused to let the slaves go.

'Warn the king that I am going to send such a heavy hail storm that any animals or people left outside will die in it,' God told Moses.

Storm clouds blew up and thunder rumbled across the sky. Lightning struck the earth. Huge hail stones beat down all the plants and killed every living thing that was still outside.

'This is the worst storm Egypt has ever had, and it's all my fault,' groaned the king. 'Moses, pray that God will stop the hail, and I'll let you all go!'

'I'll pray,' said Moses quietly, 'but I know you won't keep your promise.' Moses prayed. The storm stopped, and at once the king changed his mind and refused to let the slaves leave. So God punished Egypt again. He sent clouds of locusts to eat up all the plants that were still alive after the hail, and he sent a deep darkness which covered the land for three days, but in spite of all this the king refused to do what God wanted.

Then Moses called the Hebrews together and said, 'Because the king of Egypt won't listen to God, the eldest son in every family in Egypt is going to die! Your children will escape if you do as God says. Each family must kill a lamb and smear some of its blood over the door of their house. Then the death which God is sending will not touch your homes. And tonight you must be ready to leave, because this time the king will let us go!'

The Hebrews did as Moses told them. When they had smeared their doors with the blood they stood inside, dressed and ready for their journey, eating their supper and waiting for the order to move. At midnight they heard a sound of crying from the houses of the Egyptians. Every eldest son had died.

The king called for Moses and Aaron. 'Go
and take your people with you,' he ordered. He
was very frightened.

None of the Egyptians wanted the Hebrews
to stay. When the slaves asked their masters for
gold and silver and clothing for the journey, the
Egyptians were glad to give it to them. Anything
to get rid of the people who had brought them so
much trouble!

So, at last, the Hebrews made their way out of
Egypt and into the desert. There were no roads
to follow, but God sent a great bank of cloud
like a billowing pillar ahead of them and they
followed it each day. At night the cloud turned
to fire, giving them light for their journey. The
people were glad because they could see that
God was with them, leading them on and
looking after them.

The king wasn't going to let his slaves escape so easily, though! Already he was sorry he had let them go. 'Chase them!' he ordered his soldiers. He jumped into his war chariot. Six hundred of his best charioteers as well as the rest of his army thundered after the Hebrews.

The people had reached the sea and were wondering how to cross, when they looked up and saw the army coming. They turned on Moses in terror. 'You should have left us in Egypt! The soldiers will cut us to pieces,' they cried.

'Don't be afraid. God will fight for us,' Moses

encouraged them.

'Look!' someone pointed, 'the pillar of cloud has moved! It's hiding us from the army!'

'Stretch your hand out over the sea,' God told Moses. As Moses did so an easterly gale sprang up, pounding the sea and sweeping back the waves. A path appeared. Without wasting a minute, the Hebrews hurried across between the towering banks of water. The Egyptians charged after them, but their chariots stuck fast in the mud.

'Stretch your hand over the sea again,' God said to Moses. 'The water will come back before the Egyptians can catch you.'

'Hurry!' Moses called to the people as they scrambled up the shore. He lifted his hand. The sea foamed across the path, covering the Egyptian army. Not a soldier escaped.

The Hebrews watched in amazement, until suddenly, Miriam, Moses's sister shook her tambourine.

'Sing to our God who has won a great victory
Drowning the Egyptian army in the middle
of the sea!'

The women joined her, singing and dancing, while the men laughed and stamped and the children swayed to the music.

'The sea stood up just like a wall
The Lord our God has saved us all.'

they sang, forgetting their fear and their complaints.

In all the years ahead they never forgot the wonderful way God had saved them from the Egyptians by leading them dry footed across the middle of the sea.

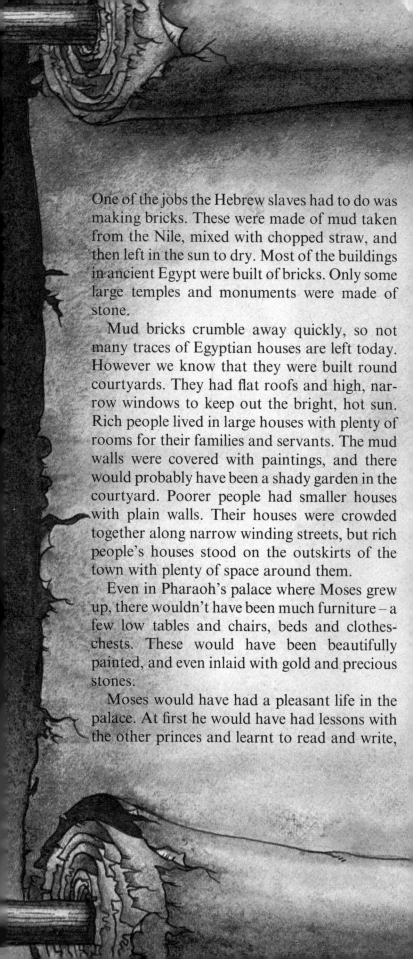

One of the jobs the Hebrew slaves had to do was making bricks. These were made of mud taken from the Nile, mixed with chopped straw, and then left in the sun to dry. Most of the buildings in ancient Egypt were built of bricks. Only some large temples and monuments were made of stone.

Mud bricks crumble away quickly, so not many traces of Egyptian houses are left today. However we know that they were built round courtyards. They had flat roofs and high, narrow windows to keep out the bright, hot sun. Rich people lived in large houses with plenty of rooms for their families and servants. The mud walls were covered with paintings, and there would probably have been a shady garden in the courtyard. Poorer people had smaller houses with plain walls. Their houses were crowded together along narrow winding streets, but rich people's houses stood on the outskirts of the town with plenty of space around them.

Even in Pharaoh's palace where Moses grew up, there wouldn't have been much furniture – a few low tables and chairs, beds and clothes-chests. These would have been beautifully painted, and even inlaid with gold and precious stones.

Moses would have had a pleasant life in the palace. At first he would have had lessons with the other princes and learnt to read and write,

Assessment of Credibility by Judges in Asylum Cases in the EU

Assessment of Credibility by Judges in Asylum Cases in the EU

Carolus Grütters, Elspeth Guild
&
Sebastiaan de Groot (eds.)

Centre for Migration Law
Radboud University Nijmegen (NL)
&
International Association of Refugee Law Judges

also containing the full text of the
"Credo Document"

Assessment of Credibility in
Refugee and Subsidiary Protection Claims
under the EU Qualification Directive:
Judicial criteria and standards
by
Allan Mackey & John Barnes
IARLJ

CMR
Centre for Migration Law

Assessment of Credibility by Judges in Asylum Cases in the EU
Carolus Grütters, Elspeth Guild & Sebastiaan de Groot (eds.)

ISBN: 978-94-6240-061-0

Published by:
Ŵolf Legal Publishers (WLP)
P.O. Box 313
5060 AH Oisterwijk
The Netherlands
E-Mail: info@wolfpublishers.nl
<www.wolfpublishers.com>

CMR
Centre for Migration Law
Radboud University Nijmegen
The Netherlands
<www.ru.nl/law/cmr>

IARLJ
International Association of Refugee Law Judges
<www.iarlj.org>

Table of Contents

Introduction

Carolus Grütters & Elspeth Guild

This book reports on the findings of a seminar on 'Judicial Scrutiny and Credibility Assessment in Asylum Procedures' organised by the Centre for Migration Law (CMR) of Radboud University Nijmegen and the International Association of Refugee Law Judges (IARLJ) and co-sponsored by the EU Jean Monnet Programme, hosted by Radboud University Nijmegen in the Netherlands on 16 April 2013.

This seminar was held for two reasons. Firstly, on the same day Dana Baldinger, a judge of the district court of Amsterdam (NL), successfully defended her doctoral thesis *Rigorous Scrutiny versus Marginal Review - Standards on judicial scrutiny and evidence in international and European Asylum law* at Radboud University. The main objective of her study was to explore what international and EU asylum law require from the national asylum judge as to: (1) the required intensity of the judicial scrutiny to be applied; and (2) evidentiary issues, such as the standard and burden of proof, the admission and evaluation of evidence and time limits for submitting evidence. Her study covers the Convention relating to the Status of Refugees and the Protocol relating to the Status of Refugees (the Refugee Convention or RC, 1951, and the Refugee Protocol or RP, 1967), the International Covenant on Civil and Political Rights (ICCPR, 1966), the Convention against Torture (CAT, 1984), the European Convention for the Protection of Human Rights and Fundamental Freedoms (ECHR, 1950), European Union primary legislation on asylum and a number of secondary EU law instruments such as the EU Qualification Directive and the EU Procedures Directive.

The results of her study are of great value to judges in national courts across the world who seek to apply the obligations of their states in respect of international protection since it brings together in one book the state of the art of the international jurisprudence. As is shown in that study, the state of the international material is not entirely consistent. There are lessons here for the members of the Treaty Bodies and the supranational judges – what do they need to provide to the national judge so that he or she can correctly apply international rule of law at the local level. In this regard, it is clear that an increasingly substantial role is required of the national judge by the international jurisdictions. They oblige the national judge to recognise a relationship of hierarchy while at the same time supporting the national judge in fulfilling that critical role fundamental to any liberal democracy of separation of powers embodied in judicial independence.

Secondly, the seminar was an opportunity to launch the so-called 'Credo-document'. This document, Assessment of Credibility in Refugee and Subsidiary Protection claims under the EU Qualification Directive - Judicial criteria and standards, was edited by the IARLJ and written by Allan Mackey and John

Barnes, both retired UK senior asylum and immigration judges. This document was prepared for the IARLJ in its role as a partner in the 'Credo Project'. In this project participated, next to the IARLJ, the Hungarian Helsinki Committee (HCC), the United Nations High Commissioner for Refugees (UNHCR) and Asylum Aid. Chapter 6 of this book contains the complete Credo-document.

The involvement of the IARLJ in the professional development of judges in this field commenced significantly in 1998 with the publication of an *International manual for new refugee law judges*. This manual included a section on 'Credibility Assessment by judges' and has been used in about 200 courses in some 50 countries, including extensive use in the EU (2000-2008) in the 'new 12' member states, EU applicant and surrounding countries. With the introduction of the *Common European Asylum System* (CEAS) an EU manual on CEAS, prepared by John Barnes, has been used extensively since published in 2007. However, with the rapid developments of both international and EU refugee and other protection law both manuals dated quickly and needed updating. The Credo Project provided an opportunity to prepare an extensive review and a judicial guidance paper on Credibility assessment in the EU. Allan Mackey and John Barnes, assisted by an editorial group of judges from all around Europe and representatives from the UNHCR, EASO and HCC, managed to finalize this document at the end of 2012.

This book not only contains the full text of this Credo-document but also some reflections of both authors of this document, Allan Mackey (chapter 4) and John Barnes (chapter 5) on certain issues handled in the Credo-document. Next to the remarks of the participants in the Credo-project, the seminar provided a stage for some experts to reflect on the issue of Credibility Assessment in asylum cases.

First, Dana Baldinger elaborated (chapter 1) on an issue that she was unable to address in depth in her dissertation but is very relevant to the work of an asylum judge, i.e. the issue of fact-finding by national courts with the assistance of the UNHCR.

Second, Egbert Myjer, former judge of the European Court of Human Rights, pointed out that it might even serve as a means of further inspiration to the ECtHR being influential in the way the Court's own interpretation evolves (chapter 2).

Thirdly, in her contribution Madeline Garlick (chapter 3) reflected on the involvement of the UNHCR in this project and the value of this document in increasing the quality of judgments and ultimately the protection of those who are in need of protection.

We hope that this book will contribute to the dissemination of knowledge on the assessment of credibility in asylum cases amongst judges and in particular assist in decreasing the risk of denying protection of those who are in need of protection.

Carolus Grütters & Elspeth Guild

Centre for Migration Law, Faculty of Law, Radboud University Nijmegen (NL)

Acknowledgements

Sebastiaan de Groot

This book is the result of a fortunate combination of events at the same time.

First of all, judge Dana Baldinger completed her dissertation 'Rigorous Scrutiny versus Marginal Review'. The successful public defence of her work was held at Radboud University, Nijmegen, on 16 April 2013.

Around the same time, the European Chapter of the International Association of Refugee Law Judges (IARLJ) completed a contribution to the EU funded CREDO Project on Credibility Assessment. This consisted of a document on the Judicial Assessment of Credibility in asylum cases, which is meant to be a guide for judges. The document was prepared by former asylum court judges John Barnes (UK) and Allan Mackey (UK and NZ) with the assistance of a review committee consisting of around 15 judges from around Europe.

The Centre for Migration Law (CMR) of Radboud University and the IARLJ then joined forces to make 16 April a full day for exchanging views on asylum law. After Dana's defence in the morning, a seminar was held in the afternoon in Nijmegen.

In this book, the contributions to the seminar and the CREDO document are bundled. We hope that this book can be of value for practitioners in asylum law, lawyers, judges and academics.

I thank the authors for agreeing in making their contributions available for this book. Also, I am thankful to Carolus Grütters of the Centre for Migration Law of Radboud University. Only thanks to Carolus's driving force, the seminar could take place and this book is published.

Sebastiaan de Groot

IARLJ President

Seminar Contributions

of a seminar
at Radboud University Nijmegen
16 April 2013 on

Judicial Scrutiny and Credibility Assessment in Asylum procedures

organised by

Centre for Migration Law
and
International Association of Refugee Law Judges

co-sponsored by the

EU Jean Monnet Programme

1. Co-operation between asylum courts and the UNHCR in the area of fact finding
Can we improve the *status quo*?

Dana Baldinger

1.1. Introduction

During the public defence of my doctoral thesis on 16 April 2013, I pointed out that international and EU asylum law require an independent and thorough national judicial scrutiny comprising both facts and law.[1] This standard requires that national courts are able to make an independent determination of the disputed facts and of the credibility of a claimant.[2] Under this standard, national courts may never be precluded from determining the 'central issue in dispute'.[3]

The topic of this chapter, which forms the basis of my presentation for the seminar of 16 April 2013, is fact-finding by national courts with the assistance of the UNHCR. National courts are, as said, required to perform a rigorous scrutiny in cases concerning expulsion of asylum seekers. In certain cases this brings along an obligation to actively engage in fact-finding. As national courts will generally not be able to conduct fact-finding missions in countries of origin of asylum seekers, these courts are largely dependent on information submitted to it by the parties or obtained *proprio motu*. Information from a wide variety of sources, compiled by Interior or Foreign Affairs Ministries of various States, UN organisations, NGO's, *et cetera*. An important supplier of information is the UNHCR. In this presentation the focus is on the UNHCR's consultative role in in relation to international and national courts.

In this chapter I will first of all briefly touch upon the theory: Article 35 of the Refugee Convention (RC), the role of the UNHCR in the Common European Asylum System (CEAS), and the ways in which the UNHCR is involved in cases before the European Court of Human Rights (ECtHR) and the Court of Justice of the European Union (CJEU).

Next, I will discuss a case from national practice in which a first instance national asylum court in the Netherlands invited the UNHCR to participate in the

---

1 See for example: ECtHR, *Muminov v. Russia*, 11 December 2008, Appl. No. 42502/06, para 101; ECtHR *Abdolkhani and Karimnia v. Turkey*, 22 September 2009, Appl. No. 30471/08, para 108; ECtHR, *Hirsi Jamaa and others v. Italy*, 23 February 2012, Appl. No. 27765/09, para 198; HRC, *Dawood Khan v. Canada*, 10 August 2006, No. 1302/2004, para 5.3; ComAT, *Agiza v. Sweden*, 20 May 2005, No. 233/2003, para 13.6 and 13.7.
The submission of the UNHCR in the case of ECtHR *Mir Isfahani v. the Netherlands,* Appl. No. 31252/03, May 2005, <www.unhcr.org/refworld/docid/454f5e484.html>, para 31-42; CJEU, *Samba Diouf*, 28 July 2011, C-69/10, paras 56, 61.
2 See, for example, ECtHR, *Koskinas v. Greece*, 20 June 2002, Appl. No. 47760/99, para 30; ECtHR, *Tsfayo v. the UK*, 14 November 2006, Appl. No. 60860/00, para 46.
3 ECtHR, *Sigma Radio Television Ltd v. Cyprus*, 21 July 2011, Appl. Nos. 32181/04 and 35122/05, para 157.

case as an expert to answer factual questions. The case concerned the planned transfer under the EU Dublin Regulation[4] of a Chechen asylum seeker from the Netherlands to Poland. The fact-finding mission failed as the UNHCR was still in the process of preparing a report and it was too early for it to respond to the court's questions.

Thirdly, I will reflect on the discussions that followed my presentation and try to provide some guidelines for the future.

1.2. Co-operation between the UNHCR and courts

Article 35 of the RC stipulates:

> *"Article 35: Co-operation of the national authorities with the United Nations*
>
> *1. The Contracting States undertake to co-operate with the Office of the United Nations High Commissioner for Refugees, or any other agency of the United Nations which may succeed it, in the exercise of its functions, and shall in particular facilitate its duty of supervising the application of the provisions of this Convention.*
>
> *2. In order to enable the Office of the High Commissioner or any other agency of the United Nations which may succeed it, to make reports to the competent organs of the United Nations, the Contracting States undertake to provide them in the appropriate form with information and statistical data requested concerning:*
>
> *a.   the condition of refugees,*
> *b.   the implementation of this Convention, and*
> *c.   laws, regulations and decrees which are, or may hereafter be, in force relating to refugees."*

As the text makes clear, Article 35 is about two things. First, an obligation for states to co-operate with the UNHCR. Second, the supervisory role of the UNHCR over the application of and adherence by States to the RC.

Part of this supervisory role of the UNHCR is a form of participation in national asylum proceedings.[5] Türk (2002), Zwaan (2005) and Bruin (2011) distinguish three different models of participation by the UNHCR in national asylum proceedings:

a. Status determination: the UNHCR makes the decision of who is a refugee.
b. Membership of the national committee or commission responsible for status determination.

---

4   Council Regulation 2003/343/EC of 18 February 2003, establishing the criteria and mechanisms for determining the Member State responsible for examining an asylum application lodged in one of the Member States by a third country national, *OJ of the EU* L 50, 25 February 2003, pp. 1-10, last amended by *OJ of the EU* L 304, 14 November 2008, p. 83.
5   R. Bruin (2011), 'UNHCR's mandaatverklaringen: de rol van UNHCR in de Nederlandse asielprocedure', *A&MR* 2011, nr. 5/6, pp. 242-248. p. 243.

c. Advising and consulting the national administrative and judicial authorities.[6]

The first two models nowadays occur only exceptionally in Europe.[7] Below the focus will therefore only be on the last type of participation, with a specific focus on the role of the UNHCR as a consultant to judicial authorities.

1.3. The UNHCR and the ECtHR

Let us first take a look at this consultative role from the perspective of the intervention of the UNHCR in proceedings before the ECtHR. Zwaan (2005) provides a list of judgments and decisions of the ECtHR in which the UNHCR is mentioned.[8] In a significant number of cases the UNHCR intervened in the proceedings before the ECtHR. By way of illustration I will mention just a few older and more recent cases here:

- *T.I. v. the United Kingdom* (2000), a case concerning the operation and application of the Dublin Convention;[9]
- *Mir Isfahani v. the Netherlands* (2008), in which case the UNHCR made a submission to the ECtHR in order to assist the ECtHR in clarifying the appropriate standard and burden of proof in asylum cases as well as the scope of judicial review, in particular in relation to credibility issues;[10]
- *M.S.S. v. Belgium and Greece* (2011), a case concerning the operation and application of the EU Dublin Regulation and the relationship with the ECHR;[11]
- *Hirsi Jamaa and others v. Italy* (2012), a case about the practice and justification of 'push-back' operations: interception and return of asylum seekers at sea by the Italian government, the situation and legal status of asylum seekers and refugees in Libya, and the extra-territorial scope of the principle of *non-refoulement* and pursuant legal obligations concerning the rescue and interception of people at sea.[12]

---

6 V. Türk (2002), *UNHCR's supervisory responsibility, New Issues in Refugee Research*, Working Paper No. 67, UNHCR 2002; <http://www.unhcr.org/3dae74b74.pdf>; K. Zwaan (2005), *UNHCR and the European Asylum Law*, Nijmegen: Wolf Legal Publishers; R. Bruin (2011), 'UNHCR's mandaatverklaringen: de rol van UNHCR in de Nederlandse asielprocedure', *A&MR* 2011, nr. 5/6, pp. 242-248.

7 Türk 2002, p. 17; Zwaan 2005, p. 51; Bruin 2011, pp. 242, 243.

8 K. Zwaan (2005), *UNHCR and the European Asylum Law*, Nijmegen: Wolf Legal Publishers, pp. 97-146.

9 ECtHR, *T.I. v. the UK*, admissibility decision, 7 March 2000, Appl. No. 43844/98. The UNHCR Submission in this case can be found at: <http://www.unhcr.org/refworld/pdfid/42f7737c4>.

10 ECtHR, *Mir Isfahani v. the Netherlands*, 31 January 2008, Appl. No. 31252/03, decision to strike the application out of the list. The UNHCR Submission in this case can be found at <http://www.unhcr.org/ref-world/docid/454f5e484.html>.

11 ECtHR, *M.S.S. v. Belgium and Greece*, 21 January 2011, Appl. No. 30696/09. See for a detailed analysis of this case W.J. van Bennekom & J.H. van der Winden (2011), *Asielrecht*, Den Haag: Boom Juridische Uitgevers, pp. 99-103; and H. Battjes, 'Subsidiaire bescherming' (2011), *A&MR* 2011, nr. 5/6, pp. 208-212. The UNHCR Submission in this case can be found at: <http://www.unhcr.org/refworld/docid/4c19e7512.html>.

12 ECtHR, *Hirsi Jamaa and others v. Italy*, 23 February 2012, Appl. No. 27765/09. The UNHCR Submission in this case can be found at: http://www.unhcr.org/refworld/docid/4d92d2c22.html.

This case-law demonstrates that the ECtHR generally gives considerable weight to information submitted by the UNHCR. In *K.R.S. v. UK* (2008), the ECtHR explicitly considered that information submitted by the UNHCR is to be regarded as independent, reliable and objective.[13] In a number of cases the ECtHR attached significant weight to refugee status determinations by the UNHCR.[14] However, the ECtHR does not blindly follow the UNHCR in its findings and there are also cases in which the ECtHR came to a different risk assessment.[15] Information on countries of origin compiled by the UNHCR is also frequently used by the ECtHR, next to other sources. The ECtHR tends to give the UNHCR's information on the situation in countries of origin substantial value because of its access to the authorities of the country of origin as well as its ability to carry out on-site inspections and assessments in a manner which States and non-governmental organisations may not be able to do.[16] The exact probative value accorded by the ECtHR to the UNHCR's country of origin information is largely determined by the specific content of this information: the more the information is couched in terms of an Article 3-ECHR risk, the more weight the ECtHR tends to give to it. When the information compiled or submitted by the UNHCR focuses more on general socio-economic and humanitarian conditions in a particular country, the ECtHR is generally inclined to accord less probative weight to it.[17]

1.4. The UNHCR and the CJEU

In proceedings concerning asylum cases before the CJEU, the role of the UNHCR is becoming more and more important. An interesting development has been going on here, which I will describe in some detail below.

So far, the UNHCR has had no possibility to intervene of its own accord in cases be-fore the CJEU. According to Article 40 of the Protocol of the Statute of

---

13 Admissibility decision of the ECtHR *K.R.S. v. UK*, 2 December 2008, Appl. No. 32733/08, p. 16.

14 See ECtHR, *Jabari v. Turkey*, 11 July 2000, Appl. No. 40035/98, para. 41; ECtHR, *Abdolkhani & Karimnia v. Turkey*, 22 September 2009, Appl. No. 30471/08, para. 82; ECtHR, *Ayatollahi and Hosseinzadeh v. Turkey*, admissibility decision, 23 March 2010, Appl. No. 32971/98; ECtHR, *Charahili v. Turkey*, 13 April 2010, Appl. No. 46605/07, para. 59; ECtHR, *Khaydarov v. Russia*, 20 May 2010, Appl. No. 21055/09, para. 109; ECtHR, *M.B. and others v. Turkey*, 15 June 2010, Appl. No. 36009/08, paras. 14 and 33-34; ECtHR, *Dbouba v. Turkey*, 13 July 2010, Appl. No. 15916/09, paras. 42, 43.

15 An example of a case in which the ECtHR did not follow the assessment made by the UNHCR is ECtHR, *Y. v. Russia*, 4 December 2008, Appl. No. 20113/07. The case concerned a Chinese Falung Gong practitioner who had fled to Moscow. The ECtHR concluded that there were insufficient grounds for assuming an Article 3-risk whereas the Moscow UNHCR office delivered refugee status. The ECtHR found it important that the refugee status had been delivered by the UNHCR before the national refugee status determination had begun, that it was not clear whether the same grounds served as a basis for both claims and, finally, that the UNHCR had not intervened in any way during the subsequent appeals or proceedings.

16 See, for example, ECtHR, *N.A. v. the UK*, 17 July 2008, Appl. No. 25904/07, para. 121.

17 ECtHR, *N.A. v. the UK*, 17 July 2008, Appl. No. 25904/07, para. 122. See also ECtHR. *F.H. v. Sweden*, 20 January 2009, Appl. No. 32621/06, para. 92, where the ECtHR stated that where reports are focused on general socio-economic and humanitarian conditions, it has been inclined to accord less weight to them, since such conditions do not necessarily have a bearing on the question of a real risk to an individual applicant of ill-treatment within the meaning of Article 3.

the CJEU[18], the right of intervention in cases before the CJEU belongs to Member States and institutions of the EU. The right of intervention is also open to any other person establishing an interest in the result of any cases submitted to the Court, save in cases between Member States, between EU institutions or between Member States and EU institutions. An important limitation is that an application to intervene shall be limited to supporting one of the parties. A third party wishing to intervene, therefore, has to have an interest in the case and has to support one of the parties. All of this means that in a large number of cases only Member States or EU institutions can intervene in proceedings before the CJEU.[19]

However, what has actually happened for some time in asylum cases before the CJEU is that the UNHCR in fact intervened in an informal and indirect way by making a statement or comment in the context of a case pending before the CJEU and issuing such a statement or comment on the internet. In fact, the UNHCR has issued such documents in the context of every asylum case before the CJEU. For example, in the context of the case of *Brahim Samba Diouf* (2011)[20] it issued its 'Statement on the right to an effective remedy in relation to accelerated asylum procedures of 21 May 2010.'[21] Advocates-General (A-Gs) have indeed taken notice of these UNHCR statements and also of other documents issued by the UNHCR and have refer to them in their opinions on cases. In this way, the UNHCR has become an informal *amicus* of the CJEU.[22]

The Statute of the CJEU allows the CJEU to entrust any individual, body, authority, committee or other organisation it chooses with the task of giving an expert opinion, and to hear witnesses. Via these routes the CJEU is able to invite the UNHCR to submit an expert opinion and hear it as a witness in asylum cases. This possibility of inviting the UNHCR to submit a statement has now for the first

---

18 Protocol of the Statute of the Court of Justice of the EU, 30 March 2010, OJ 2010, C 83/210, <http://curia.europa.eu> under Statute of the Court of Justice of the EU. Article 40 stipulates: 'Member States and institutions of the Union may intervene in cases before the Court of Justice. The same right shall be open to the bodies, offices and agencies of the Union and to any other person which can establish an interest in the result of a case submitted to the Court. Natural or legal persons shall not intervene in cases between Member States, between institutions of the Union or between Member States and institutions of the Union. Without prejudice to the second paragraph, the States, other than the Member States, which are parties to the Agreement on the European Economic Area, and also the EFTA Surveillance Authority referred to in that Agreement, may intervene in cases before the Court where one of the fields of application of that Agreement is concerned. An application to intervene shall be limited to supporting the form of order sought by one of the parties.'

19 See on the limited possibilities for the UNHCR to participate in proceedings before the CJEU also Zwaan (2005), p. 50 and K. Pollet (2011), 'De Definitierichtlijn en het Vluchtelingenverdrag, bedenkingen bij een Europees Experiment', *A&MR* 2011, nr. 5/6, p. 220.

20 CJEU, *Brahim Samba Diouf*, 28 July 2011, C-69/10.

21 These statements are readily accessible on RefWorld, the UNHCR's database, via the query UNHCR, name of the case, under the heading 'related documents'.

22 See the Opinion of A-G Sharpston delivered on 4 March 2010 in Case C-31/09, *Bolbol v. Bevándorlási és állampolgársági Hivatal*, para. 16, where she stated: 'The UNHCR occasionally makes statements which have persuasive, but not binding, force. His Office has published various statements which relate to the interpretation of Article 1D of the 1951 Convention: a commentary in its Handbook (...), a note published in 2002 (and re-vised in 2009) and a 2009 statement (also subsequently revised) which relates expressly to Ms Bolbol's case. I intend to treat this last as an unofficial amicus curiae brief.'

time been used by the CJEU in three pending joined cases concerning the level of protection for homosexual asylum seekers under the EU Qualification Directive. These cases were referred to the CJEU by the Dutch Council of State by interim judgments of 18 April 2012.[23]

1.5. The UNHCR and national asylum courts in the EU: a case study

Let us now shift the focus to the subject of UNHCR's consultative role in relation to national courts.

In the past, the Dutch Council of State, which in the period between 1976 and 1994 functioned as the court of first and final instance performing judicial review in asylum cases, used to invite the UNHCR representative in the Netherlands to submit its view, during a hearing open to the public, in every asylum case coming before it. Jaap Hoeksma, former legal advisor of the UNHCR branch office in the Netherlands, has collected the UNHCR Submissions to the Council of State in his book 'De Menselijke maat, zienswijzen in asielzaken' of 1990.[24] However, this practice of consulting the UNHCR was, however, not taken up again in 2001, the year in which – after a period of absence of jurisdiction – the Council of State became the higher appeal instance in asylum cases.

Article 21 of the EU Asylum Procedures Directive stipulates in its first paragraph at sub c that the UNHCR is entitled 'to present its views, in the exercise of its supervisory responsibilities under Article 35 of the Geneva Convention, to any competent authorities regarding individual applications for asylum at any stage of the procedure'.[25] This provision entails that the UNHCR is entitled to make submissions to national courts in the form of *amicus curiae* briefs, statements or letters.[26]

This right of the UNHCR to intervene entails that national courts cannot refuse the UNHCR leave to intervene with reference to national law. Article 21 of the EU Procedures Directive cannot be seen in isolation from Articles 8, second paragraph, sub b, and 38, of the EU Asylum Procedures Directive, which also concern the advisory role of the UNHCR and stipulate, in short, that decision makers in asylum cases must have access to and gather accurate actual information from different sources, including the UNHCR, about the general

---

23   See for the full text of the judgments: Council of State (ABRvS) 201109928/1/V2 (Senegal), LJN BW3076; ABRvS 201012342/1/T1/V2 (Sierra Leone), LJN BW3078; and ABRvS 201106615/1/T1/V2 (Uganda), LJN BW3077.

24   J.A. Hoeksma (1990), *De menselijke maat, zienswijzen in asielzaken*, Nijmegen: Ars Aequi Libri 1990.

25   The supervisory role of the UNHCR is also laid down in a number of provisions contained in other EU asylum directives. Zwaan (2005) provides a list of these provisions on pp. 84-88; see also the table on pp. 26-27.

26   V. Türk (2002), *UNHCR's supervisory responsibility, New Issues in Refugee Research*, Working Paper No. 67, UNHCR 2002; <http://www.unhcr.org/3dae74b74.pdf>, p. 11; K. Zwaan (2005), *UNHCR and the European Asylum Law*, Nijmegen: Wolf Legal Publishers, p. 7; C.W. Wouters (2009), *International Legal Standards for the Protection from Refoulement, a legal analysis of the prohibitions on refoulement contained in the Refugee Convention, the European Convention on Human Rights, the International Covenant on Civil and Political Rights and the Convention against Torture*, Antwerp-Oxford-Portland: Intersentia, p. 41.

situation in the countries of origin, and that information compiled by or submitted by the UNHCR must also be taken into account in decision making concerning the revocation of refugee status.

In theory the consultative role of the UNHCR in relation to national courts is very well arranged. However, practice is more capricious, and it may sometimes be very difficult for the UNHCR to reply to questions of national courts. The following case study is used to illustrate this.

1.5.1.   Case study: judicial fact-finding in a Dublin-transfer case

In the spring and summer of 2012 the court of Den Bosch where I was working at the time as an asylum judge was of inundated with appeals and requests for interim measures lodged by asylum seekers from Chechnya, Russia, who had applied for asylum in the Netherlands after an earlier application for asylum in Poland. In these cases decisions were taken that the applicants were to be transferred to Poland under the EU Dublin Regulation. The main ground of appeal in these cases was that transfer under the EU Dublin Regulation could not take place and the Netherlands should take responsibility for processing the asylum claim on the basis of Article 3(2) of the EU Dublin regulation, because of serious deficiencies in the asylum procedure in Poland and because of extremely bad living conditions, including very poor health care.

In cases of transfers of asylum seekers under the EU Dublin Regulation to another EU Member State, the transferring EU Member State's authorities, including the national courts, are, to a certain extent, allowed to presume that the authorities of the intermediary EU Member State will respect their international obligations (the presumption of treaty compliance by EU Member States). From the judgment of the ECtHR in the case of *M.S.S. v. Belgium and Greece* (2011) and the judgment of the CJEU in the case of *N.S.* (2011) it appears, however, that both international courts have put a firm restriction on the presumption of treaty compliance. As soon as some information to the contrary becomes available – either because the applicant has submitted this information or because the authorities are familiar with it or should be familiar with it – the national authorities must assess whether the asylum procedure and living conditions in the intermediary EU Member State afford 'sufficient guarantees' and are not at variance with Article 3 ECHR and EU law standards on living conditions.[27]

The applicant in the case I will describe below is Ms Muratova (not her real name but an invented one), female, of Russian nationality, from Chechnya. She applied for asylum in the Netherlands on 1 May 2012. The Dutch Immigration and Naturalisation Service (IND) determined, with the aid of the EURODAC system, that the applicant submitted a request for asylum in Poland on 8 December 2011. The applicant stayed in Poland until March 2012. In that month she travelled to the Netherlands, entering the country on 9 March 2012. On 13 March 2012 the IND forwarded a request to Poland on the basis of EU Resolution 343/2003 (the Dublin), requesting the Polish authorities to take the applicant back as it was in Poland that she lodged a first claim for asylum protection. Poland approved this

---

27 CJEU, *N.S. and Others*, 21 December 2011, C-411/10 and C-493/10, paras 86, 94; ECtHR, *M.S.S. v. Belgium and Greece*, 21 January 2011, Appl. No. 30696/09, paras 342-358.

request on 19 March 2012. On 9 May 2012, the IND refused the applicant's request for protection on the ground that, in accordance with the EU Dublin Regulation, not the Netherlands, but Poland was responsible for processing the asylum application. The applicant lodged an appeal against this decision with the Court of 's-Hertogenbosch. She also applied for a provisional measure with the aim of staying a transfer to Poland under the Dublin Regulation until the judgment of the District Court on the appeal would be issued.

The applicant stated that there are major shortcomings in the asylum procedure in Poland and also major problems in living conditions of asylum seekers in Poland. According to the applicant, in the centres in which she lived in Poland, there were very poor hygienic conditions. According to the applicant herself, she lived in an asylum seekers centre in Horbow; according to her lawyer, she also stayed in a centre in Lublin. The applicant also stated that she was in very bad medical shape and that she urgently needed medical care, which was refused. She expressed her fear that she would not receive medical care if returned to Poland as a Dublin claimant. She mentioned furthermore that she received threats from Chechens while she was staying in Poland and that the Polish authorities were unable to protect her against these threats. The applicant's lawyer furthermore pointed at a number of other problems in the Polish asylum procedure, being unreasonably short time limits, insufficient access to interpreters and legal aid, very limited judicial scrutiny of asylum refusals, and, finally, homelessness of refugees in Poland.

The applicant's lawyer corroborated these statements by referring to a number of reports:

- A report of the Belgian Committee for Aid to Refugees of December 2011;
- A report of the Gesellschaft führ bedrohte Völker: the situation of Chechen Refugees in Poland of January 2011,
- A report of UNHCR: Refugee Homelessness in Poland – Results of a Pilot Study, 2010.

The District Court found it difficult to determine what probative value could be attached to these reports. The UNHCR report was not very recent and pertained to recognised refugees or subsidiary protection status holders, not to asylum seekers. The other two reports were rather specific about various problems in the asylum procedure in Poland and shortcomings in living conditions, but the exact status of the organisations that had issued the reports was not entirely clear and it was therefore not certain whether the information contained in the reports was objective. However, given the judgments of the ECtHR in *M.S.S. v. Belgium and Greece* (2011) and of the CJEU in the case of *N.S.* (2011), the District Court was on the alert. It was therefore decided that more factual information on the situation in Poland would be needed in order to come to a sound judgment. The first step we therefore took was take interim measure so that transfer under the Dublin Regulation would be stayed. The appeal was referred to a grand chamber of three judges. In preparation of the grand chamber court hearing, the District Court requested both parties to answer a number of questions, mainly aimed at bringing more clarity to the medical condition of the applicant, and to the alleged problems in the asylum procedure and living conditions of asylum seekers in Poland. Unfortunately, the parties to the case could initially not provide the District Court with any other sources of information then the sources listed above.

We (the involved judges and court clerks) then decided to approach the UNHCR to answer a number of factual questions on the situation in Poland. Given the prominent role of the UNHCR in the CEAS, and the importance attached to information submitted by the UNHCR to the ECtHR, it seemed a good plan to turn to this very organisation and not, for example, to NGO's. Of course we first consulted the parties about our plan to involve the UNHCR in fact-finding. We then made informal inquiries with the UNHCR about the feasibility of posing questions. After a careful positive response that the UNHCR would try to answer our questions, we sent out official letters of the District Court in which we requested the UNHCR, in the capacity of expert, to respond to a number of factual questions. The questions are listed below.

1.5.2.   Questions to UNHCR

1.   Questions concerning living conditions and detention of asylum seekers in Poland
1a.   Living conditions in open reception centres and closed detention centres

The report of the Gesellschaft führ bedrohte Völker "The situation of Chechen Refugees in Poland of January 2011" mentions on p. 4 that in Poland asylum seekers are hosted in open reception centres and in closed detention centres, and are sometimes accommodated for outside a centre. The report mentions that severe living conditions prevail in the closed detention centres.

- *The applicant states, and this has so far not been disputed, that the Polish authorities took a negative decision on her application for asylum. She has also stated that she stayed in an open centre in Horbow; her lawyer mentioned in addition a reception centre in Lublin. If the applicant is transferred to Poland under the Dublin Regulation, where will she be placed: in an open or closed centre for asylum seekers? Is it possible that she will again be placed in the centre in Horbow or in Lublin as she stayed there before? Is it possible that the applicant will end up without shelter because of the fact that the Polish authorities have negatively decided upon her asylum request?*
- *Does UNHCR know anything about the quality of living conditions in the reception centres in Horbow and Lublin?*
- *Does UNHCR know anything about living conditions in the closed detention centres?*

1b.   Medical care

The report of the Gesellschaft führ bedrohte Völker "The situation of Chechen Refugees in Poland of January 2011" mentions on p. 5 a number of problems concerning access of asylum seekers to medical care. It is mentioned in particular that there is insufficient psychological / psychiatric care for traumatised asylum seekers.

- *Is UNHCR familiar with problems of access to medical care for asylum seekers?*
- *If so, what types of problems occur?*
- *If so, what is the scale of these problems?*
- *Are certain groups of asylum seekers, or certain individuals, affected in particular?*
- *Do problems in the medical health care system in Poland affect the Polish population in a similar way, or are asylum seekers treated differently compared to Poles?*

1c. Threats of Chechen asylum seekers by representatives of the Chechen authorities or by … ?

The report of the Gesellschaft führ bedrohte Völker "The situation of Chechen Refugees in Poland of January 2011" mentions on p. 9 that "There are numerous reports that the Russian secret service and ally of the Chechen President Kadyrov put pressure on refugees in Poland." The applicant herself stated that, while awaiting the decision on her asylum application, she received a written threat from a Chechen man who knew about her role in the Chechen war. The applicant also stated that she did not report this to the Polish authorities in the reception centre as she was sure that she would not be offered protection.

- *Is UNHCR familiar with threats of Chechen asylum seekers in Poland by representatives of the Russian authorities / Chechen authorities / others?*
- *Can UNHCR say anything about the nature, the frequency and the scale of such threats?*
- *Do the Polish authorities offer protection against this? If not, what are the reasons for not offering protection?*

1d. Assaults and racist attacks from local populace against asylum seekers?

The report of the Gesellschaft führ bedrohte Völker "The situation of Chechen Refugees in Poland of January 2011" mentions on p. 9 that "Mass media report assaults and racist attacks against refugees, which dispirit the centre residents."

- *Is UNHCR familiar with this? Can UNHCR mention specific incidents?*
- *On what scale do assaults and racist attacks occur?*
- *Are certain individuals or (ethnic or other) groups of individuals affected in particular?*

2. Questions concerning the asylum procedure
2a Legal assistance

The report of the Gesellschaft führ bedrohte Völker "The situation of Chechen Refugees in Poland of January 2011" mentions on p. 5 that there is no access to public legal assistance for asylum seekers.

- *Is there a system of legal assistance to asylum seekers in Poland, and, if there is a system, how is it organised? Can UNHCR say anything about the quality of legal assistance to asylum seekers?*

The report of the Belgian Committee for Aid to Refugees of December 2011 mentions that it is difficult to obtain legal assistance because lawyers are situated in the bigger cities, whereas asylum seekers are placed in centres far away from these cities.

- *Is UNHCR familiar with this problem? If so, does this problem affect a large number of asylum seekers?*

2b. Interpretation of the refugee definition / definition for subsidiary protection

The report of the Belgian Committee for Aid to Refugees of December 2011 mentions that different components of the refugee definition and of the definition for subsidiary protection are interpreted incorrectly by the Polish administrative and judicial authorities and that, as a result, individuals who are in fact refugees or qualify for subsidiary protection, are refouled to their countries of origin.

- *Can UNHCR confirm that the Polish (administrative and/or judicial) authorities interpret a number of constituent components of the refugee definition in an incorrect way?*
- *Does this occur on a large scale (is it constant administrative practice / constant case-law) or do incorrect interpretations occur on a limited scale only?*
- *Is UNHCR familiar with cases in which the Polish authorities, as a result of incorrect interpretation, refused protection claims to asylum seekers who were in fact refugees and sent these individuals back to their countries of origin?*

2c. Interpreters

The report of the Belgian Committee for Aid to Refugees of December 2011 mentions that there is insufficient assistance of translators and interpreters.

- *Is UNHCR familiar with this problem?*
- *What is the scale of this problem: does it affect (almost) all asylum seekers or only a limited number of individuals?*

2d. Recognition rates

The report of the Gesellschaft führ bedrohte Völker "The situation of Chechen Refugees in Poland of January 2011" mentions on p. 6 that refugee recognition rates have dropped significantly in Poland during the past few years and that in 2010, in only 1.9% of all decisions refugee status was granted.

- *Can UNHCR confirm the trend signalled by the Gesellschaft führ bedrohte Völker?*
- *Can UNHCR give refugee recognition rates and rates of granting subsidiary protection over the past few years (2009, 2010, 2011)?*
- *If there is a significant drop in recognition rates, are certain (ethnic or other) groups affected in particular by it?*
- *If there is a significant drop in recognition rates, what are reasons for this change?*

3. Position of UNHCR concerning Dublin transfers of asylum seekers to Poland

In its Submission in the case of M.S.S. v. Belgium and Greece (European Court of Human Rights, 2011) UNHCR has pointed at a number of situations in which EU Member States should consider themselves responsible for taking a material decision on the protection claim instead of sending the asylum seeker to another Dublin State:

> *"In UNHCR's view, Dublin II transfers should not take place when there is evidence showing:*
> *(1)   a real risk of return/expulsion to a territory where there may be a risk of persecution or serious harm;*
> *(2)   obstacles limiting access to asylum procedures, to a fair and effective examination of claims or to an effective remedy; or*
> *(3)   conditions of reception, including detention, which may lead to violations of Article 3 ECHR.*
>
> *In these cases, UNHCR considers a State should apply Article 3(2) of the Dublin II Regulation, even if it does not bear responsibility under the criteria laid down in Articles 5–14 of the Regulation."[28]*

> -   *Is UNHCR of the opinion that one of the situations mentioned in its Submission in M.S.S. v. Belgium and Greece, or a combination thereof, prevails in Poland, and that Dublin transfers of asylum seekers to Poland should not take place for that reason / for these reasons?*
> -   *If this is UNHCR's position, does this position cover all asylum seekers transferred under Dublin or only (a) particular (ethnic or other) group(s) of individuals?*
> -   *Does it make a difference whether the individual concerned has or has not applied for asylum in Poland before travelling on to another EU Member State? Does it make a difference whether or not the individual concerned has received a negative decision of the Polish authorities on an asylum request?*

Unfortunately, six weeks after the request to provide expert information had been sent out, the UNHCR informed the District Court that the questions posed could not be answered at this point in time. The reason was that the UNHCR was still in the process of preparing a report on the situation in Poland and that at the point in time, insufficient information was available to answer the questions. It was not clear when the report on Poland would be ready.

In the meantime, in preparation for the grand chamber court hearing, the representative of the Minister for immigration and asylum provided additional information on the situation of asylum seekers in Poland. This information was obtained via the Ministry of Foreign Affairs.

Two weeks after the UNHCR had informed the District Court about its inability to answer the questions, applicant Muratova left the Netherlands for

---

28 UNHCR Submission in *M.S.S. v. Belgium and Greece*, para 5.2.

France. The lawyer informed us that she was no longer in touch with her client and that her whereabouts and intentions were not clear.

This so being, the District Court declared the appeal inadmissible for loss of interest in a material judgment. A case, which started out as a difficult one and required our special attention, had all of a sudden become very small.

1.6. Reflections

The case study presented above clearly demonstrates that thorough fact-finding can indeed be very difficult for national asylum courts to undertake, and that involving the UNHCR in this does not always lead to the desired result of obtaining clarity on the facts.

In the discussions following my presentation it became clear that from the perspective of the UNHCR, there are, in fact, two problems. The first problem is that the UNHCR does not always have the means and resources to answer factual questions posed by national first instance asylum courts, such as the ones posed by the District Court of Den Bosch in the case studied above. The UNHCR's capacity and possibilities to answer legal - and not factual - questions seem to be somewhat better, though. The second problem is that the UNHCR logically also has to protect certain interests relating to protection of refugees in the different countries involved, in the particular case at hand, Poland. As a result, the UNHCR may not always be fully free to comment on the situation.

In the particular case at hand, an unfortunate factor was that, when the questions rose with the District Court, the UNHCR was still in the middle of preparing a report on the situation in Poland. As the UNHCR phrased it: 'your questions arrived too early'.

At the same time, however, the discussions during the seminar also made clear that national courts should not take the above example as an indication that the UNHCR is never able and willing to answer questions of either factual or legal nature. When the national court wishes to consult the UNHCR, the best route to take is to first make informal inquiries with the UNHCR whether it would at all be feasible to pose questions, after consultation with the parties to the case. To conclude, national courts and the UNHCR must remain in contact with each other and try to find each other where necessary.

Dana Baldinger

Judge at the District Court of Amsterdam, The Netherlands.

2. The European Court of Human Rights is no European Asylum Court
Notes on the European Court, Judicial Scrutiny and Credibility Assessment in Asylum Procedures

Egbert Myjer

"It must be underlined that, according to its case-law and practice, the Court will only request a member State not to deport, extradite or expel a person where, having reviewed all the relevant information, it considers that he or she faces a real risk of serious, irreversible harm if removed. An interim measure requested in this way has binding legal effect on the State concerned. The Court is not an appeal tribunal for the asylum and immigration tribunals of Europe, any more than it is a court of criminal appeal in respect of criminal convictions. Where national immigration and asylum procedures carry out their own proper assessment of risk and are seen to operate fairly and with respect for human rights, the Court should only be required to intervene in truly exceptional circumstances."[29]

2.1. Introductory comment

When I read an academic comment on a judgment in a case where I was one of the judges, it sometimes happens that I feel completely lost: did we really reason in the manner as explained and did we really mean to say what is suggested in the comment? Every now and then I even feel obliged to reread the original text of the judgment in order to make sure that nothing is wrong with my short-term memory. Needless to say that such comments are mostly of little value to the court, which rendered the judgment. At the most it causes the judges in future cases to repeat the reasoning in more simple wording. That however has not been the case when I read the dissertation by Dana Baldinger.

It was refreshing to read the way she managed to summarise the relevant case-law on judicial scrutiny. Thus her thesis may be of great interest to her fellow judges in the field of migrant law.

The same applies to the research paper '*Assessment of Credibility in Refugee and Subsidiary Protection claims under the EU Qualification Directive – Judicial criteria and standards*'. Especially the part, which sets out judicial guidance on criteria and standards for credibility assessment, may indeed be of great help to national judges and even to everyone else involved in the daily practice of migration cases. Moreover, it may even serve as a means of further inspiration to

---

29 Statement issued on 11 February 2011 by the President of the European Court of Human Rights, Jean-Paul Costa, concerning Requests for Interim Measures.

the European Court. Codes of Conduct and standard setting by the profession itself can indeed be influential in the way the Court's own interpretation evolves.[30]

Still, one should not expect even a beginning of dialogue from my part today. I have chosen to only make some general remarks about the Court itself in relation to asylum cases. In doing so I will pay some extra attention to recent judgments in the field, which were not or could not be included in the doctoral thesis of Dana Baldinger. I mainly stick to what can be found in official documents, in the text of the Convention and in the case-law of the Court. The blame for any shortcomings in the choice of the – sometimes lengthy – quotes belongs to me alone.

2.2. Principle of Subsidiarity: it should be done at the national level

I will start with pointing to some open doors. Human Rights protection should be done at the national level. That is laid down in the very first provision in the Convention, Article 1 (Obligation to respect human rights):

The High Contracting Parties shall secure to everyone within their jurisdiction the rights and freedoms defined in Section 1 of this Convention.

It is also clear from Article 13 (Right to an effective remedy):

Everyone whose rights and freedoms as set forth in this Convention are violated shall have an effective remedy before a national authority notwithstanding that the violation has been committed by persons acting in an official capacity.

Besides: the Court shall only deal with the matter after all domestic remedies have been exhausted (Article 35). Once the Court finds a violation of the Convention, the State concerned has undertaken to abide by the final judgment of the Court (Article 46).

The Court itself was established 'to ensure the observance of the engagements undertaken by the High Contracting Parties in the Convention and the Protocols thereto' (Article 19). The jurisdiction of the Court extends to 'all matters concerning the interpretation and application of the Convention and the Protocols thereto' (Article 32).

In the Brighton Declaration, adopted at the High Level Conference on the Future of the European Court of Human Rights (19-20 April 2012), some interesting remarks were made in relation to the implementation of the Convention at the national level:

"A. Implementation of the Convention at national level

7. The full implementation of the Convention at national level requires States Parties to take effective measures to prevent violations. All laws and policies should be formulated, and all State officials should discharge their responsibilities, in a way that gives full effect to the Convention. States Parties must also provide means by which remedies may be sought for alleged

---

30 See for instance para 104-110 in the judgment of 20 November 2012 in the case *Harabin* v. Slowakia. In the judgment the Court referred to the Bangalore Principles of Judicial Conduct and other codes of conduct on the judiciary.

violations of the Convention. National courts and tribunals should take into account the Convention and the case-law of the Court. (...)

B. Interaction between the Court and national authorities

10. The State Parties to the Convention are obliged to secure to everyone within their jurisdiction the rights and freedoms defined in the Convention, and to provide an effective remedy before a national authority for everyone whose rights and freedoms are violated. The Court authoritatively interprets the Convention. It also acts as a safeguard for individuals whose rights and freedoms are not secured at the national level.

11. The jurisprudence of the Court makes clear that the States Parties enjoy a margin of appreciation in how they apply and implement the Convention, depending on the circumstances of the case and the rights and freedoms engaged. This reflects that the Convention system is subsidiary to the safeguarding of human rights at national level and that national authorities are in principle better placed than an international court to evaluate local needs and conditions. The margin of appreciation goes hand in hand with supervision under the Convention system. In this respect, the role of the Court is to review whether decisions taken by national authorities are compatible with the Convention, having due regard to the State's margin of appreciation. (...)"

This Declaration lead to the adoption of a Draft Protocol No. 15 amending the Convention for the Protection of Human Rights and Fundamental Freedoms:

Preamble

The member States of the Council of Europe and the other High Contracting Parties to the Convention for the Protection of Human Rights and Fundamental Freedoms, signed at Rome on 4 November 1950 (hereinafter referred to as "the Convention"), signatory hereto,

Having regard to the declaration adopted at the High Level Conference on the Future of the European Court of Human Rights, held in Brighton on 19 and 20 April 2012, as well as the declarations adopted at the conferences held in Interlaken on 18 and 19 February 2010 and İzmir on 26 and 27 April 2011; (...),

Have agreed as follows:

Article 1

At the end of the preamble to the Convention, a new recital shall be added, which shall read as follows:

"Affirming that the High Contracting Parties, in accordance with the principle of subsidiarity, have the primary responsibility to secure the rights and freedoms defined in this Convention and the Protocols thereto, and in doing so enjoy a margin of appreciation, subject to the supervisory jurisdiction of the European Court of Human Rights established by this Convention," (...)

Explanatory report

(...) 7. A new recital has been added at the end of the Preamble of the Convention containing a reference to the principle of subsidiarity and the doctrine of the margin of appreciation. It is intended to enhance the transparency and accessibility of these characteristics of the Convention system and to be consistent with the doctrine of the margin of appreciation as developed by the Court in its case-law. In making this proposal, the Brighton Declaration also recalled the High Contracting Parties' commitment to give full effect to their obligation to secure the rights and freedoms defined in the Convention.

8. The States Parties to the Convention are obliged to secure to everyone within their jurisdiction the rights and freedoms defined in the Convention, and to provide an effective remedy before a national authority for everyone whose rights and freedoms are violated. The Court authoritatively interprets the Convention. It also acts as a safeguard for individuals whose rights and freedoms are not secured at the national level.

9. The jurisprudence of the Court makes clear that the States Parties enjoy a margin of appreciation in how they apply and implement the Convention, depending on the circumstances of the case and the rights and freedoms engaged. This reflects that the Convention system is subsidiary to the safeguarding of human rights at national level and that national authorities are in principle better placed than an international court to evaluate local needs and conditions. The margin of appreciation goes hand in hand with supervision under the Convention system. In this respect, the role of the Court is to review whether decisions taken by national authorities are compatible with the Convention, having due regard to the State's margin of appreciation.

Notwithstanding the subsidiarity principle, the Court's task (Article 19) remains the same: to ensure the observance of the engagements undertaken by the High Contracting Parties. And the scope of the Court's jurisdiction (Article 32) has not altered either: all matters concerning the interpretation and application of the Convention. So the Court still has a task to perform in all cases where it is of the opinion that the Convention was not applied at the national level in a correct way. To think otherwise would be nonsense, like former president of the Court Jean-Paul Costa convincingly said in his *Raymond and Beverly Sackler Distinguished Lecture in Human Rights* at Leiden Law School[31]:

"(...) (T)here is a deep misunderstanding about this notion. For the Strasbourg Court, playing a subsidiary role – which is correct – obviously does not mean playing no role at all, and for instance confirming all the rulings made by the national judiciary. Otherwise, the supervisory part granted to the Court by Article 19 of the Convention would be illusory. Exhaustion of domestic remedies, which is a prerequisite for the applications being declared admissible, most of the time implies judgments made by the high national tribunals. If the Court were bound to systematically confirm them, practically

---

31 Jean-Paul Costa, *Current challenges for the European Court of Human Rights*, Leiden University 2011, p. 12.

all applications to Strasbourg would be either inadmissible on grounds of non-exhaustion, or ill-founded for having been rejected at domestic level. This is simply nonsense."

2.3. The European Court is no fourth instance:

In its case-law the Court has constantly made it clear that it is no fourth instance court. So in the Grand Chamber judgment of 21 January 1999 in the case *Garcia Ruiz* v. Spain, the Court ruled:

> *"28. (...) the Court reiterates that, according to Article 19 of the Convention, its duty is to ensure the observance of the engagements undertaken by the Contracting Parties to the Convention. In particular, it is not its function to deal with errors of fact or law allegedly committed by a national court unless and in so far as they may have infringed rights and freedoms protected by the Convention. Moreover, while Article 6 of the Convention guarantees the right to a fair hearing, it does not lay down any rules on the admissibility of evidence or the way it should be assessed, which are therefore primarily matters for regulation by national law and the national courts (see the Schenk v. Switzerland judgment of 12 July 1988, Series A no. 140, p. 29, §§ 45-46). (...)"*

And in the Grand Chamber judgment of 18 February 1999 in the case *Waite and Kennedy* v. Germany, the Court said:

> *"54. The Court would recall that it is not its task to substitute itself for the domestic jurisdictions. It is primarily for the national authorities, notably the courts, to resolve problems of interpretation of domestic legislation (see, inter alia, the Pérez de Rada Cavanilles v. Spain judgment of 28 October 1998, Reports 1998-VIII, p. 3255, § 43). This also applies where domestic law refers to rules of general international law or international agreements. The Court's role is confined to ascertaining whether the effects of such an interpretation are compatible with the Convention. (...)".*

In the Grand Chamber judgment of 15 January 2007 in the case *Sisojeva and Others* v. Latvia, the Court added that that might be different when there is clear evidence of arbitrariness:

> *"89. (...) In other words, the Court cannot question the assessment of the domestic authorities unless there is clear evidence of arbitrariness, (...)."*

2.4. Limits to interpretation

In performing its task, the Court is limited by the General Rules of Interpretation as laid down in Articles 31 (General Rule of Interpretation) and Article 32 (Supplementary Rules of Interpretation) of the 1969 Vienna Convention on the Law of Treaties:

Article 31 (General Rule of Interpretation)

1. A treaty shall be interpreted in good faith in accordance with the ordinary meaning to be given to the terms of the treaty in their context and in the light of its object and purpose.

2. The context for the purpose of the interpretation of the interpretation of a treaty shall comprise, in addition to the text, including its preamble and annexes:

(a) any agreement relating to the treaty which was made between all parties in connection with the conclusion of the treaty;

(b) any instrument which was made by one or more parties in connection with the conclusion of the treaty and accepted by the other parties as an instrument related to the treaty.

3. There shall be taken into account, together with the context:

(a) any subsequent agreement between the parties regarding the interpretation of the treaty or the application of its provision;

(b) any subsequent practice in the application of the treaty which establishes the agreement of the parties regarding its interpretation;

(c) any relevant rules of international law applicable in the relations between the parties.

4. A special meaning shall be given to a term if it is established that the parties so intended.

Article 32 (Supplementary means of interpretation)

Recourse may be had to supplementary means of interpretation, including the preparatory work of the treaty and the circumstances of its conclusion, in order to confirm the meaning resulting from the application of article 31, or to determine the meaning when the interpretation according to article 31:

(a) leaves the meaning ambiguous or obscure; or
(b) leads to a result which is manifestly absurd or unreasonable.

In its Grand Chamber judgment of 12 November 2008 in the case *Demir and Baykara* v. Turkey, the Court elaborated on its interpretation methods:

> "65. In order to determine the meaning of the terms and phrases used in the Convention, the Court is guided mainly by the rules of interpretation provided for in Articles 31 to 33 of the Vienna Convention on the Law of Treaties (...). In accordance with the Vienna Convention the Court is required to ascertain the ordinary meaning to be given to the words in their context and in the light of the object and purpose of the provision from which they are drawn (... and Article 31 § 1 of the Vienna Convention). Recourse may also be had to supplementary means of interpretation, either to confirm a meaning determined in accordance with the above steps, or to establish the meaning where it would otherwise be ambiguous, obscure, or manifestly absurd or unreasonable (Article 32 of the Vienna Convention) (...).
>
> 66. Since the Convention is first and foremost a system for the protection of human rights, the Court must interpret and apply it in a manner, which renders

its rights practical and effective, not theoretical and illusory. The Convention must also be read as a whole, and interpreted in such a way as to promote internal consistency and harmony between its various provisions (...).

67. In addition, the Court has never considered the provisions of the Convention as the sole framework of reference for the interpretation of the rights and freedoms enshrined therein. On the contrary, it must also take into account any relevant rules and principles of international law applicable in relations between the Contracting Parties (... see also Article 31 § 3 (c) of the Vienna Convention).

68. The Court further observes that it has always referred to the "living" nature of the Convention, which must be interpreted in the light of present-day conditions, and that it has taken account of evolving norms of national and international law in its interpretation of Convention provisions (...)."

2.5. Does the Court act as a European Asylum Court?[32]

Practice shows that between 90 and 95% of the complaints submitted to the Court will be declared inadmissible. Among these cases there are many cases where the single judge will find no clear evidence of arbitrariness in the final decisions of the national courts. All these fourth-instance cases are manifestly ill-founded. Although the statistics of the Court do not show a subdivision in civil, criminal, administrative or immigration cases, one may assume that from all asylum-related cases introduced in Strasbourg, in more than 90% there was no prima facie evidence of the national immigration-law court not acting according to the minimum European level of protection. That in itself is an important conclusion: from all immigration cases submitted to the Court only a very small percentage will give rise to a consideration on the merits.

Still, the question may be asked: did the founding fathers of the Convention ever intend to let the Court decide on immigration cases? The consistent answer of the Court itself has been clear:

"a State is entitled, as a matter of international law and subject to its treaty obligations, to control the entry of aliens into its territory and their residence there. The Convention does not guarantee the right of an alien to enter or to reside in a particular country'.

However, once a migrant finds himself within the jurisdiction of a Contracting State to the Convention, he or she is entitled to the protection afforded by the Convention. In its judgment of 7 July 1989 in the case of *Soering v. the United Kingdom* the Court established for the first time that the decision by a Contracting State to extradite a fugitive may give rise to an issue under Article 3 and hence engage the responsibility of that State under the Convention, where substantial grounds have been shown for believing that the person concerned, if extradited, faces a real risk of being subjected to torture or to inhuman or degrading treatment or punishment in the requesting country. That judgment, I add, was not a matter of

---

32 See for a concise summary of the relevant case-law: Nuala Mole, *Asylum and the European Convention on Human Rights*, Council of Europe Publishing 2008.

judicial activism; the Court merely ensured the effectiveness of the safeguard provided by Article 3 and explained why this was the only decision possible in view of the serious and irreparable nature of the alleged suffering risked. In doing so the Court acted within the General Rule of Interpretation as laid down in Article 31 of the Vienna Convention:

"88. Article 3 makes no provision for exceptions and no derogation from it is permissible under Article 15 in time of war or other national emergency. This absolute prohibition of torture and of inhuman or degrading treatment or punishment under the terms of the Convention shows that Article 3 enshrines one of the fundamental values of the democratic societies making up the Council of Europe. It is also to be found in similar terms in other international instruments such as the 1966 International Covenant on Civil and Political Rights and the 1969 American Convention on Human Rights and is generally recognised as an internationally accepted standard.

The question remains whether the extradition of a fugitive to another State where he would be subjected or be likely to be subjected to torture or to inhuman or degrading treatment or punishment would itself engage the responsibility of a Contracting State under Article 3. That the abhorrence of torture has such implications is recognised in Article 3 of the United Nations Convention Against Torture and Other Cruel, Inhuman or Degrading Treatment or Punishment, which provides that "no State Party shall ... extradite a person where there are substantial grounds for believing that he would be in danger of being subjected to torture". The fact that a specialised treaty should spell out in detail a specific obligation attaching to the prohibition of torture does not mean that an essentially similar obligation is not already inherent in the general terms of Article 3 of the European Convention. It would hardly be compatible with the underlying values of the Convention, that "common heritage of political traditions, ideals, freedom and the rule of law" to which the Preamble refers, were a Contracting State knowingly to surrender a fugitive to another State where there were substantial grounds for believing that he would be in danger of being subjected to torture, however heinous the crime allegedly committed. Extradition in such circumstances, while not explicitly referred to in the brief and general wording of Article 3 would plainly be contrary to the spirit and intendment of the Article, and in the Court's view this inherent obligation not to extradite also extends to cases in which the fugitive would be faced in the receiving State by a real risk of exposure to inhuman or degrading treatment or punishment proscribed by that Article 3.

89. What amounts to "inhuman or degrading treatment or punishment" depends on all the circumstances of the case (...). Furthermore, inherent in the whole of the Convention is a search for a fair balance between the demands of the general interest of the community and the requirements of the protection of the individual's fundamental rights. As movement about the world becomes easier and crime takes on a larger international dimension, it is increasingly in the interest of all nations that suspected offenders who flee abroad should be brought to justice. Conversely, the establishment of safe havens for fugitives would not only result in danger for the State obliged to harbour the protected person but also tend to undermine the foundations of extradition. These considerations must also be included among the factors to be taken into account in the interpretation and application of the notions of inhuman and degrading treatment or punishment in extradition cases.

90. It is not normally for the Convention institutions to pronounce on the existence or otherwise of potential violations of the Convention. However, where an applicant claims that a decision to extradite him would, if implemented, be contrary to Article 3 by reason of its foreseeable consequences in the requesting country, a departure from this principle is necessary, in view of the serious and irreparable nature of the alleged suffering risked, in order to ensure the effectiveness of the safeguard provided by that Article (...).

91. In sum, the decision by a Contracting State to extradite a fugitive may give rise to an issue under Article 3, and hence engage the responsibility of that State under the Convention, where substantial grounds have been shown for believing that the person concerned, if extradited, faces a real risk of being subjected to torture or to inhuman or degrading treatment or punishment in the requesting country. The establishment of such responsibility inevitably involves an assessment of conditions in the requesting country against the standards of Article 3 of the Convention. Nonetheless, there is no question of adjudicating on or establishing the responsibility of the receiving country, whether under general international law, under the Convention or otherwise. In so far as any liability under the Convention is or may be incurred, it is liability incurred by the extraditing Contracting State by reason of its having taken action which has as a direct consequence the exposure of an individual to proscribed ill-treatment."

The reasoning in the *Soering* judgment – a case concerning extradition – was ever since reaffirmed by the Court, also in cases concerning refused asylum seekers. Thus, as a recent example, in the judgment of 23 February 2012 in the case *Hirsi Jamaa and Others* v. Italy, the Court ruled:

"General principles

(a) Responsibility of Contracting States in cases of expulsion

113. According to the Court's established case-law, Contracting States have the right, as a matter of well-established international law and subject to their treaty obligations, including the Convention, to control the entry, residence and expulsion of aliens (...). The Court also notes that the right to political asylum is not contained in either the Convention or its Protocols (...).

114. However, expulsion, extradition or any other measure to remove an alien may give rise to an issue under Article 3, and hence engage the responsibility of the expelling State under the Convention, where substantial grounds have been shown for believing that the person in question, if expelled, would face a real risk of being subjected to treatment contrary to Article 3 in the receiving country. In such circumstances, Article 3 implies an obligation not to expel the individual to that country (see Soering, cited above), (...)

115. In this type of case, the Court is therefore called upon to assess the situation in the receiving country in the light of the requirements of Article 3. In so far as any liability under the Convention is or may be incurred, it is liability incurred by the Contracting State, by reason of its having taken action, which has as a direct consequence the exposure of an individual to the risk of proscribed ill-treatment (...).

(β) Factors used to assess the risk of being subjected to treatment in breach of Article 3 of the Convention

116. In determining whether it has been shown that the applicant runs a real risk of suffering treatment proscribed by Article 3, the Court will assess the issue in the light of all the material placed before it, or, if necessary, material obtained proprio motu (...). In cases such as the present the Court's examination of the existence of a real risk of ill-treatment must necessarily be a rigorous one (...).

117. In order to ascertain whether or not there was a risk of ill-treatment, the Court must examine the foreseeable consequences of the removal of an applicant to the receiving country in the light of the general situation there as well as his or her personal circumstances (...).

118. To that end, as regards the general situation in a particular country, the Court has often attached importance to the information contained in recent reports from independent international human-rights-protection associations such as Amnesty International, or governmental sources (...).

119. In cases where an applicant alleges that he or she is a member of a group systematically exposed to a practice of ill-treatment, the Court considers that the protection of Article 3 of the Convention enters into play when the applicant establishes, where necessary on the basis of the sources mentioned in the previous paragraph, that there are substantial grounds for believing in the existence of the practice in question and his or her membership of the group concerned (...).

120. Owing to the absolute character of the right guaranteed, the Court does not rule out the possibility that Article 3 of the Convention may also apply where the danger emanates from persons or groups of persons who are not public officials. However, it must be shown that the risk is real and that the authorities of the receiving State are not able to obviate the risk by providing appropriate protection (...).

121. With regard to the material date, the existence of the risk must be assessed primarily with reference to those facts which were known or ought to have been known to the Contracting State at the time of removal."

It is in principle for the applicant to adduce evidence capable of proving that there are substantial grounds for believing that he would be exposed to a real risk of being subjected to treatment contrary to Article 3. When this initial burden of proof is met, it is for the government to dispel any doubts about it. National courts have the duty to conduct a proper investigation into the alleged Article 3 risk. As long as the national courts have applied an independent and rigorous scrutiny of the claim that there exist substantial grounds for fearing a real risk of treatment contrary to Article 3, the Court will generally accept the findings of the national court.[33] There are however occasions that the Court is nevertheless triggered to proceed to an independent assessment of the credibility of the applicant. I follow the subdivision made by Dana Baldinger in her dissertation:

1. *Insufficient national proceedings, for example, evidence was overlooked or not taken seriously, or the assessment made at the national level was insufficiently supported by relevant country of origin materials;*

2. *New facts, circumstances or developments, including evidence thereof, or new information which cast doubt on the information relied on by the government; and*

3. *The absolute nature of Article 3 was disrespected, for example, a weighing of national security considerations against the Article 3-risk took place, or an incorrect application of the standard of proof or another evidentiary standard took place. For example, a too strict standard on individualisation.*

I have the feeling that 1 and 3 can be accepted more easily by the national authorities. If it is clear that at the national level relevant evidence was overlooked or when there are major conflicting reports[34] on the situation in the country of origin, or when the wrong standards were applied at the national level[35], it is only fair to conclude that something went wrong at that national level. In this respect it is also useful to know that applicants sometimes draw the attention of the Court to conflicting country-of-origin information compiled by other States[36] or to judgments rendered in another State where – unlike the national judgment at issue – it is accepted that for the particular group to which also the applicant belongs, there exists a real risk in a particular country. Moreover, since the Court deals with cases in relation to the 47 Contracting States, it is able *proprio motu* to collect and compare relevant country-of-origin information. As was indicated above, the Court will assess the issue in the light of all the material placed before it, or, if necessary, material which it has collected itself. In a case where there is conflicting information the Court's examination of the existence of a real risk of

---

33 Dana Baldinger, *Rigorous Scrutiny versus Marginal Review; standards on judicial scrutiny and evidence in international and European asylum law*, Nijmegen: Wolf Legal Publishers 2013.

34 Baldinger, o.c. p. 267, mentions: four main sources of country information used by the Court: (1) Information compiled by organs, organizations and agencies of the United Nations and the Council of Europe; (2) Information compiled by States (whether respondent in a particular case or any other Contracting or non-Contracting State such as the US); (3) Information from independent international human rights protection organizations such as Amnesty International, Human Rights Watch; and (4) Information from the media and other sources.

35 Much will depend on the assessment of the credibility of the account given by the asylum seeker. The (2013) initiative taken by the International Association of Refugee Law Judges to publish a document on the *Assessment of Credibility in Refugee and Subsidiary Protection claims under the EU Qualification Directive; Judicial criteria and standards*, can be of great help in carrying out the proper credibility assessment at the national level.

36 In this respect it might be useful if at least at least at the EU-level, the Malta based EASO (European Asylum Support Office) would be able to help the member states to ensure that individual asylum cases are dealt with in a coherent way and thus contributes to the establishment of a European asylum and immigration policy.

ill-treatment must necessarily be a rigorous one. Like in all cases where there may be an issue on the merits, the Court will, in accordance with the Rules of Court, communicate a case to the government concerned and will ask for their observations. Practice shows that in their observations a government sometimes indicate that the new information has given rise to a decision to allow the applicant to introduce a new request at the national level. Such cases will normally lead to a striking out of the application (Article 37).

I guess that the national misgivings mainly lie in 2: the Court taking into account new facts, circumstances or developments. In this respect it is important to keep in mind that in cases where the applicant has not yet been expelled to his country of origin the Court will assess the existence of the real risk on an *ex nunc-*basis[37]. It means that the material point in time is the moment that the Court examines the case. As said above: when the national courts have sufficiently applied an independent and rigorous scrutiny of the applicant's claim that, if expelled, he will face a real risk of treatment in breach of Article 3, and no relevant new facts have been adduced or found by the Court *proprio motu*, that will be normally be the end of the case. But it may happen that at the national level the applicant was time-barred from submitting new relevant facts, and that he thus has no other choice than to submit them to the Court. In this type of cases the Court has ruled that 'the formal requirements and time-limits laid down in domestic law should normally be complied with, such rules being designed to enable the national jurisdictions to discharge their caseload in an orderly manner'. In its case-law the Court has nevertheless accepted that it may be difficult for asylum seekers to provide evidence within a short time frame and it has adopted a flexible approach.[38, 39] The Court may not only take into account the new

---

37 It may happen that an ex nunc assessment is not beneficial for the applicant if, for instance, in the meantime a civil war in the country of origin, has ended. See for instance the admissibility decision of 14 October 2003 in the case Tomic v. the United Kingdom.

38 In its judgment in the case of Bahaddar v. the Netherlands, the Court mentioned in this respect: "(...) 45. The Court notes at the outset that, although it has (...)held the prohibition of torture or inhuman or degrading treatment contained in Article 3 of the Convention to be absolute in expulsion cases as in other cases (...), applicants invoking that Article are not for that reason dispensed as a matter of course from exhausting domestic remedies that are available and effective. It would not only run counter to the subsidiary character of the Convention but also undermine the very purpose of the rule set out in Article 26 of the Convention if the Contracting States were to be denied the opportunity to put matters right through their own legal system. It follows that, even in cases of expulsion to a country where there is an alleged risk of ill-treatment contrary to Article 3, the formal requirements and time-limits laid down in domestic law should normally be complied with, such rules being designed to enable the national jurisdictions to discharge their caseload in an orderly manner.

Whether there are special circumstances, which absolve an applicant from the obligation to comply with such rules, will depend on the facts of each case. It should be borne in mind in this regard that in applications for recognition of refugee status it may be difficult, if not impossible, for the person concerned to supply evidence within a short time, especially if – as in the present case – such evidence must be obtained from the country from which he or she claims to have fled. Accordingly, time-limits should not be so short, or applied so inflexibly, as to deny an applicant for recognition of refugee status a realistic opportunity to prove his or her claim. (...)"

39 It is interesting to note that the Rules of Court are also strict in applying time-limits. Rule 38 stipulates that no written observations or documents may be filed after the time –limit fixed, unless the President of the Chamber decides otherwise. As far as the six-month rule is concerned

information, it can – according to the Rules of Court – also ask the Contracting State or the applicant to provide further information. When, however, the Contracting State or the applicant fails to provide information requested by the Court or fails to divulge relevant information, the Court may draw such inferences as it deems appropriate.

2.6. The Court's evaluation of the facts

As a recent authority I refer to the judgment of 13 December 2012 in the case *El-Masri* v. Former Yugoslav Republic of Macedonia:

> *"General principles*
>
> *151. In cases in which there are conflicting accounts of events, the Court is inevitably confronted when establishing the facts with the same difficulties as those faced by any first-instance court. It reiterates that, in assessing evidence, it has adopted the standard of proof "beyond reasonable doubt". However, it has never been its purpose to borrow the approach of the national legal systems that use that standard. Its role is not to rule on criminal guilt or civil liability but on Contracting States' responsibility under the Convention. The specificity of its task under Article 19 of the Convention – to ensure the observance by the Contracting States of their engagement to secure the fundamental rights enshrined in the Convention – conditions its approach to the issues of evidence and proof. In the proceedings before the Court, there are no procedural barriers to the admissibility of evidence or pre-determined formulae for its assessment. It adopts the conclusions that are, in its view, supported by the free evaluation of all evidence, including such inferences as may flow from the facts and the parties' submissions. According to its established case-law, proof may follow from the coexistence of sufficiently strong, clear and concordant inferences or of similar unrebutted presumptions of fact. Moreover, the level of persuasion necessary for reaching a particular conclusion and, in this connection, the distribution of the burden of proof, are intrinsically linked to the specificity of the facts, the nature of the allegation made and the Convention right at stake. The Court is also attentive to the seriousness that attaches to a ruling that a Contracting State has violated fundamental rights (...).*
>
> *152. Furthermore, it is to be recalled that Convention proceedings do not in all cases lend themselves to a strict application of the principle affirmanti incumbit probatio. The Court reiterates its case-law under Articles 2 and 3 of the Convention to the effect that where the events in issue lie within the exclusive knowledge of the authorities, as in the case of persons under their control in custody, strong presumptions of fact will arise in respect of injuries and death occurring during that detention. The burden of proof in such a case may be regarded as resting on the authorities to provide a satisfactory and convincing explanation (...). In the absence of such explanation the Court can*

(Article 35) , the Court is strict. See as a recent authority: the judgment of 29 June 2012 in the case of Sabri Günes v. Turkey.

draw inferences, which may be unfavourable for the respondent Government (...).

153. The Court has already found that these considerations apply also to disappearances examined under Article 5 of the Convention, where, although it has not been proved that a person has been taken into custody by the authorities, it is possible to establish that he or she was officially summoned by the authorities, entered a place under their control and has not been seen since. In such circumstances, the onus is on the Government to provide a plausible and satisfactory explanation as to what happened on the premises and to show that the person concerned was not detained by the authorities, but left the premises without subsequently being deprived of his or her liberty (...). Furthermore, the Court reiterates that, again in the context of a complaint under Article 5 § 1 of the Convention, it has required proof in the form of concordant inferences before the burden of proof is shifted to the respondent Government (...)."

2.7.   A real risk of ill treatment [40]

The case-law shows that the Court has mainly found an individualised real risk of ill treatment in the country of origin, in cases of political opponents, members of illegal organisations, persons accused of terrorism, and people belonging to a stigmatised ethnic or religious minority group. Also circumstances relating to a death sentence or prison conditions could lead to establishing the real risk. The Court has found a risk of ill-treatment in the event of removal (*refoulement*) under the Dublin II Regulation to Greece (*M.S.S.* v. Belgium and Greece). A risk of ill treatment may also come from third parties, where the local authorities are not capable to be of help to prevent the ill treatment. In very exceptional circumstances health issues may also cause a real risk. The graver the general human rights situation in the country of origin, the more significant this situation becomes in assessing the risk and the less individual facts and circumstances are required.

2.8.   In relation to the real risk, when will diplomatic assurances suffice?

The Court has accepted that the existence of diplomatic assurances may suffice in preventing the real risk from taking place. There is however an obligation at the national level to examine whether the assurances provide, in their practical application, a sufficient guarantee that the applicant will be protected against the risk of ill-treatment. The weight to be given to assurances from the receiving State depends, in each case, on the circumstances prevailing at the material time In its judgment of 17 January 2012 in the case *Othman (Abu Quatada)* v. United Kingdom, the Court ruled:

---

40 See for a comprehensive factsheet with further references to relevant case-law: European Court of Human Rights, *Factsheet – Expulsions and extraditions* <www.echr.coe.int> – Press – Information Sheets – Factsheets.

"183. First, the Court wishes to emphasise that, throughout its history, it has been acutely conscious of the difficulties faced by States in protecting their populations from terrorist violence, which constitutes, in itself, a grave threat to human rights (...). Faced with such a threat, the Court considers it legitimate for Contracting States to take a firm stand against those who contribute to terrorist acts, which it cannot condone in any circumstances (...).

184. Second, as part of the fight against terrorism, States must be allowed to deport non-nationals whom they consider to be threats to national security. It is no part of this Court's function to review whether an individual is in fact such a threat; its only task is to consider whether that individual's deportation would be compatible with his of her rights under the Convention (...).

185. Third, it is well-established that expulsion by a Contracting State may give rise to an issue under Article 3, and hence engage the responsibility of that State under the Convention, where substantial grounds have been shown for believing that the person concerned, if deported, faces a real risk of being subjected to treatment contrary to Article 3. In such a case, Article 3 implies an obligation not to deport the person in question to that country. Article 3 is absolute and it is not possible to weigh the risk of ill-treatment against the reasons put forward for the expulsion (...).

186. Fourth, the Court accepts that, as the materials provided by the applicant and the third party interveners show, there is widespread concern within the international community as to the practice of seeking assurances to allow for the deportation of those considered to be a threat to national security (...). However, it not for this Court to rule upon the propriety of seeking assurances, or to assess the long term consequences of doing so; its only task is to examine whether the assurances obtained in a particular case are sufficient to remove any real risk of ill-treatment. Before turning to the facts of the applicant's case, it is therefore convenient to set out the approach the Court has taken to assurances in Article 3 expulsion cases.

187. In any examination of whether an applicant faces a real risk of ill-treatment in the country to which he is to be removed, the Court will consider both the general human rights situation in that country and the particular characteristics of the applicant. In a case where assurances have been provided by the receiving State, those assurances constitute a further relevant factor, which the Court will consider. However, assurances are not in themselves sufficient to ensure adequate protection against the risk of ill-treatment. There is an obligation to examine whether assurances provide, in their practical application, a sufficient guarantee that the applicant will be protected against the risk of ill-treatment. The weight to be given to assurances from the receiving State depends, in each case, on the circumstances prevailing at the material time (...).

188. In assessing the practical application of assurances and determining what weight is to be given to them, the preliminary question is whether the general human rights situation in the receiving State excludes accepting any assurances whatsoever. However, it will only be in rare cases that the general situation in a country will mean that no weight at all can be given to assurances (...).

189. More usually, the Court will assess first, the quality of assurances given and, second, whether, in light of the receiving State's practices they can be relied upon. In doing so, the Court will have regard, inter alia, to the following factors:

(i)   *whether the terms of the assurances have been disclosed to the Court (...);*

(ii)   *whether the assurances are specific or are general and vague (...);*

(iii)   *who has given the assurances and whether that person can bind the receiving State (...);*

(iv)   *if the assurances have been issued by the central government of the receiving State, whether local authorities can be expected to abide by them (...);*

(v)   *whether the assurances concerns treatment which is legal or illegal in the receiving State (...)*

(vi)   *whether they have been given by a Contracting State (...);*

(vii)   *the length and strength of bilateral relations between the sending and receiving States, including the receiving State's record in abiding by similar assurances (...);*

(viii)   *whether compliance with the assurances can be objectively verified through diplomatic or other monitoring mechanisms, including providing unfettered access to the applicant's lawyers (...);*

(ix)   *whether there is an effective system of protection against torture in the receiving State, including whether it is willing to cooperate with international monitoring mechanisms (including international human rights NGOs), and whether it is willing to investigate allegations of torture and to punish those responsible (...);*

(x)   *whether the applicant has previously been ill-treated in the receiving State (...); and*

(xi)   *whether the reliability of the assurances has been examined by the domestic courts of the sending/Contracting State (...)."*

2.9. Rule 39: interim measures

The Court may, under Rule 39 of its Rules of Court, indicate Interim Measures to any State Party to the Convention. Interim measures are urgent measures which, according to the established practice of the Court, apply only when there is an imminent risk of irreparable damage (judgment of 4 February 2005 in the case *Mamatkulov and Askarov* v. Turkey and judgment of 10 March 2009 in the case *Paladi* v. Moldova). Interim measures are applied only in limited situations: the most typical cases are ones in which there is fear of

a. threat to life (situation falling under Article 2) and

b. ill-treatment prohibited by Article 3.

In highly exceptional cases they can also be applied in respect of certain requests relating to the right to respect for private and family life (Article 8). The vast majority of interim measures indicated concern expulsion and extradition cases. In these cases the Court can request the State concerned to suspend a deportation order against the applicant. Interim measures may be indicated for the duration of the proceedings before the Court or for a more limited period of time. An order under Rule 39 may be lifted at any time by a decision of the Court. In particular, as an order under Rule 39 is linked to the proceedings before the Court, an interim measure may be lifted if the application is not maintained.

2.10. Expulsion-issues related to other Articles of the Convention.

2.10.1. Expulsion which interferes with rights protected under Article 8, must be in accordance with the conditions set out in Article 8 paragraph 2. Need for effective national remedy (Article 13). In article 3 cases: remedy with automatic suspensive effect.

For completeness sake I refer in this respect to the recent judgment of 13 December 2012 in the case *De Souza Ribeiro* v. France:

> "77. *In cases concerning immigration laws the Court has consistently affirmed that, as a matter of well-established international law and subject to their treaty obligations, the States have the right to control the entry, residence and expulsion of aliens. The Convention does not guarantee the right of an alien to enter or to reside in a particular country and, in pursuance of their task of maintaining public order, Contracting States have the power to expel an alien convicted of criminal offences. However, their decisions in this field must, in so far as they may interfere with a right protected under paragraph 1 of Article 8, be in accordance with the law, pursue a legitimate aim and be necessary in a democratic society (...).*
>
> *By virtue of Article 1 of the Convention, the primary responsibility for implementing and enforcing the guaranteed rights and freedoms is laid on the national authorities. The machinery of complaint to the Court is thus subsidiary to national systems safeguarding human rights. This subsidiary character is articulated in Article 13 and Article 35 § 1 of the Convention (...).*
>
> 78. *The Court has reiterated on numerous occasions that Article 13 of the Convention guarantees the availability at national level of a remedy to enforce the substance of the Convention rights and freedoms in whatever form they are secured in the domestic legal order. The effect of this Article is thus to require the provision of a domestic remedy allowing the competent national authority both to deal with an "arguable complaint" under the Convention and to grant appropriate relief. The scope of the Contracting States' obligations under Article 13 varies depending on the nature of the applicant's complaint. The States are afforded some discretion as to the manner in which they conform to their obligations under this provision (...). However, the remedy required by Article 13 must be "effective" in practice as well as in law (...).*
>
> 79. *The effectiveness of a remedy within the meaning of Article 13 does not depend on the certainty of a favourable outcome for the applicant. Nor does the "authority" referred to in that provision necessarily have to be a judicial authority. Nevertheless, its powers and the procedural guarantees which it*

affords are relevant in determining whether the remedy before it is effective (...). When the "authority" concerned is not a judicial authority, the Court makes a point of verifying its independence (...) and the procedural guarantees it offers applicants (...). Also, even if a single remedy does not by itself entirely satisfy the requirements of Article 13, the aggregate of remedies provided for under domestic law may do so (...).

80. In order to be effective, the remedy required by Article 13 must be available in practice as well as in law, in particular in the sense that its exercise must not be unjustifiably hindered by the acts or omissions of the authorities of the respondent State (...).

81. In addition, particular attention should be paid to the speediness of the remedial action itself, since it is not inconceivable that the adequate nature of the remedy can be undermined by its excessive duration (...).

82. Where a complaint concerns allegations that the person's expulsion would expose him to a real risk of suffering treatment contrary to Article 3 of the Convention, in view of the importance the Court attaches to that provision and given the irreversible nature of the harm that might occur if the risk of torture or ill-treatment alleged materialised, the effectiveness of the remedy for the purposes of Article 13 requires imperatively that the complaint be subject to close scrutiny by a national authority (...), independent and rigorous scrutiny of a claim that there exist substantial grounds for fearing a real risk of treatment contrary to Article 3 (...) and reasonable promptness (...). In such a case, effectiveness also requires that the person concerned should have access to a remedy with automatic suspensive effect (see ...). The same principles apply when expulsion exposes the applicant to a real risk of a violation of his right to life safeguarded by Article 2 of the Convention. Lastly, the requirement that a remedy should have automatic suspensive effect has been confirmed for complaints under Article 4 of Protocol No. 4 (...).

83. By contrast, where expulsions are challenged on the basis of alleged interference with private and family life, it is not imperative, in order for a remedy to be effective, that it should have automatic suspensive effect. Nevertheless, in immigration matters, where there is an arguable claim that expulsion threatens to interfere with the alien's right to respect for his private and family life, Article 13 in conjunction with Article 8 of the Convention requires that States must make available to the individual concerned the effective possibility of challenging the deportation or refusal-of-residence order and of having the relevant issues examined with sufficient procedural safeguards and thoroughness by an appropriate domestic forum offering adequate guarantees of independence and impartiality."

2.10.2.   No expulsion when there is the real risk of flagrant breach of Article 5.

I refer in this respect to the reasoning in the judgment of 17 January 2012 in the case *Othman (Abu Quatada)* v. United Kingdom:

"Does Article 5 apply in an expulsion case?

231. The Court accepts that, in Tomic, cited above, it doubted whether Article 5 could be relied on in an expulsion case. However, it also recalls that in Babar Ahmad and Others, §§ 100-116, cited above, the applicants complained that if they were extradited to the United States of America and either designated as enemy combatants or subjected to rendition then there would be a real of risk of violations of Articles 3, 5 and 6 of the Convention. The United States Government had given assurances that the applicants would not be so designated and would be tried before federal courts. Before both the domestic courts and this Court, the applicants' complaints were examined on the premise that they met the criteria for designation as enemy combatants and that, if such a designation were made, there would be a real risk of a violation of Articles 3, 5 and 6 of the Convention. Ultimately, the complaints were rejected as manifestly ill-founded because the assurances given by the United States were sufficient to remove any real risk of designation or rendition. Equally, the Court recalls that, while examining the applicant's Article 6 complaint in Al-Moayad, cited above, § 101, it found that:

"A flagrant denial of a fair trial, and thereby a denial of justice, undoubtedly occurs where a person is detained because of suspicions that he has been planning or has committed a criminal offence without having any access to an independent and impartial tribunal to have the legality of his or her detention reviewed and, if the suspicions do not prove to be well-founded, to obtain release (references omitted)."

Given that this observation was made in the context of the applicant's complaint that he would be detained without trial at Guantánamo Bay, the Court finds that these observations must apply with even greater force to Article 5 of the Convention.

232. The Court also considers that it would be illogical if an applicant who faced imprisonment in a receiving State after a flagrantly unfair trial could rely on Article 6 to prevent his expulsion to that State but an applicant who faced imprisonment without any trial whatsoever could not rely on Article 5 to prevent his expulsion. Equally, there may well be a situation where an applicant has already been convicted in the receiving State after a flagrantly unfair trial and is to be extradited to that State to serve a sentence of imprisonment. If there were no possibility of those criminal proceedings being reopened on his return, he could not rely on Article 6 because he would not be at risk of a further flagrant denial of justice. It would be unreasonable if that applicant could not then rely on Article 5 to prevent his extradition (...).

233. The Court therefore considers that, despite the doubts it expressed in Tomic, it is possible for Article 5 to apply in an expulsion case. Hence, the Court considers that a Contracting State would be in violation of Article 5 if it removed an applicant to a State where he or she was at real risk of a flagrant breach of that Article. However, as with Article 6, a high threshold must apply. A flagrant breach of Article 5 would occur only if, for example, the receiving State arbitrarily detained an applicant for many years without any intention of bringing him or her to trial. A flagrant breach of Article 5 might also occur if an applicant would be at risk of being imprisoned for a substantial period in the receiving State, having previously been convicted after a flagrantly unfair trial."

2.10.3.   *No expulsion when there is the risk of a flagrant denial of justice (Article 6).*

See the same judgment of 17 January 2012 in *Othman (Abu Quatada)* v. United Kingdom:

"a.   The "flagrant denial of justice" test

258.   It is established in the Court's case-law that an issue might exceptionally be raised under Article 6 by an expulsion or extradition decision in circumstances where the fugitive had suffered or risked suffering a flagrant denial of justice in the requesting country. That principle was first set out in Soering v. the United Kingdom, 7 July 1989, § 113, Series A no. 161 and has been subsequently confirmed by the Court in a number of cases (...).

259.   In the Court's case-law, the term "flagrant denial of justice" has been synonymous with a trial which is manifestly contrary to the provisions of Article 6 or the principles embodied therein (...). Although it has not yet been required to define the term in more precise terms, the Court has nonetheless indicated that certain forms of unfairness could amount to a flagrant denial of justice. These have included:

- *conviction in absentia with no possibility subsequently to obtain a fresh determination of the merits of the charge (...);*
- *a trial which is summary in nature and conducted with a total disregard for the rights of the defence (...);*
- *detention without any access to an independent and impartial tribunal to have the legality the detention reviewed (...);*
- *deliberate and systematic refusal of access to a lawyer, especially for an individual detained in a foreign country (....).*

260.   It is noteworthy that, in the twenty-two years since the Soering judgment, the Court has never found that an expulsion would be in violation of Article 6. This fact, when taken with the examples given in the preceding paragraph, serves to underline the Court's view that "flagrant denial of justice" is a stringent test of unfairness. A flagrant denial of justice goes beyond mere irregularities or lack of safeguards in the trial procedures such as might result in a breach of Article 6 if occurring within the Contracting State itself. What is required is a breach of the principles of fair trial guaranteed by Article 6 which is so fundamental as to amount to a nullification, or destruction of the very essence, of the right guaranteed by that Article.

261.   In assessing whether this test has been met, the Court considers that the same standard and burden of proof should apply as in Article 3 expulsion cases. Therefore, it is for the applicant to adduce evidence capable of proving that there are substantial grounds for believing that, if he is removed from a Contracting State, he would be exposed to a real risk of being subjected to a flagrant denial of justice. Where such evidence is adduced, it is for the Government to dispel any doubts about it (...).

262. Finally, given the facts of the present case, the Court does not consider it necessary to determine whether a flagrant denial of justice only arises when the trial in question would have serious consequences for the applicant. It is common ground in the present case that the sentences which have already been passed on the applicant in absentia, and to which he would be exposed on any retrial, are substantial terms of imprisonment.

b. Does the admission of evidence obtained by torture amount to a flagrant denial of justice?

263. The Court agrees with the Court of Appeal that the central issue in the present case is the real risk that evidence obtained by torture of third persons will be admitted at the applicant's retrial. Accordingly, it is appropriate to consider at the outset whether the use at trial of evidence obtained by torture would amount to a flagrant denial of justice. In common with the Court of Appeal (...), the Court considers that it would.

264. International law, like the common law before it, has declared its unequivocal opposition to the admission of torture evidence. There are powerful legal and moral reasons why it has done so.

It is true, as Lord Phillips observed in the House of Lords' judgment in the present case, that one of the reasons for the prohibition is that States must stand firm against torture by excluding the evidence it produces. Indeed, as the Court found in Jalloh, cited above, § 105, admitting evidence obtained by torture would only serve to legitimate indirectly the sort of morally reprehensible conduct which the authors of Article 3 of the Convention sought to proscribe.

There are, however, further and equally compelling reasons for the exclusion of torture evidence. As Lord Bingham observed in A and others no. 2, § 52, torture evidence is excluded because it is "unreliable, unfair, offensive to ordinary standards of humanity and decency and incompatible with the principles which should animate a tribunal seeking to administer justice." The Court agrees with these reasons: it has already found that statements obtained in violation of Article 3 are intrinsically unreliable (...). Indeed, experience has all too often shown that the victim of torture will say anything – true or not – as the shortest method of freeing himself from the torment of torture.

More fundamentally, no legal system based upon the rule of law can countenance the admission of evidence – however reliable – which has been obtained by such a barbaric practice as torture. The trial process is a cornerstone of the rule of law. Torture evidence damages irreparably that process; it substitutes force for the rule of law and taints the reputation of any court that admits it. Torture evidence is excluded to protect the integrity of the trial process and, ultimately, the rule of law itself.

265. These reasons underscore the primacy given to the prohibition on torture evidence in the Convention system and international law. For the Convention system, in its recent judgment in Gäfgen v. Germany [GC], no. 22978/05, §§ 165-167, ECHR 2010-..., the Court reiterated that particular considerations apply in respect of the use in criminal proceedings of evidence obtained in breach of Article 3. It observed:

> "The use of such evidence, secured as a result of a violation of one of the core and absolute rights guaranteed by the Convention, always raises serious issues as to the fairness of the proceedings, even if the admission of such evidence was not decisive in securing a conviction.
>
> Accordingly, the Court has found in respect of confessions, as such, that the admission of statements obtained as a result of torture or of other ill-treatment in breach of Article 3 as evidence to establish the relevant facts in criminal proceedings rendered the proceedings as a whole unfair. This finding applied irrespective of the probative value of the statements and irrespective of whether their use was decisive in securing the defendant's conviction.
>
> As to the use at the trial of real evidence obtained as a direct result of ill-treatment in breach of Article 3, the Court has considered that incriminating real evidence obtained as a result of acts of violence, at least if those acts had to be characterised as torture, should never be relied on as proof of the victim's guilt, irrespective of its probative value (references omitted)".
>
> Gäfgen reflects the clear, constant and unequivocal position of this Court in respect of torture evidence. It confirms what the Court of Appeal in the present case had already appreciated: in the Convention system, the prohibition against the use of evidence obtained by torture is fundamental. Gäfgen also confirms the Court of Appeal's view that there is a crucial difference between a breach of Article 6 because of the admission of torture evidence and breaches of Article 6 that are based simply on defects in the trial process or in the composition of the trial court (...)"

266. Strong support for that view is found in international law. Few international norms relating to the right to a trial are more fundamental than the exclusion of evidence obtained by torture. There are few international treaties which command as widespread support as UNCAT. One hundred and forty-nine States are party to its provisions, including all Member States of the Council of Europe (see paragraph 125 above). UNCAT reflects the clear will of the international community to further entrench the ius cogens prohibition on torture by taking a series of measures to eradicate torture and remove all incentive for its practice. Foremost among UNCAT's provisions is Article 15, which prohibits, in near absolute terms, the admission of torture evidence. It imposes a clear obligation on States. As the United Nations Committee Against Torture has made clear, Article 15 is broad in scope. It has been interpreted as applying to any proceedings, including, for instance, extradition proceedings (P.E. v. France; G.K. v. Switzerland; ..). P.E. and G.K. also show that Article 15 applies to "any statement" which is established to have been made as a result of torture, not only those made by the accused (...). Indeed, the only exception to the prohibition that Article 15 allows is in proceedings against a person accused of torture.

267. For the foregoing reasons, the Court considers that the admission of torture evidence is manifestly contrary, not just to the provisions of Article 6, but to the most basic international standards of a fair trial. It would make the whole trial not only immoral and illegal, but also entirely unreliable in its outcome. It would, therefore, be a flagrant denial of justice if such evidence were admitted in a criminal trial. The Court does not exclude that similar considerations may apply in respect of evidence obtained by other forms of ill-treatment which fall short of torture. However, on the facts of the present case (...), it is not necessary to decide this question."

2.11. Concluding remarks

I am deeply aware that the above reads like much Court and little of this author.

Still, even in the choice of the citations, one can try to express ones private opinions. What I wanted to indicate is that the Court's reasoning in asylum cases is a logical consequence of the Convention system as such. Everyone within the jurisdiction of the Contracting States has the right that his or her Convention rights are secured.

Practise shows that in 9 out of 10 cases introduced in Strasbourg by a failed asylum seeker, the application will simply fail because the national authorities did what they are supposed to do: applying an independent and rigorous scrutiny. In some cases the Court is forced to do its own rigorous examination whether there exists the alleged real risk. Taking into account what might be at stake: the life and limbs of a fellow human being, there are some cases in which one cannot be rigorous enough.

Egbert Myjer

Former Judge of the European Court of Human Rights

3. Selected aspects of UNHCR's research findings and analysis in the 'Beyond Proof' report

Madeline Garlick

3.1. Credibility assessment: its central role in asylum claim determination

Credibility assessment is a key part of the adjudication of asylum applications. Deciding on a claim for international protection requires the decision-maker first to establish the material facts in the case, and credibility assessment is an integral part of this first stage. It involves a determination of whether and which of the applicant's statements and other evidence relating to the material elements of the claim can be accepted. Those parts of the evidence which are accepted as credible will generally be taken into account in determining whether the applicant has a well-founded fear of persecution in terms of the 1951 Convention relating to the Status of Refugees (1951 Convention) or faces a real risk of suffering serious harm, including in the European Union (EU) context under the Qualification Directive[41] (or QD), if returned to his or her country of origin, or in the case of a stateless person, to his or her country of former habitual residence.

In 2012, the United Nations High Commissioner for Refugees (UNHCR) conducted research and analysis into the practice of credibility assessment in EU asylum processes, as part of a joint project involving the Hungarian Helsinki Committee, UNHCR and the International Association of Refugee Law Judges and Asylum Aid (UK). The project, *Towards Improved Asylum Decision-Making in the EU* (also known as 'CREDO' sought to promote a harmonized approach, reflecting relevant provisions from EU law and international and regional standards. The final report from UNHCR's component of the project, entitled *Beyond Proof: Credibility Assessment in EU asylum systems*[42], was published in May 2013. This piece highlights selected elements emerging from that report.

In its research, UNHCR noted a trend across EU Member States indicating that many negative decisions on applications for international protection at first instance are based on findings that key elements of the applicants' statements were not credible. While recognizing the different national legal traditions within the EU, UNHCR also noted that there is not a common understanding of, nor approach to, the credibility assessment among Member States.

---

41 Directive 2011/95/EU of the European Parliament and of the Council of 13 December 2011 on standards for the qualification of third-country nationals or stateless persons as beneficiaries of international protection, for a uniform status for refugees or for persons eligible for subsidiary protection, and for the content of the protection granted.

42 UNHCR, *Beyond Proof: Credibility Assessment in EU asylum systems,* May 2013. The full report is available at <http://www.unhcr.org/51a8a08a9.html> and an Executive Summary at <www.unhcr.org/eu>.

Apart from limited guidance on some aspects of credibility assessment in Article 4 QD and some relevant provisions in the Asylum Procedures Directive,[43] the EU asylum *acquis* provides little guidance on this core aspect of asylum claim determination. The UNHCR Handbook on Procedures and Criteria for Determining Refugee Status, (UNHCR, Handbook), and the UNHCR Note on Burden and Standard of Proof, offer some additional guidance. Given the complexity of the issue and its importance for asylum procedures, it would appear that further clarification, analysis and guidance would be valuable for asylum decision-makers at first instance, in Europe and elsewhere.

3.2. Challenges arising in the credibility assessment in asylum procedures

The task of gathering relevant information to substantiate an application, and determining whether the applicant's statements relating to the material facts of the claim can be accepted, is extremely complex. The challenges of credibility assessment in the asylum procedure are often compounded by cultural and other differences between the applicant and the interviewer and/or decision-maker, among other things. In addition, the reality facing determining authorities is that there is often a paucity of documentary and other evidence confirming or supporting an applicant's statements. Evidence, which is available, may be fragmentary and unclear.

It is apparent that multi-lingual and cross-cultural communication in the asylum procedure increases the scope for misunderstandings and errors. The decision-maker's ability to conduct a fair assessment of credibility is affected by the quality of first instance asylum procedures, including the opportunity for and quality of personal interview(s); the accuracy of interpretation and translation; the accuracy and detail of written interview reports; the pro-activity and quality of the determining authority's independent fact-finding enquiries; and country of origin information (COI) and other information resources available to the decision-maker. It is also affected by the length of the procedure, procedural rules, and the availability and competence of human resources.

In light of these widely recognized challenges, it was surprising to note that many decision-makers interviewed in the research stated that the credibility assessment was not one that they found particularly difficult, and that it was a straightforward task.

3.3. Principles and standards relevant to credibility assessment

Despite relatively little explicit guidance, decision-makers do not have unfettered discretion in the assessment of credibility in the asylum procedure. They are required to adhere to fundamental principles and standards, derived from the legislative instruments of international human rights treaties and EU law, as expressed in the decisions and guidance of international and regional bodies such

---

43 Directive 2005/85/EC of 1 December 2005 on minimum standards on procedures in Member States for granting and withdrawing refugee status.

as the CJEU, the ECtHR, CAT and UNHCR. At the national level, courts have also contributed to the development of standards for credibility assessment in their jurisprudence. Moreover, some states and judicial bodies have produced specific guidance on credibility assessment.

The following are key principles and standards that have been identified in the course of UNHCR's research as relevant for the credibility assessment:

a. Shared duty: The duty to substantiate the application lies 'in principle' with the applicant. However, as the CJEU has stated in the 2012 case of *M.M. v. Minister for Justice*, Equality and Law Reform, Ireland, Attorney General, "the fact remains that it is the duty of the Member State to cooperate with the applicant at the stage of determining the relevant elements of that application."

b. Individual assessment: The credibility assessment must be conducted on an individual basis, taking into account the individual and contextual circumstances of the applicant.

c. Objective and impartial assessment: Decision-makers should neither prejudge the case nor approach the task with scepticism or a "refusal" mind-set. Decision-makers should be aware that their own values, prejudices and views, emotional and physical state can all affect the objectivity of their assessments, and should strive to minimize these.

d. Evidence-based assessment: Credibility findings have to be supported by the evidence. Adverse credibility findings should not be based on unfounded assumptions, subjective speculation, conjecture, stereotyping, intuition, or gut feelings.

e. Focus on the material facts: The credibility assessment should focus on those facts asserted by the applicant that are identified as material for qualification for international protection. Adverse credibility findings must be substantial in nature and not relate only to minor matters.

f. Opportunity for applicant to comment on potentially significant adverse credibility findings: The applicant should have an opportunity to clarify and/or provide explanations to address any potential adverse credibility findings. This stems from the right to be heard and of defence.

g. Credibility assessment based on entire evidence: The credibility assessment must be based on the entirety of the available relevant evidence as submitted by the applicant and gathered by the determining authority by its own means, including additional explanations and documentary or other evidence provided by the applicant.

h. Close and rigorous scrutiny: The assessment of the credibility of the asserted material facts must be carried out with close and rigorous scrutiny, paying due attention to the observations submitted by the applicant. Decision-makers are required to dispel any doubts they may retain.

i. Benefit of the doubt: The principle of the benefit of the doubt reflects recognition of the considerable difficulties applicants face in obtaining and providing evidence to support their claim, as well as the potentially grave consequences of a wrongful denial of international protection. Applying the benefit of the doubt allows the decision-maker to reach a clear conclusion to accept an asserted material fact as credible where an element of doubt remains.

j. Clear and unambiguous credibility findings and a structured approach: The decision-maker should reach clear and unambiguous findings on the credibility of the identified material facts and explicitly state whether the asserted material fact is accepted as credible or not accepted. A structured approach to the assessment of credibility supports the appropriate application of the above-mentioned standards.

Some of these elements and standards are explained further below, and discussed in detail in the *Beyond Proof* report.

3.4.   A multidisciplinary approach

Expectations regarding the applicant's ability to substantiate his or her application, the indicators used to assess the credibility of the applicant's statements and the criteria applied in determining whether to afford the applicant the benefit of the doubt are all based on assumptions about human memory, behaviour, values, attitudes, perceptions of and responses to risk, as well as on how a genuine account is presented. However, scientific research has shown that many of these assumptions do not accord with what is now known about human memory, behaviour, and perceptions. It confirms that human memory, behaviour and perceptions vary widely and unpredictably as they are affected by a wide range of factors and circumstances.

For this reason, the credibility assessment must be conducted taking into account fully the individual and contextual circumstances of the applicant. This requires the decision-maker to try to bridge geographical, cultural, socio-economic, gender, educational and religious gaps, and take account of different individual experiences, temperaments and attitudes. Decision-makers also need to be aware of the factors that may influence their own approaches to credibility. His or her assessment will benefit greatly from an awareness of factors, processes and elements in different disciplinary fields, including psychology, the science of human memory, gender and sociology, among others, relating to the perception and expression of experiences of persecution and serious harm. These should not be perceived as aspects separate from or opposed to the legal requirements of asylum decision-making. Indeed, taking elements relevant to the individual and contextual circumstances principles can constitute a legal requirement. Some of these aspects are discussed below.

3.4.1.   The applicant's individual and contextual circumstances

The applicant's individual and contextual circumstances should be taken into account in an integrated manner in all aspects of the credibility assessment. This includes, for instance, in determining whether the applicant has made a genuine effort to substantiate the application; whether the authority has discharged its duty to cooperate in this process; whether specific indicators are reliable indicators of the credibility of the applicant's information; whether explanations given for credibility problems are reasonable; whether the applicant's reasons for any lack of supporting evidence are satisfactory; or whether the principle of the benefit of the doubt should be applied to facts for which an element of doubt remains.

UNHCR's research revealed some good practice in this regard in EU Member States. Relevant factors that need to be taken into account include:

a. the limits and variations of human memory, in particular the wide-ranging variability in people's ability to record, retain, and retrieve memories; in the accuracy of memories for dates, times, appearance of common objects, proper names, and verbatim verbal exchanges (the recall of which is nearly always reconstructed from inference, estimation and guesswork). Directly relevant are also the impact of high levels of emotion on the encoding of any memory; and the influence on memory of the questioning and the way questions are asked;

b. the impact of trauma and other mental ill-health on memory, behaviour and testimony;

c. the influence of factors such as disorientation, anxiety, fear, lack of trust in authorities or interpreters on the disclosure of material facts and submission of other evidence;

d. the influences of stigma, shame, fear of rejection by family and community, which may also inhibit disclosure. Stigma may also account for the lack of documentary or other evidence, including under- reporting of incidents of violence, and limits on their inclusion in country of origin information (COI);

e. the influence on knowledge, memory, behaviour and testimony of aspects of the applicant's background, such as age, culture, education, gender, sexual orientation or gender identity, profession, socio-economic status, religion, values, and past experiences.

UNHCR's research has shown that international and national jurisprudence and judicial guidance recognize that the need to cope with traumatic experiences affects memory. These also acknowledge the consequent impact on an applicant's testimony and behaviour, even with regard to inconsistencies about material facts. Fear or lack of trust in state authorities can also explain a failure to disclose some evidence in an interview.

UNHCR's review of practice in several Member States revealed some helpful references to the need to consider the individual and contextual circumstances of the applicant. However, in general, UNHCR's research suggested that the credibility assessment undertaken by determining authorities may not be sufficiently informed by and/or in line with the substantial body of scientific evidence in the relevant fields. UNHCR's research revealed that often written internal notes and decisions in individual cases did not acknowledge relevant individual and contextual circumstances that might affect aspects of credibility assessment. As such, it was not always clear from the case-file materials whether the applicant's individual and contextual circumstances had been taken into account.

3.5. Factors affecting the decision-maker

Just as the individual and contextual circumstances of an applicant are crucial to the credibility assessment, so too is an awareness on the part of decision-makers of the influence of their own individual and contextual circumstances on the decision-making process. The need for objectivity and impartiality requires decision-makers to be aware of the extent to which their own thought processes, emotional and physical state, background, values, beliefs and life experiences may influence their decision-making.

One way in which decisions can be inappropriately subjective is through the unacknowledged influence of the decision-maker's background and culture. Societal, political and institutional pressure to prevent abuse of the asylum system may also subconsciously influence the mind-set of the decision-maker, so that decision-makers approach the credibility assessment with scepticism. UNHCR found that although decision-makers expressed their intention to start the examination with an open mind, some also expressed the view that the majority of asylum applicants are economic migrants. Scepticism or a "refusal" mind-set may prejudice and distort the gathering of facts and the assessment of the applicant's statements. The decision-maker's task is to uphold fundamental human rights through the recognition of applicants who are in need of international protection. Determining authorities can assist individual decision-makers in this task by taking appropriate steps to ensure an institutional mind-set that is protection-oriented and an institutional culture that is protection-sensitive.

Decision-makers also need to be aware of situations in which their fact-finding, reasoning and decisions might be guided primarily by intuition rather than by consideration of all available evidence. Given the repetitive nature of the task, UNHCR's research highlighted a risk that decision-makers may, consciously or unconsciously, categorize applications into generic case-profiles with pre-determined assumptions regarding credibility. Of the decision-makers interviewed in one Member State, a majority stated that when they heard similar stories over and over again, they concluded the stories were false.

Previous findings of credibility or non-credibility with regard to similar applications concerning the same country of origin or habitual residence should not result in predetermined assumptions about credibility. Conversely, the fact that one application is substantively different from other applications relating to the same country of origin should also not result in such assumptions. Routine exposure to narratives of torture, violence, inhuman and degrading treatment can also take its psychological toll on examiners. Examiners may suffer psychological distress due to their exposure to such evidence - so-called vicarious trauma - and employ natural coping strategies, which can involuntarily compromise their impartiality. They may find the content of the evidence so horrific that they are tempted to reject it as unimaginable, fabricated and therefore lacking credibility. Disbelief is a very human coping strategy, but it undermines objectivity and impartiality. Emotional detachment may be viewed as essential to maintain objectivity. However, decision-makers must ensure that such detachment does not translate into reluctance to engage with the applicant's narrative, and/or disbelief. UNHCR's research revealed that self-awareness existed among some decision-makers of case-hardening, credibility fatigue and burn-out.

UNHCR's research underlined the importance of decision-makers understanding how their thought processes, individual background and physical and mental state affect their assessments of credibility. Moreover, it underlined the importance of adequate and accessible support mechanisms for decision-makers, as well as strategies that address the psychological impact of their tasks. The research also highlighted that while jurisprudence and guidance acknowledges the relativity of culture, few court rulings have articulated the impact of the other factors on decision-making. This emerges in contrast to academic research examining those factors.

3.6. Gathering the facts

The task of gathering relevant information to substantiate the application and examining it in light of the individual and contextual circumstances of the applicant enables the decision-maker to determine whether and which of the statements and other evidence relating to core elements of the application can be accepted. It is, therefore, essential that as much relevant information as possible is gathered in each case. Both the applicant and the determining authority must cooperate in this process.

Under Article 4 (1) QD, "Member States may consider it the duty of the applicant to submit as soon as possible all the elements needed to substantiate the application for international protection.." However, where Member States do consider that it is the duty of the applicant to substantiate the application, this duty rests only 'in principle' on the applicant. While the relevant facts will have to be furnished in the first place by the applicant, through provision of statements and other evidence, the process of gathering information with respect to the application should thereafter be collaborative.

It is important to recall that the first instance determination of eligibility for international protection is not an adversarial process. Bearing this in mind, in some cases it may be for the determining authority to gather evidence by its own means, including any evidence that supports the application. This flows from several factors inherent in the asylum process: the manifest difficulties for applicants in providing information and supporting their statements with documentary and other evidence; the gravity of the possible consequences of a wrong determination; the fact that the duty to ascertain and evaluate all relevant facts is shared; the duty of the determining authority to conduct a close and rigorous examination; the requirement that the determining authority's credibility findings have an evidentiary basis; and the greater resources that will generally be available to the determining authority to gather evidence compared with the applicant.

UNHCR's research considered state law and practice relating to the nature and extent of the applicant's duty in principle to substantiate the application; the responsibilities of the determining authority to facilitate and assist the applicant in the substantiation of the application and to gather evidence by its own means including, where necessary, in support of the application; and how these relate to the credibility assessment.

3.6.1. The applicant's duty in principle to substantiate the application

Article 4(2) QD lists the relevant elements required for the substantiation of an application, which:

> "consist of the applicant's statements and all the documentation at the applicant's disposal regarding the applicant's age, background, including that of relevant relatives, identity, nationality(ies), country(ies) and place(s) of previous residence, previous asylum applications, travel routes, travel documents and the reasons for applying for international protection."

It is important to emphasize that the applicant's duty to substantiate the application does not entail a duty to provide documentary or other evidence in support of every asserted fact. Some asserted facts are not susceptible to support from documentary or other evidence; the applicant may have arrived with the barest necessities and without documentary or other evidence; the applicant's circumstances may make it impossible to obtain relevant documentary or other evidence. Therefore, an applicant is only required to make an effort to support his or her statements by any available evidence; and to the extent practically possible. The applicant's statements, which in any case are a key source of evidence, may be the only evidence that the applicant is able to furnish. In some cases, the applicant's statements alone may suffice to substantiate the application.

With regard to credibility assessment, a decision-maker cannot disbelieve the statements of an applicant merely because he or she furnishes no documentary or other evidence to support his or her testimony. Under Article 4(5)(a) and (b) QD, where aspects of the applicant's statements are not supported by documentary or other evidence, those aspects shall not need confirmation when, inter alia:

> "the applicant has made a genuine effort to substantiate his application; and all relevant elements at the applicant's disposal have been submitted, and a satisfactory explanation has been given regarding any lack of other relevant elements."

UNHCR's research highlighted the need to stress that the applicant's statements constitute evidence capable of substantiating the application. Evidence may be oral or documentary, from the applicant or experts, family members and other witnesses. Documentary evidence includes written, graphic, digital, and visual materials. The research revealed some good practice where the applicant's statements were clearly regarded as evidence capable of substantiating the application and were accordingly assessed for credibility. However, some written decisions appeared indicative of a lack of consideration of the applicant's statements as evidence and/ or recognition that each asserted material fact need not necessarily be supported by documentary or other evidence.

Some applicants may, however, be placed in a 'catch-22' situation whereby it may be considered adverse to their case if they provide no documentary evidence. They may, however, also be disadvantaged if they provide documentary evidence in support of some of the facts of the application, as they are then expected to provide evidence in support of *all* the asserted facts. In cases such as these, which were identified in UNHCR's research, the applicant's inability to produce further documentary evidence in support of a material fact was seen to undermine the credibility of the asserted fact. Moreover, on the whole, decision-makers in these cases did not seek an explanation from the applicant for the lack of specific documentary evidence. Therefore, they appeared to base their finding on a non-evidence based on an assumption that the specific evidence was available, but not furnished by the applicant.

3.6.2. Documentation and other evidence 'at the applicant's disposal'

Article 4(1) QD provides that Member States may consider it the duty of the applicant to submit '*all the documentation at the applicant's disposal*'. UNHCR's research sought to understand what interpretation is given to this term, as well as to the term '*satisfactory explanation*' (for a lack of relevant elements) used in Article 4(5) QD. In general, where a decision-maker finds that an explanation for a lack of evidence is not satisfactory, the decision-maker considers the evidence is at the applicant's disposal, but has not been submitted. Such a finding may be seen as bearing on the credibility of the applicant's statements.

UNHCR's research confirmed that evidence '*at the applicant's disposal*' is understood to mean more than documentation in the applicant's possession. For example, legislation and policy guidance indicate that evidence is considered to be at the applicant's disposal when the applicant may reasonably be expected to be able to obtain it. In one Member State, applicants are required to do everything *in their power* to gather evidence in support of the application, if need be with the assistance of family members or other contacts.

However, UNHCR's research revealed that some determining authorities have onerous expectations regarding what documentary or other evidence applicants should possess, and/or can be reasonably expected to obtain and submit in support of applications. These high expectations seem to stem, in part, from unfounded theories or preconceptions about human behaviour and interaction. They seem to assume that those in need of international protection, for example, will:

- know in advance of flight from the country of origin, or place of habitual residence, that documentary or other evidence will be relevant if he or she applies for international protection in another country;
- know what specific documentary evidence will be relevant, and take this evidence with them on the journey to the putative country of asylum, looking after it carefully and keeping it in their possession at all times, regardless of the needs of family remaining in the country of origin, the hazards of the journey or advice or instructions from others;
- not place trust in the advice of agents or others - but place trust in national authorities;
- not willingly dispose of or surrender any documentary or other evidence unless subject to coercion or force.

Such assumptions raise empirical questions about what people actually do know and how they actually behave when fleeing in fear, as well as how they decide who to trust. Unreasonably high expectations that an applicant can submit documentary evidence may unwittingly encourage applicants to submit documentary evidence, including false documents, in support of all asserted material facts at all costs. UNHCR's research highlighted the importance of awareness on the part of decision-makers that the applicant's statements constitute evidence capable of substantiating the application. Determining whether an explanation is satisfactory, in effect, means assessing the credibility of any explanation offered in accordance with relevant credibility indicators (discussed below and in the *Beyond Proof* report), and in light of the individual and contextual circumstances of the applicant.

3.6.3. Duty of the applicant to substantiate the application 'as soon as possible'

The first sentence of Article 4(1) QD states that:

> *"Member States may consider it the duty of the applicant to submit* **as soon as possible** *all the elements needed to substantiate the application for international protection"* (emphasis added).

It is widely recognized that corroboration is one of the most effective means of supporting the credibility of an applicant's statements. In the interests of ensuring a correct credibility assessment, it is therefore important that determining authorities offer applicants sufficient time to obtain documentary or other evidence, when this can reasonably be obtained and could help in the assessment of credibility.

The interpretation of '*as soon as possible*' needs to be informed by an understanding of the applicant's circumstances – including those that may inhibit disclosure of information and affect the possibility of obtaining supporting evidence. The term '*as soon as possible*' should also be interpreted with reference to the point in time at which the applicant is informed in a language and a manner he or she understands of his or her duty to substantiate the application and how to fulfil this obligation; and also, if relevant, the when he or she is requested to obtain any further specific or additional evidence.

Based on the *Beyond Proof* research, it appears some Member States consider that it is the duty of the applicant to submit evidence 'as soon as possible'. What this means in practice is intrinsically linked to the timeframes and arrangements in national procedures. As these vary from state to state, from procedure to procedure, and from decision-maker to decision-maker (who may or may not wish to exercise discretion and flexibility), some applicants have greater time than others within which to substantiate their applications. Across the Member States participating in UNHCR's research, some applicants had three months or more within which to substantiate their applications, while other applicants were required to substantiate their applications within just a few weeks of registration of the application. In one Member State, stakeholders expressed concern regarding the time pressures within the procedure and considered that this negatively affected the credibility assessment.

UNHCR understands that determining authorities and decision-makers may work under political and institutional imperatives to meet targets for decision-making. However, expediency should not be achieved at the expense of fairness, justice and fundamental human rights. The credibility assessment is, by nature, extremely difficult and challenging, and the task is seriously hampered when timeframes are so short and/ or procedures are such that they do not allow the applicant to present his or her case as fully as possible. This is so also where they do not allow the applicant to obtain documentary or other evidence that would support an asserted material fact. In the interests of ensuring a correct credibility assessment, it is important that determining authorities have as much available and relevant information as possible. Flexibility is in the interests both of the determining authority and the applicant with regard to time frames.

3.7. The duty of the determining authority with regard to substantiation of the application

The second sentence of Article 4(1) QD states that:

> *"in cooperation with the applicant, it is the duty of the Member State to assess the relevant elements of the application." The Court of Justice of the EU, in its MM decision, has stated that "the fact remains that it is the duty of the Member State to cooperate with the applicant at the stage of determining the relevant elements of that application."*

The determining authority has a duty to provide information and guidance to the applicant on his or her duty to substantiate the application, and how to discharge this duty; provide guidance through the use of appropriate questioning during the interview; give the applicant an opportunity to clarify any potential adverse credibility findings; and use all means at its disposal to gather relevant evidence, including where necessary in support of the application, and base the credibility assessment on all materials submitted by the applicant and gathered by its own means.

3.7.1. *Provision of information and guidance to the applicant*

The applicant cannot be expected to know that he or she has a duty to substantiate the application, how to discharge this duty, and what facts and type of documentary or other evidence may be relevant. The determining authority, therefore, must ensure that the applicant is assisted in this regard. In the Member States surveyed, applicants are generally informed via information brochures of their duty to substantiate the application. Applicants are further informed of this duty by legal advisers and/or by interviewers. In some Member States, brochures also indicated some of the documentary or other evidence that might be useful to support the application. In one Member State, if an applicant is identified as illiterate, the content of the information brochure should also be explained to him or her at the personal interview.

UNHCR observed some examples of good guidance where the interviewer is encouraged to invite the applicant to submit specific documentary evidence. However, UNHCR also reviewed a number of cases in which an absence of specific documentary evidence was considered to undermine the credibility of an asserted material fact; even though other supporting documentary evidence of the fact had been submitted, and the applicant had neither been advised to submit that specific evidence, nor asked to explain its absence.

3.7.2. Provision of guidance through the use of appropriate questioning during the interview

In its research, UNHCR found that questioning generally was coherent. A technique known as 'signposting' to indicate shifts in the focus of the questioning was observed. For example: *"Now I'm going to ask you some questions about (...)"*. This may usefully be considered by decision-makers to avoid changing abruptly the focus of the questioning from one question to the next, an approach that may result in inconsistencies in the applicant's statements.

UNHCR's research also indicated that in some cases, interviewing techniques sufficed to elicit the relevant facts in sufficient detail to provide a basis for the credibility assessment. However, there were some notable exceptions. For example, UNHCR observed cases in which a lack of detail was used as an indicator of non-credibility, notwithstanding the fact that questioning during the personal interview was not tailored to elicit the relevant detail.

The personal interview is an essential component of the credibility assessment. It should provide the opportunity for the applicant to present all the necessary information related to the core elements of the claim, and the decision-maker to probe the credibility of the asserted material facts. Contradictions, inconsistencies, a lack of detail and omissions in the applicant's statements may be indicative of shortcomings in the conduct and environment of the interview rather than indicative of the non-credibility of the applicant. UNHCR's research underlined the need to emphasize that credibility of asserted facts should not be impugned on grounds of a lack of detail if the context of or questioning during the interview was not conducive to or hampered disclosure of details.

3.7.3. Providing the applicant with an opportunity to clarify potential adverse credibility findings

It is very possible that a perceived lack of detail, omission, inconsistency or implausibility in the information provided by the applicant may legitimately be explained. As credibility assessments should be based, as far as possible, on reliable evidence, it is crucially important that the determining authority affords applicants a reasonable opportunity to clarify issues that may lead to adverse credibility findings. Moreover, explanations offered by the applicant should be duly considered before a final decision is taken.

UNHCR's research indicated that the extent to which applicants are afforded such an opportunity varies from Member State to Member State, and from application to application. However, UNHCR noted a number of decisions in which negative credibility findings were based on inconsistencies and discrepancies that the applicant was not given the opportunity to address during the procedure. As such, the applicant was not able to provide an explanation or mitigating circumstance before a final decision was taken.

UNHCR welcomes national guidance, which requires interviewers to raise matters that may be the source of adverse credibility findings during the personal interview. However, an examiner may only become aware of a lack of detail, an inconsistency and/or implausibility *after* the personal interview. The failure on the part of interviewers to identify inconsistencies, discrepancies and implausibilities at interview and to put them all to the applicant may be due to insufficient time for, or poor, preparation; a lack of focus on the details of the applicant's account during the interview; and/or a tendency to defer identification of adverse credibility indicators until after the interview.

UNHCR understands that Member States are mindful of the time and financial resources required to conduct the examination of applications for international protection. However, it is in the interests both of applicants and Member States to ensure that first instance decision-making is fair and that relevant standards are upheld. This may require determining authorities to offer a further personal interview or otherwise provide a means for applicants to explain apparent indications of non-credibility before a final decision.

3.7.4.   The determining authority's duty to gather by its own means evidence bearing on the application

The duty to submit elements in support of an application for international protection lies in principle with the applicant, but it may be for the examiner to use all the means at his disposal to produce the necessary evidence in support of the application. Moreover, due to the individual and contextual circumstances of some applicants, the determining authority may need to assume greater responsibility to gather evidence with respect to the application. Case-law of the European Court of Human Rights has established that it is the duty of national authorities to conduct a thorough and rigorous assessment in order to dispel any doubt regarding the credibility of asserted facts, given the importance of Article 3 ECHR and the irreversible nature of the harm in case of return to ill treatment. This may require national authorities to take proactive steps to obtain evidence, which includes but is not limited to COI, expert evidence, witness statements or other information from reliable sources.

The need to gather relevant COI is recognized in the laws and guidance of Member States. In general, UNHCR's research indicated awareness among decision-makers of the need to gather COI. However, in some cases in UNHCR's research, no COI was referred to or included in the case file by the decision-maker, beyond information obtained from the applicant, when relevant COI was available. In some cases, only COI supporting the decision-maker's credibility findings was added to the case file. UNHCR's research also indicated notable variations between Member States in the gathering of other evidence such as expert evidence (for example, document verification, language analysis etc.) or specific information.

It is clear that the quality of the credibility assessment is affected by the extent to which the determining authority fulfils its duty objectively and impartially to gather evidence bearing upon asserted material facts. The determining authority must ensure that it gathers any available evidence, including COI or other material that might confirm (and not just refute) the facts or the credibility of the applicant's statements. A failure to gather specific or general information or expert evidence bearing on a material fact, when this is possible, may be at odds with the requirement of close and rigorous scrutiny, and undermines the validity of the credibility assessment.

3.7.5.   Basing the credibility assessment on the entire evidence

The credibility assessment should be based on the entirety of the available relevant evidence as submitted by the applicant and gathered by the determining authority by its own means. It was sometimes difficult to deduce with certainty from UNHCR's review of case files whether the credibility assessment had been conducted in the light of all available evidence relevant to the application. Some internal notes and written decisions did not mention whether specific documentary or other evidence submitted by the applicant had been taken into account or not.

However, UNHCR's research highlighted several cases in which it appeared that the credibility assessment was, or may have been, based on only a portion of the available relevant evidence. In one Member State, UNHCR observed that although the written decisions referred to the documentary and other evidence adduced by the applicant, further evidence submitted in support of an asserted material fact was often not assessed. This was done on the basis that the applicant's statements alone were considered credible (or not credible). Rather than assessing the other evidence together with the oral statements and reaching a credibility conclusion on the basis of all available evidence, non-credibility findings were sometimes based solely on the oral evidence, and this finding was given as the reason for not assessing the other available evidence. Written decisions often stated that submitted documentation was accorded no value because it had not been supported by credible statements. UNHCR reiterates that the assessment of the credibility of asserted material facts is likely to be flawed if it is based on a portion of the available evidence relating to a particular fact, rather than on the entirety of the available evidence.

3.8.   A structured approach to the credibility assessment

UNHCR's observation of state practice suggests the need for a structured approach to ensure that the credibility assessment adheres to relevant principles and standards. UNHCR favours a structured approach underpinned by a focus on the material facts presented by the applicant, taking into account his or her individual and contextual circumstances as informed by evidence from the relevant disciplinary fields. UNHCR has identified the following key steps in the credibility assessment:

a. In cooperation with the applicant, gather the information to substantiate the application.
b. Determine the material facts, taking into account the applicant's experiences or fear of ill-treatment, torture, persecution, harm, or other serious human rights violations, as well as the wider legal, institutional, political, social, religious and cultural context of his or her country of origin, or place of habitual residence, the human rights situation, the level of violence, and available state protection.
c. Assess the credibility of each material fact. Each material fact should be assessed, taking into account the applicant's statements and all other evidence that bears on the fact, through the lens of the following   five credibility

indicators, taking into account the applicant's individual and contextual circumstances and the reasonableness of his or her explanations:

- Sufficiency of detail and specificity;
- Internal consistency;
- Consistency with information provided by any family members and/or other witnesses;
- Consistency with available specific and general information, including country of origin information (COI); and
- Plausibility.

UNHCR's research found that in some Member States, in practice, demeanour was also considered as an additional indicator of credibility. However, there are important limitations on the utility and reliability of demeanour as a credibility indicator, which are set out in further detail in the *Beyond Proof* report. UNHCR also underlines, in its analysis of credibility indicators and their application in practice, that no single credibility indicator is a certain determinant of credibility or non-credibility.

d. Determine which material facts can be:

- accepted as credible;
- rejected as not credible; and
- those material facts for which an element of doubt remains.

An asserted fact may be accepted because it is sufficiently detailed, internally consistent and consistent with information provided by family members and witnesses; consistent with available specific and general objective information; and plausible when considered in light of the applicant's individual and contextual circumstances. Such facts may be accepted without reference to the principle of the benefit of the doubt.

An asserted fact may be rejected because, taking into account the reasonableness of the explanations provided by the applicant with regard to the potentially adverse credibility findings and the applicant's individual and contextual circumstances, the applicant's statements about that fact are not sufficiently detailed, consistent, and plausible and/or are contradicted by other reliable objective evidence. Again, such facts may be rejected without reference to the principle of the doubt because the principle cannot be applied to remedy what is clearly not credible based on all the available evidence.

e. Consider the application of the principle of the benefit of the doubt for those material facts for which an element of doubt remains, taking into account the applicant's individual and contextual circumstances.
f. Determine on the basis of all the information at hand, and the applicant's effort to substantiate the application, as well as his or her explanations for any apparent lack of credibility, whether the applicant's statements are on the whole coherent and plausible, and do not run counter to generally known facts.
g. Decide to accept the remaining facts as credible; or to reject the remaining facts as not credible.

h. State in the written decision all the material facts that have been accepted as credible and will inform the assessment of risk in stage two of the examination, and all the material facts that have been rejected as not credible, as well as the reasons underpinning these findings of facts.

3.9. Conclusion

UNHCR has aimed, through the *Beyond Proof* report and its participation in the CREDO project more broadly, to identify key concepts and insights into specific aspects of practice in relation to credibility assessment in European Union asylum procedures. The complexity of the subject and limited time and resources mean that it has not been possible to provide a comprehensive overview or comparative analysis of evidentiary rules and practices in the EU. UNHCR considers there are however some important issues emerging from the research that warrant further analysis, dialogue, research and consideration, including for asylum practitioners, decision-makers at first and later instances, judges, EU institutions, EASO, policy-makers and legislative bodies at European and national level, as well as academia and civil society.

Among UNHCR's observations from this research, variations in the three Member States under review were apparent in practically all aspects of the credibility assessment. These discrepancies could be indicative of wider variations and challenging issues across the EU Member States.

In some Member States, there may be a disparity between policy and practice in the credibility assessment. The research suggests that some decision-makers are unaware of the content of guidance, or that their content is unclear or mis-understood. This calls, in addition to further research, discussion and scrutiny of the issue (including by courts), and for enhanced training on credibility assessment for decision-makers across the EU.

Further reflection and discussion in the area of credibility assessment will be of value to all stakeholders involved in asylum systems in the EU. It would also assist states and other concerned bodies for whom credibility assessment continues to represent a major challenge in seeking to establish and reinforce quality and consistency in asylum decision-making in the EU.

Madeline Garlick

Head of Unit, Policy and Legal Support, Bureau for Europe, UNHCR

4.   Introduction to the Credo Project

Allan Mackey

4.1.   Background

The involvement of the IARLJ in professional development of judges in this field is a major objective of the association. It commenced significantly in 1998 with the publication of an 'International manual for new refugee law judges.' That manual, which included a section on Credibility Assessment by judges, has, with adaptation and improvement, been used by 'trainer' judges from the IARLJ with 'trainee' judges and others in about 200 courses in some 50 countries,. This included extensive use in the EU (2000-2008) in the 'new 12' member states, EU applicant and surrounding countries. An EU manual on CEAS, prepared by John Barnes, has been used extensively since published in 2007. With the rapid developments of both international and EU refugee and other protection law both manuals have dated quickly and need updating.

When the opportunity arose in late 2010, to join in the Credo project, with the Hungarian Helsinki Committee (HHC) and UNHCR, to prepare an extensive review, and a judicial guidance paper on Credibility assessment in the EU, the IARLJ (EU) quickly agreed to participate. I was later tasked as project director. It soon proved to be a much larger task than originally envisaged! However, I was soon hugely benefited by my co-author, John Barnes and an Editorial group of some 10 IARLJ (EU) members who are all highly experienced judges. Later an excellent consultation group of judges from all around Europe, and representatives from the UNHCR and EASO and HHC, were able to meet in Madrid in September 2012 and extensively review an advanced draft of the paper.[44]

4.2.   Who for, What for, What is included and Why?

4.2.1.   Who for?

It was agreed that this paper, whilst directed to judges considering refugee and subsidiary protection cases should aim to be instructive and relevant to all decision-makers, counsel and claimants in this unique field of law. The paper should provide guidance in best practices, criteria and standards for credibility assessment. The guidance is for judges determining both 'full merits reviews', and error of law only appeals. We trust the paper also provides assistance to: government first instance decision makers, claimants, counsel, the UNHCR, European Asylum Support Office (EASO), academics and NGOs working with claimants.

---

44   The full text of the Credo-document can be found on p. 89 ff.

4.2.2.   Main aims?

A fundamental aim of this paper is to set out, and explain for EU judges a set of substantively agreed judicial criteria and standards of best practice in credibility assessment within the EU. By using these we hope our paper may assist to ensure sound assessments of 'accepted past and present facts', about each claimant and these can be established as an essential first step in the full asylum assessment procedure. These accepted facts can be conveniently referred to as the claimant's 'accepted profile'.[45]

4.2.3.   What's included?

The full paper is divided into six parts. An abridged version, with hyperlinks to other parts of the full paper, is to be translated by HHC into French and German.

In Part I we set out the background to refugee and other protection law by first discussing the unique nature of decision-making in this arcane and highly specialised area of law, before exploring its comparatively recent origins. We then outline briefly the way in which the CEAS is both structured and works in practice and the role of the judge in these appeals. Part II then sets out, in nine steps, our suggested structured approach to judicial determination of appeals or reviews in which the full merits of the claimant's case require consideration. This is in chart form, with an explanation of each step to follow. Part III, is the heart of the paper. Here we set out judicial guidance on criteria and standards for credibility assessment, which are derived from best judicial practice both, within the EU and internationally. Parts IV and V then explore in greater detail the CEAS and the role of the judge, which were briefly introduced in Part I of the paper. Part VI is a discussion paper only on the highly relevant, but vexed, issues of burdens and standards of proof that may be applicable in credibility assessment of refugee and subsidiary protection claims.[46]

The criteria and standards recorded are primarily concerned with credibility issues which may arise in the consideration of refugee and subsidiary protection claims and appeals made under Directive 2004/83/EU (the 2004 QD). It is to be noted that Directive 2011/95/EU (the 2011 QD), in substitution for the 2004 Directive, was passed in December 2011, but comes fully into operation on 21 December 2013 (see Art 40, 2011 QD). References in the text are, however, generally to the 2004 Directive.[47]

---

45 The words 'accepted profile' used in this paper should not be confused with the terms 'profile' or 'profiling' commonly used in the criminal law or policing context. Its use here is to cover, holistically, all factors about a claimant accepted by the judge in the context of refugee and other international protection claims only.

46 Those who attended the Madrid workshop, that reviewed this paper in September 2012, agreed that these topics required much more debate and study by the IARLJ (European chapter) and others. A working party within the IARLJ (European chapter) to continue work on credibility assessment, (along with the optional approaches permitted to residual or "benefit" of the doubt issues by Article 4 QD) was established to direct this further study and will publish its findings through the IARLJ.

47 These both relate to minimum standards for the qualification and status of third-country nationals or stateless persons as refugees or persons who otherwise need international protection and the content of the protection granted. Neither Directive applies to Denmark and the later Directive applies to all Member States with the exception of Ireland and the United Kingdom who continue

4.2.4. Why?

Detailed analysis by the EC of the application of the QD and Procedures Directive 2005/85/EC (APD), as well as independent assessments by the UNHCR, academics and NGOs, have pointed to marked differences in the outcome of refugee and subsidiary protection claims (often where the factual situations are markedly similar) between member states (MS) throughout the EU. It also shows the highly important part that domestic MS methods, procedures and approaches to credibility assessment can play in creating those differences. Clearly to be effective, meaningful, and indeed 'credible', the QD, APD and all parts of the CEAS need to be seen to be harmoniously applied and interpreted such that similar cases should be treated alike and result in similar outcomes. Also so called 'asylum shopping' between MS should be minimised and thus the judiciary of each MS should be moving as closely as possible to common interpretations and assessment approaches.

4.3. The contextual use of the word 'credibility/credible' and contextual disambiguation

The first observation we found in our research was that there is actually little written in major decisions from higher EU or MS courts, or indeed academic commentary, on the issue of judicial guidance or commentary on credibility in the EU refugee assessment context. (Although there is some excellent MS and EAC/EASO first instance training material on the subject.) Thus finding, contextually, how the term 'credibility' is actually used in Courts' practices and decisions was a starting point. We found, particularly in the common law countries, the term is often used indiscriminately in two different contexts. (And serious confusion often arises because both uses are valid in lay, if not legal, usage.)

The first context, and the legally correct one, we argue, relates to: 'the *credibility* of a claimant's evidence, presented as their past and present factual background'. In the second context, we noted 'credibility' is often used 'loosely' to cover the 'credibility of the *claim* for recognition as a refugee or protected person'. In this second context the term 'credibility' is used as meaning *all* the evidence and assessment relevant to the claim for protection status (including the accepted past and present facts as found *and* all the COI, *and* expert *and* other evidence, *and* the actual assessment of a well-founded fear (real risk) of being persecuted on return etc.).

We address 'credibility' in the first context only in the paper both for clarity and also because the second contextual use is, we consider, wrong in law. As judges will be aware Art. 1A(2) of the Refugee Convention does not refer to the *credibility of the claim* but rather to whether there is a 'well-founded fear of being persecuted'. Thus reliance on a concept of the 'credibility of the claim for recognition as a refugee or a protected person' (or the wider second context) is, in

---

to be bound by the earlier 2004 Directive (see Recitals 50, 51 of 2011 QD). The differences between the two Directives are nevertheless, for our purposes, comparatively minor so that the general thrust of this paper is relevant to all EU Member States with the exception of Denmark.

our view, erroneous in law. (It appears the two contextual usages do arise in many EU languages, however in many jurisdictions the confusion is greatly reduced, in practice, by the manner and accepted procedure, in which issues are addressed and/or where there is always reference back to the GC/QD wording itself in the assessment process.

4.4.   Setting the scene

As can be seen above, and from the knowledge of those well experienced in refugee law and practice, it would not be of great benefit to judges and others, new to, or largely unfamiliar to the subject, to present a bald set of criteria and guidance standards on credibility assessment unless this was proceeded by a sound background explanation of the unique and arcane nature of refugee and other forms of complementary or subsidiary protection law, in the EU and internationally (recognising the primacy of the GC accorded in the CEAS). Hence we had to: 'Set the scene'. This required us to explain:

A. The unique character of decision-making in refugee and other international protection claims;
B. The legal framework and the CEAS;
C. The role of the judge in refugee and subsidiary protection cases and structured approach to decision making; and
D. The burden and standard of proof in refugee and subsidiary protection claims and appeals.

4.4.1.   Sub A

Within A. we noted:

- One party is a non-national individual claimant while the other is a state;
- The factual substance of every claim will be difficult to check and thus reference to the country information in other states will be needed;
- The focus of the case is significantly on the future, not the past.
- The core treaties, such as ECHR and GC, are living instruments;
- The decision-making is international rights-based, not domestic privilege-based;
- The principles of surrogate protection arise from international and EU treaty obligations;
- Refugee and subsidiary protection status are declaratory, not constitutive;
- Judicial independence and impartiality can be put under pressure from anti-refugee/migrant or societal pressures;
- Many claimants will have vulnerabilities inherent in their situation, thus the psychological and trauma dimensions affecting them must be considered;
- Claimants will often have difficulties in presenting corroborative evidence and thus careful attention is needed in the use and abuse of 'supporting' documentation, including web-sourced material; and
- Cross-cultural awareness and challenges of working through interpreters are the norm.

Whilst the first three are self-evident, the others needed explanation which we set out in the paper.

4.4.2.   Sub B

To explain B we needed to provide an overview of the historical development of refugee law, the CEAS and relevant EU law. This we have set out in Part IV of the paper.

4.4.3.   Sub C

Similarly with C 'The role of the judge', we have gone into in some depth in Part V of the full paper. In Part II we suggest a logical structure for decision making. Briefly summarised we see the judge's role, in a full merits review appeal, after 'credibility assessment' and making their findings of the accepted past and present facts (Steps 2 and 3 below), is:

- To decide whether the claimant is entitled to recognition as a person in need of international protection;
- As at the date of the hearing;
- By reference to the relevant provisions of the QD governing recognition of refugee and subsidiary protection status;
- On the totality of the evidence before the court;
- Including that obtained by the court of its own volition;
- Considered and assessed objectively;
- So as to establish whether;
- If then immediately returned to his country of origin;
- There is a well-founded fear of the claimant being persecuted (Article 13 refugee status recognition) or;
- If not recognised as a refugee pursuant to Article 13 of the QD;
- Whether, if so returned, substantial grounds have been shown for believing there is;
- A real risk that the claimant will suffer serious harm as defined in the QD (Article 18 subsidiary protection status recognition).

4.4.4.   Sub D

For D we considered that whilst Burden and Standard of Proof issues were not perhaps strictly part of credibility assessment it was essential for judges, working in this field, to understand the background to the issues of Proof in refugee and other protection law so the approaches taken to credibility assessment could be taken in the right overall context. Burden of Proof issues are probably widely understood across most MS jurisdictions; however the 'standard of proof' issue is a far more vexed one. Accordingly, and as all the judges involved in this project agreed, it needed more study and debate. We have thus prepared what we term a 'Discussion paper' only and this is set out in Part VI of the full paper.

4.5. A structured approach to decision making in status determination

We considered as important background for judges, new, or unfamiliar, to this area of law, who need, as a first step in assessment to establish the past and present facts about a claimant, that setting out the full structure of decision making, and an explanation of each step in decision making, would greatly assist them. Hence we suggest the nine steps in the Chart attached. We were able (with assistance from someone with far greater IT skills than us) to put a summary of the structure into a, hopefully useful, one page chart.

It will be seen that we place the 'credibility assessment' task is Issue 1-Step 2: *'Establishing the accepted facts of the claimant's past and present story'*. We term this the *'believability box'*. We then set out seven guidance factors that need to be taken into account in reaching conclusions at each step, including the criteria and standards set out in Part III — which is the core of the paper.

4.6. Judicial guidance for the assessment of credibility under the EU QD - Basic Criteria and Standards of Good Practice

4.6.1. Assumptions

We considered that, before setting out what we considered are the basic criteria applicable, a number of preliminary points of need recognition. These are:

a. It is the duty of claimants[48] to present their own applications for recognition of their status and each application is to be assessed on an individual basis (Article 4.1-4.5 QD).

b. The determination of eligibility for protection within the EU is an onerous and specialist task.[49] Whilst the initial source of judicial reference will be the national law of the Member State transposing the applicable EU Directives in the CEAS, it must always be borne in mind that this will be informed by the GC and other European and international human rights conventions themselves, together with judicial interpretation by courts over the past sixty years.[50]

c. Because the issues involved (for both claimants and states) are so serious in nature and involve fundamental principles of justice, only the highest standards of fairness are applicable.

d. The assessment of credibility of past and present facts (evidence) presented by a claimant is a tool used to establish the 'accepted profile' of the claimant and to determine their international protection needs. Thus, as shown in Part II

---

48 See discussion on burden of proof in Part VI (on p. 89 ff.).

49 See Part I.1 of full paper (on p. 89 ff.).

50 Certain national legislation of MS seeks to prescribe issues, which are to be reflected in the assessment of the claimant's credibility – e.g., s. 8 of the UK Asylum and Immigration (Treatment of Claimants, etc.) Act 2004. Such national legislation cannot be relied upon as a substitute for assessment of credibility being made on an *'individual, objective and impartial'* basis in order to comply with both EU and internationally recognised standards of decision-making – see, e.g., Article 47 EU Charter and Article 8 APD.

('The structured approach'), it is necessary to decide Issue 1 before moving on to Issue 2 ('the prospective risk').

e. This Guidance is based on EU administrative law principles, including the right to a fair and public hearing, equality of arms (*audi alteram partem*), proportionality, legal certainty, and the right to an effective remedy. These principles are set out in the core instruments of the EU (including the TFEU and the EU Charter) and the ECHR.[51]

f. The principles contained in this Guidance are derived from EU legislative instruments, the jurisprudence of relevant courts and the experience of the judges who have participated in this project.[52] In addition we have had regard to guidance from the UNHCR Handbook and Guidelines (2011 reprint) and leading academic publications.

g. In EU, and wider international law, there are some basic criteria (as set out below), applied in all valid judicial reasoning, to evaluate the 'lawfulness' of credibility assessment. These criteria, and the detailed standards of good practice that expand on them, specifically in the assessment of credibility in refugee and subsidiary protection cases, have been developed in asylum law and practice over the past 60 years. The explanatory memoranda of the EC make it clear that EU legislative principles are drawn largely from accepted international practices in the field of asylum and international human rights law and that in many instances the EU legislation is partly declaratory of the best international practice. A failure to apply these criteria and/or meet the standards, will, on judicial review, lead to consideration of whether an error of law in the decision making has rendered it unsustainable.

h. This Guidance is non-exhaustive. It includes, often with overlap between them, standards of good practice based on fundamental fairness, including procedural requirements and recognition of the specialised needs of vulnerable sub-groups of claimants.

4.6.2. Basic Criteria

a. Internal consistency: These are findings on consistencies or discrepancies within the statements and other evidence presented by claimants from their first meetings, applications, and personal interviews and examination at all stages of processing their application/appeal until final disposal.

b. External consistency: These are findings on consistencies or discrepancies between the statements of the claimants and all the external objective evidence, including duly weighted COI, expert and any other relevant evidence.

c. Impossibility: These are findings, which when set against objective internal or external evidence, show alleged 'facts', presented by a claimant, as impossible,

---

51 For further elaboration, see Parts IV to VI of the full paper (on p. 89 ff.).

52 The legislative instruments include both the primary legislation, such as TEC, TFEU, and the EU Charter, and secondary legislation comprising regulations and directives concerned with the implementation of the CEAS, with particular reference to the QD and APD. The jurisprudence includes not only that of the CJEU and ECtHR but also that of the national courts of MS and internationally recognised case-law dealing with IP law principles. That hierarchy has been adopted in the sources quoted in the text.

(or near thereto) of belief. For example: relevant dates, locations, and timings, mathematical, scientific or biological facts.

d. Plausibility: These are findings on the plausibility of the claims including explanations by the claimant of alleged past and present 'facts', and whether they add to or subtract from acceptance of those facts as being able to be believed. Within this criterion several specific issues may be relevant, such as: a lack of satisfactory or logical detail in explanation, explanations for the use of false or misleading documentation, delays in presentation of claims; and reasons/evidence given in previous claims and appeals. Plausibility will, to some extent, often overlap with external consistency findings.53

e. 'In the round': Overall credibility conclusions should not be made only on 'non-material', partially relevant or perhaps tangential findings only. Thus the substantive findings in the assessment of accepted credibility profiles, including the weight accorded to the above issues, should be made 'in the round' based on the totality of the evidence and taking into account that findings on a, b, and c (above) criteria will logically have more weight than those solely relying on 'implausibility'.54

f. Sufficiency of detail: With rare exceptions, based on a claimant's incapacity, a claim should be substantively presented and sufficiently detailed, at least in respect of the most material facts of the claim, to show it is not manifestly unfounded.

g. Timeliness of the claim: Late submission of statements and late presentation of evidence may negatively affect general credibility, unless valid explanations are provided.55

h. Personal involvement: If all the above criteria are met it is still important to ensure the claimant has been personally involved in the 'story' or evidence presented.

4.7.   EU judicial standards of good practice in credibility assessment

Many of the following standards of good practice are often to be found in the Codes of Administrative Procedure in several Member States. Additionally they have been developed by EU and international judges on a wide range of issues that are applicable in credibility assessment. The list that follows is not exhaustive and experienced judges may indeed consider applying many of them 'goes without saying'. However this list aims to be as extensive as possible, especially to assist and guide those judges, and all others, unfamiliar with this area of law, to

---

53 See M. Kagan (2003) 'Is Truth in the Eye of the Beholder? Objective Credibility Assessment in Refugee Status Determinations', 17(3) *Georgetown Immigration Law Journal,* pp. 367-415. Especially section on plausibility at pp. 390-391 where he argues that plausibility "adds very little" to external consistency.

54 See, e.g., *Cruz Varas and Others v Sweden* (1991) 14 EHRR 1; *Vilvarajah v UK* (1991) 14 EHRR 248; *A v SSHD* (2006) EWCA Civ 973; Article 80 Polish Code of Administrative Procedure (CAP); Section 108(1) and (2) German Code of Administrative Court Procedure.

55 See ECtHR in *B v Sweden* (28 October 2004) Appl. No. 16578/03; *Khan v Canada* (15 October 1994) Convention Against Torture Committee CATC No. 015/1994; *Kaoki v Sweden* (8 May 1996) No. 041/1996.

carry out the challenging task of credibility assessment, with the assistance of the cumulative experience reflected in these suggested standards.

Also, it must be said that, while appropriate deference to skill and experience will normally be accorded to experienced, first instance decision-makers, or full merits review judges, a material failure to adhere to one or more of these standards will often lead to a finding of a material error of law on judicial review. The approach we have taken to expressing each standard follows that of some well-known academic texts and is:

- The Standard or 'Rule' in brief summary.
- An explanation.
- Examples where the standard may not be self-evident.
- Authorities from EU, national MS courts, non EU courts, and academic or UNHCR material.[56]

For ease of use the standards are grouped in the four categories that follow:

A. Treatment of Substantive Evidence
B. Procedural Standards
C. Treatment of Vulnerable Claimants
D. Residual doubts and Article 4 QD

4.8. Treatment of Substantive Evidence (A)

We have identified 25 substantive evidence standards that arise in the case-law and correlate with the basis criteria we note above. The principle ones, with explanations on some, are:

4.8.1. *Consistency (A.1)*

Past or present facts should be presented by claimants in an internally and externally consistent manner.

4.8.2. *Plausibility (A.2)*

The plausibility of factual evidence will be reflected in the assessment of credibility of the claimant's history.

Explanation: These are not ends in themselves. Plausibility may potentially reflect the subjective view of the judge. Awareness of the judge's own personal theories of 'truth' and 'risk' should be noted by the judge to ensure objectivity is maximised. It is a fundamental characteristic of refugee and subsidiary protection claims that their proper consideration requires that specific conditions applicable in the claimant's country of origin be understood and reflected in the assessment. Rejections of evidence for implausibility must be fully reasoned, including explanations provided by claimants in regard to the potentially implausible parts of their evidence. Decisions based solely on implausibility are likely to be less persuasive than those based on a wider range of basic criteria.

---

56 We were greatly assisted here by the judges, who assisted in the project, and by Judge Dana Baldinger (NL) who kindly allowed us access to excerpts from her thesis before its publication.

4.8.3.   Coherence (A.3)

Coherently presented evidence by claimants is *prima facie* more likely to be accepted as credible.

4.8.4.   Audi alteram or Equality of Arms (A.4)

The 'other side' must be heard. Potentially negative material evidence, in respect of which a claimant is not afforded the opportunity for explanation or rebuttal, should not be taken into account in assessment of credibility.

4.8.5.   Reasons (A.5)

Judges must provide substantive, objective and logical reasons, founded in the evidence, for rejecting past or present facts presented by claimants in support of their claim.

4.8.6.   Materiality (A.6)

Judges must reach credibility conclusions on facts material to the claimant's case that go to the core of the fundamental issues.

4.8.7.   Speculation (A.7)

Judges must not engage in subjective speculation in their reasons for rejecting the credibility of claimants' evidence as to do so would be to rely on unfounded assumptions.

4.8.8.   Objective approach (A.8)

All credibility assessments in refugee and subsidiary protection claims must be undertaken with a balanced and objective approach.

4.8.9.   Delayed claims (A.11)

A delay in the presentation of a claim should not be treated as a presumption that the whole claim lacks credibility.

Explanation: Claimants should be expected to give good reasons for their delay and failure to do this *may* contribute to a lack of credibility. However, there should be recognition of situations where avoidance of disclosure may have arisen through shame, possibly associated with sexual violence, cultural/wider family and indirect personal 'costs' of disclosure.

4.8.10.   Past persecution (A.12)

Judges must make specific findings on evidence of past persecution or serious maltreatment.

4.8.11.   Use of COI (A.14)

Judges must refer to reliable COI as a vital part of testing the internal and external consistency of a claimant's asserted past and present facts. (Indeed judges should see the obtaining and use of COI as part of 'shared burden' approach to credibility assessment.)

4.8.12.   Findings made in previous claims (A.16)

When judges are determining second or subsequent claims from the same claimant, findings from the earlier claim, whether of positive or negative credibility, must be taken into account.

4.8.13.   Corroboration (A.17)

Because of the particular nature of refugee and subsidiary protection assessment, there is no specific requirement for corroboration of the claimant's accepted account.

4.8.14.   Partly credible claimants (A.18)

Rejection of some evidence, material or peripheral, relating to past or present facts will not necessarily lead to a rejection of all of the claimant's evidence.

4.8.15.   Demeanour (A. 24)

Caution must always be exercised in using aspects of the claimant's demeanour, and the manner in which a claimant presents his or her evidence, as a basis for not accepting credibility.

Explanation: The basic principle here is that using demeanour as a basis for credibility assessment should be avoided in virtually all situations. If demeanour is used as a negative factor the judge must give sustainable reasons as to why and how the demeanour and presentation of the claimant contributed to the credibility assessment, taking into account relevant capacity, ethnicity, gender and age factors. Additionally it should only be used in a context of evidenced understanding of the relevant culture, and in acknowledgment of culture as a repertoire of possible behaviours, which are not binding on any individual.

However, it must be recognised that in reality, demeanour can always have some impact in an oral hearing. A major reason for having an 'oral hearing' (as happens in most European jurisdictions) is so that judges can 'see and hear' the claimant, and witnesses and claimants can see, hear and address the judge(s).

4.8.16.   Behaviour modification as a means of avoiding risks, as indicated by COI (A.25)

Explanation: It can be an error of law to conclude that real risks of claimants being persecuted on return may be avoided by them modifying their behaviour. It is vital for judges to make sound findings, on their past and present behaviour, and the depth of a claimant's current convictions. As the best indicators of future forms of behaviour (fundamental to the exercise of core human rights) will be found in the past and present behaviour (that are accepted by the judge), sound and well-reasoned findings must be made, and set out as part of the claimant's accepted profile.

4.9.   Procedural Standards - General guidance on procedure (B)

Credibility assessments may be fundamentally flawed where, through faulty or inappropriate procedures, claimants do not have the opportunity to present their claims and supporting evidence fairly and reasonably. At the first instance decision stage, the APD contains extensive provisions designed to ensure procedural fairness. At the appeal or review stage, the requirements are governed by Article 39 APD but, as appears from other parts of this paper, the requirement for granting an 'effective remedy' also requires observance of a number of related concepts for a fair disposal.

4.9.1. *Interpreters (B.1)*

So far as is reasonably possible, claimants must have access to competent and unbiased interpreters. There must be an ability to communicate effectively.

4.9.2. *Legal representation (B.2)*

Recognising that legal aid/representation is not available in some Member States and/or at all levels of status determination or judicial review, judges should ensure (wherever possible) that claimants have access to competent legal or other suitable representation, with or without legal aid.

4.9.3. *Effect of time limits (B.3)*

Unreasonable time limits upon claimants to respond to contradictory or provide fresh evidence of changed circumstances or COI, can breach basic fairness principles which can render a whole determination/assessment unsustainable.

4.9.4. *Bias, incompetence and conflict of interest (B.5)*

Procedural and substantive issues will involve the application of the maxim that manifestly justice must be seen to be done, and where any of these issues do arise potentially any findings on credibility, and indeed all other issues, will *prima facie* be wrong in law.

4.10. Treatment of Vulnerable Claimants (C)

One general standard of good judicial practice only is provided, rather than setting a list of separate standards for every known type of vulnerability or sensitivity. This is done as, not only would it be impossible for such a list to be exhaustive, but also it is frequently the case that the vulnerability of individual claimants may have a number of overlapping causes. It is the totality of the claimants' physical and psychological predicament that must be taken into account in the assessment of their evidence.

In the assessment of the credibility of the evidence from a vulnerable or sensitive claimant, a failure to take into account appropriately their specific vulnerabilities can lead to an error of law.

Explanation: The need for refugee or subsidiary international protection by vulnerable people is at the heart of the humanitarian nature of international protection determination assessment. The predicament of particularly vulnerable or sensitive claimants requires careful understanding and reflection in the credibility assessment (Article 13.3 APD).

Although some individuals are by definition vulnerable or sensitive (for example: children, victims of trafficking, individuals who suffer from psychiatric illnesses or who have sustained serious harm, torture, sexual and gender based violence, and some women), others can be less readily identifiable. Factors to be taken into account in assessing the level of vulnerability, the degree to which an individual is affected and the impact on assessment of credibility include:

- Mental health problems
- Social or learning difficulties
- Sexual orientation (the LGBTI claimants)
- Ethnic, social and cultural background
- Domestic, education and employment circumstances
- Physical impairment or disability.

4.11. Residual doubts and Article 4 QD (D)

Where residual doubts are held by judges, in the assessment of the credibility of claimant's facts and circumstances, due to unsupported evidence, it will be, *prima facie*, an error of law not to adopt, at least, the minimum provisions of Article 4 QD.

The issue of residual and /or benefit of the doubt proved to be a vexed one where the impact and interpretation of Article 4 QD, and in particular 4.1 and 4.5, appears to have resulted in many member states implementing the optional approach set out in Article 4.5 into their domestic implementation legislation and/or guidelines to assessors. This has, in some MS, meant, in practice, a move away from the UNHCR approach known as 'benefit of the doubt' which is set out in the UNHCR Handbook that may have been used in the past.

From a judicial viewpoint we considered either approach is correct in EU law terms. Thus the Standard suggested is that the minimum approach acceptable is that in Article 4 QD . However in MS where domestically they follow a 'UNHCR-benefit of the doubt approach' or a somewhat similar approach to this, it will not be an error of law to do so. We were unable to find decisions in appeal cases, taken to higher courts by the state, where applying the 'UNHCR- benefit of the doubt approach' rather than strict adherence to the terms of Art 4.5, when the domestic legislative or regulatory implementation specifically states it is to be followed. It is accordingly one of the reasons why the judges involved in this project considered far more discussion and working party consideration was needed.

Allan Mackey

IARLJ Past President
Former Senior Asylum and Immigration Judge in the United Kingdom and New Zealand

5. Comments on the Credo Project and CEAS

John Barnes

5.1. The operation of the APD and QD in the CEAS[57]

Doubts have been expressed as to whether this topic should have been dealt with at length, or included at all, in the Paper.[58] I respectfully disagree.

It is not directly concerned with the assessment of credibility. But it overarches the individual national jurisdiction of Member States, whilst its single most important 'legal' component (the QD) is derived in part from treaty obligations already binding on Member States.

In its present stage of development, the APD and QD are based on minimum requirements to be observed by Member States thus leaving it open, subject to compatibility with the Directives, to apply more generous standards under national law if they choose to do so.

Being Directives, they also require transposition into the national law of each Member State and this leaves room for divergences of practice legitimately based upon existing national laws, particularly in the area of Procedural Law. Significantly, The EC Green Paper of 2008 states at paragraph 3.2 that:

"Diverse procedural arrangements and qualified safeguards produce different results when applying common criteria for the identification of persons genuinely in need of international protection. This can damage the very objective of ensuring access to protection under equivalent conditions across the EU. (...) This requires a fundamentally higher level of alignment between Member States' asylum procedures."

It continues, in discussing the proposed recast APD, which still awaits re-enactment that primary aims will include:

"setting up of a single, common asylum procedure leaving no space for the proliferation of disparate procedural arrangements in Member States, thus providing for a comprehensive examination of protection needs under both the Geneva Convention and the EU's subsidiary protection regime;

establishing obligatory procedural safeguards (...) which will consolidate the asylum process and ensure equal access to procedures throughout the Union."

The 2009 recast APD has not yet been enacted although this now finally appears imminent. Of direct interest to the judiciary is the recast Article 39 APD (now proposed Article 46). This retains the basic requirement of provision of a 'right to an effective remedy before a court or tribunal' and then expands on the scope of an effective remedy at sub-paragraph 3 as follows:

---

57 See further Part IV of the Credo Document, pp. 155 ff.
58 The full text of the Credo-document can be found on pp. 89 ff.

"Member States shall ensure that the effective remedy (...) provides for a full examination of both facts and points of law, including an ex nunc examination of the international protection needs pursuant to [the QD], at least in appeal procedures before a court or tribunal of first instance."

That provision requires careful analysis of the meaning of 'full examination of both facts and points of law'. It does not require there to be a full rehearing and the recast APD already provides that the administrative decision must set out 'the reasons in fact and in law' leading to rejection of a protection application. Arguably, an appeal or review court would provide an effective remedy if, at least as far as past facts relied on are concerned, it limited its consideration to whether that part of the decision challenged was reasonably open to a decision-maker whose decision demonstrated that he had considered all relevant evidence and provided sustainable reasons for his findings of fact. The requirement of an *ex nunc* examination of current international protection needs does not arguably imply any need for reconsideration of past facts as found by the initial decision-maker.

The level of judicial review required may arguably be affected by the general procedural law of the Member State and legitimately differ between States. In particular, state provisions may limit the role of a reviewing court or tribunal to issues of the lawfulness of the initial decision. Limitations as to the circumstances of admission of new evidence on appeal or review may be relevant to that part of the decision concerning the past history of the claimant.

The authority of initial decision-makers is likely to be enhanced if it is shown that they have been properly trained in protection law and decision-making. To that end, Member States who are members of DISC have facilitated the independent production of the European Asylum Curriculum (EAC), which is now owned by the European Asylum Support Office (EASO). One of their priority tasks is to expand the numbers of decision-makers who pursue this course so that, in time, review or appeal will increasingly be from the decision of someone who has qualified under an EU accredited training programme.

5.2.   The role of the national judge within the CEAS[59]

It has been an area of concern for me that the division of the fact-finding process between the past history of the claimant and the current existence of a well-founded fear of persecution or real risk of suffering harm proscribed by Article 15 QD might lead to a failure to consider the effect of the totality of the evidence at both stages and would place undue emphasis on past facts as opposed to the prospective risk which is the ultimate determinant of the need for protection.

Part V therefore is intended to counter these two concerns by reviewing the role of the national judge in the entire full rehearing process. In other words, to present a holistic account of the judge's role in such a case.

---

59 See further Part V of the Credo Document, pp. 187 ff.

5.3. Discussion paper on the burden and standard of proof in refugee and subsidiary protection claims and appeals in the EU[60]

Part VI is concerned with the fundamental issue of the burden and standard of proof applicable in protection cases under the QD. It is an area where the importance of Member States' national law is likely to be of most influence and to render impossible the goal of consistent decision-making throughout the EU.

Part VI was not originally intended to be classified as a discussion paper but my research made it ever clearer that it was not possible to treat this subject adequately within the terms of the Credo Project and that it needed to be the subject of more intensive research, with particular reference to the practice of Member States and the way in which decisions of the CJEU and the ECtHR impacted on them in laying down principles of general application. But it does lead to the final, perhaps controversial, point I wish to make.

5.4. The elements of conflict between the Executive and the Judiciary and their effect on the CEAS

Becoming a signatory to international treaty obligations leads to a ceding to some extent of the individual State's power of control of its own affairs in order to comply with its treaty obligations, This is potentially particularly problematic in relation to the obligations under the Geneva Convention and the ECHR which affect the state's power to determine under its own law which of non-citizens shall be entitled as of right to remain in that State.

In Part I we quoted Sedley LJ's address to the New Zealand Association World Conference in 2002, when he said:

"Asylum law, however, has an aspect which I think makes it unique: the need for it to deal in outcomes which are publicly perceived as having a direct and often unwelcome effect on the lives of the settled population. Asylum judges consequently handle facts and topics which, unlike those addressed by any other branch of the law except crime, are a matter of often passionate daily debate.

What affects judges in such a situation is not a targeted critique of their own role but an ambient pressure to stem the tide, to stop the rot, to reject the stories they hear from asylum-seekers so that they can be sent home."

That is probably a reasonably accurate reflection of the position some 10 years ago, but it seems to me from newspaper reports and articles that the position has intensified since then. The pressure of demographic changes within the populations of states have made it easy to single out for public criticism those who are potentially the most vulnerable entrants – those who are in need of international protection.

Such reports and articles seem to me, however, to reflect a genuine tension, which exists between the executive and the legislature on the on hand and the judiciary on the other.

---

60 See further Part VI of the Credo Document, on page 195 ff.

The delays in the progress of the recast APD are symptomatic of such tension and the reluctance of Member States to cede further their powers of control of entry of non-citizens. The diminution of the traditional deference afforded by the Courts to the Executive in administrative decisions, largely derived from an accretion of judicial powers of adjudication where human rights law concepts have evolved to place the burden of determination on the Courts rather than the Executive, have lead to real differences which have fuelled this tension. The imposition of the ultimate over-riding jurisdiction of supra-national European Courts appears further to have exacerbated the position, at least in the public mind.

Whilst the judiciary has not sought this additional power, there can be little doubt that the extent of its jurisdiction has and is continuing to increase by reason of the emphasis now placed upon individual rights and their protection. We are, I suggest, in the midst of one of the most fundamental changes in the balance between individual rights affected by government decisions and deference to the state function that has occurred in the law for many years. Although this may apply with differing intensity in the Member States, I suggest it is nevertheless a worldwide phenomenon.

So long as states retain their international obligations and their judges are charged with the duty of securing their observance, the present tensions are likely to continue.

Some Member States have already put in place statutory directions as to ways in which certain matters are to be considered as having an adverse impact on credibility – section 8 of the UK Asylum and Immigration (Treatment of Claimants, etc) Act 2004 is a well-known example which states its purpose uncompromisingly at sub-section (1):

> *"In determining whether to believe a statement made by or on behalf of a person who makes an asylum claim or a human rights claim, a deciding authority shall take account, as damaging the claimant's credibility, of any behaviour to which this section applies"*

before going on to set out a disparate list of the behaviour referred to.

'Deciding authority' is defined to include not only the administrative decision maker but also the Asylum and Immigration Tribunal and Special Immigration Appeals Commission so that the provision is intended to direct judges also as to how they should make their findings of fact in these cases.

In those circumstances, it seems likely that many Member States may ensure in their transposition of the recast Directives that they are treated as restrictively as is permissible. The pressures which already exist in relation to the assessment of credibility of claimants' past history in relation to their claimed prospective fear are likely to be maintained and, perhaps, enhanced. Ultimately, the disbelief of a claimant's asserted history will in the majority of cases lead to rejection of the claim for recognition as being in need of protection.

The recast Article 46(3) arguably does little to ensure that assessment of past credibility will be revisited unless the first instance decision is found to be unsustainable as a matter of law.

Moreover, our research indicates that, at least until very recently, the European Courts have maintained the traditional deference to factual findings by the state in the applications made to them by individual claimants.

I would suggest that, for all these reasons, there is doubt as to the existence of the political will necessary to enhance the scope of the CEAS in the manner envisaged by the TFEU and the European Commission – namely, the adoption of uniform standards of qualification assessed by common procedures. The effect of the fundamental principles of judicial fairness inherent in the EU and the provisions of the Charter of Fundamental Rights of the European Union are, in those circumstances, together with the jurisprudence of the European Courts, likely to achieve more significance and consideration in the future in determining the essential elements of an effective remedy.

John Barnes

Former Senior Asylum and Immigration Judge in the United Kingdom and author of IARLJ manual on the CEAS

6.   Concluding Remarks

Elspeth Guild

Asylum for refugees and others in need of international protection is a central plank of the international and regional human rights systems within which European states participate fully. States' human rights obligations regarding asylum for those in need of international protection are found in multiple treaties as Baldinger's book demonstrates. However, the translation of those obligations into national law and the procedures regarding the assessment of the need for international protection as incorporated into national law has not resulted in a convergence of outcomes for asylum seekers from the same countries in different European Union states. According to the UNHCR Yearbook 2011, protection rates for Syrian nationals in the EU vary from 83.1% in Austria to 2.7% in Greece and 3.4% in Cyprus.[61]

From the perspective of the judge who hears appeals against refusal of asylum, there are many issues to be taken into account. Three are of utmost importance.

First, the independence of the judge at first instance to review the facts and evidence is central. In this context, as the work of Baldinger shows, assistance from supra national judicial instances and UN Treaty Bodies regarding the intensity of the review is fundamental to ensuring that the human rights engaged are fully protected. Simple procedural issues like time limits on the submission of fresh evidence can make the difference between a full review which may result in recognition of refugee status and a partial review with important evidence excluded on grounds of procedural rules.

In the second case the result may be a confirmation of the refusal of recognition of the need for asylum. One can only wonder to what extent such procedural rules account for differences in recognition rates of Syrian nationals in Austria, Greece and Cyprus.

Secondly, the assessment of the credibility of the applicant is always vital to the determination of his or her need for international protection. By the time the judge comes to hear the evidence of the individual, the state authorities have usually already made a negative assessment of the person's credibility. Thus the procedural rules around the judge's obligation to review any assessment on credibility and to determine the evidence on which such an assessment is undertaken is critical.

National procedural rules which privilege the state authorities' negative assessment of credibility of the asylum seeker or obstacles to the ability of the asylum seeker to present in person his or her evidence before the judge to enable the judge to make a full and independent assessment of credibility, taking into

---

61 UNHCR Statistical Yearbook 2011, Annex, Table 12 <http://www.unhcr.org/51628f589.html> visited 12 June 2013.

account of course the state authorities' perspective, are problematic and diminish the fairness of any procedure.

Thirdly, country of origin evidence must be complete and accurate so that the judge can have as full an understanding of the risk of persecution, torture or inhuman or degrading treatment or punishment as possible.

In this book, we have focused on the first two issues, which are so important to the credibility of the asylum system of any country and its compatibility with the international obligations of its state.

Elspeth Guild

Centre for Migration Law, Faculty of Law,
Radboud University Nijmegen, The Netherlands

The Credo Document

John Barnes & Allan Mackey

Assessment of Credibility in Refugee and Subsidiary Protection Claims under the EU Qualification Directive: Judicial criteria and standards

A document edited by the IARLJ, written by Allan Mackay and John Barnes, and prepared in the framework of the EU-funded CREDO-project, which was led by the Hungarian Helsinki Committee with co-partners UNHCR and IARLJ

Table of Contents of the Credo Document

About the Authors

Authors, list of judicial editorial group, other judges, and participants consulted in the preparation of this document

The authors[1] were greatly assisted throughout the project by an Editorial group of IARLJ members who are all European judges, highly experienced in this field of law, and by all the other judges and participants who took part in a two day workshop on this paper in Madrid (20-21 September 2012). Country reports from all of the countries represented and commentary from UNHCR, together with feedback on the many draft versions of this paper, also contributed significantly.

The Editorial group members were: Judges: Nicolas Blake (UK), Eamonn Cahill (Ireland), Jacek Chlebny (Poland), Jane Coker (UK), Bernard Dawson (UK), Katelijne Declerck (Belgium), Sebastiaan de Groot (Netherlands), Harald Dörig (Germany), Joseph Krulic (France), Hugo Storey (UK), Boštjan Zalar (Slovenia).

The wider judicial consultation group who attended in Madrid were: All the Editorial group (except Judges Blake and Storey), Judges Anne Bruland (Norway), Maureen Clark (Ireland), Maria Contini (Italy), Dora Virág Dudas (Hungary), Bent Jespersen (Denmark), Dirk Maresch (Germany), Judith Putzer (Austria), Juha Rautiainen (Finland), Umberto Luigi Scotti (Italy), Jolien Schukking and Liesbeth Steendijk (Netherlands), Walter Stöckli (Switzerland), Karolina Tylova (Czech Republic), Juan Carlos Fernández de Aguirre, Celestino Salgado Carreo, Nieves Buisán García, Jesús Nicolás García Paredes and Isabel Perello (all from Spain), also Ms Anna Bengtsson (Sweden), Laurent Dufour (France) and Mike Ross (Canada/IARLJ). From UNHCR: Cornelis (Kees) Wouters (DIP, Geneva), Madeline Garlick and Fadela Novak (Bureau for Europe, Brussels), Maricela Daniel, Juan Carlos Arnaiz and Marta Garcia (all from Madrid) and Laura Cantarini (Rome). From EASO: Marta Ballestero Beltrán (Malta). From HHC: Gábor Gyulai and Tudor Roşu (Budapest).

A particular debt is owed to Liesbeth van de Meeberg, IARLJ office manager in Haarlem, who provided excellent support services to the authors and all others involved throughout the project. Also our thanks to: Judge Dana Baldinger, Netherlands, for allowing us the use of parts of her doctoral research studies, Dr Jane Herlihy, Chartered Clinical Psychologist, London for her comments and to Maya Bozovik and Hannah Cochrane (Legal Associates IPTNZ) who did the final editing.

---

1   Allan Mackey and John Barnes, are both retired UK Senior Immigration Judges
     Allan Mackey is Project director of the International Association of Refugee law Judges (IARLJ), a former IARLJ President, Senior Immigration Judge (UK), Chair of the Refugee Status Appeal Authority (NZ), and Deputy Chair, Immigration and Protection Tribunal (NZ).
     John Barnes is a project expert for IARLJ and their liaison officer with EASO in Malta. Previously he was a Senior Immigration Judge (UK). He is the author of the IARLJ (EU Chapter) Training manual on the CEAS.

EU legislation

Article 78 TFEU
> Article on the development of a common policy on asylum, subsidiary protection and temporary protection with a view to offering appropriate status to any third-country national requiring international protection and ensuring compliance with the principle of non-refoulement; Treaty on the Functioning of the European Union (TFEU).

Article 63 TEC
> Article on (the intention to adopt within a period of five years) measures on asylum in accordance with the Geneva Convention of 28 July 1951 and the Protocol of 31 January 1967 relating to the status of refugees and other relevant treaties; Treaty Establishing the European Community (TEC).

EU Charter
> Charter of Fundamental Rights of the European Union (2000)

Qualification Directive (QD) 2004
> Council Directive 2004/83/EC of 29 April 2004 on minimum standards for the qualification and status of third country nationals or stateless persons as refugees or as persons who otherwise need international protection and the content of the protection granted, *Official Journal* L 304, 30/09/2004 p. 12-23.

Qualification Directive (QD) 2011
> Directive 2011/95/EU of the European Parliament and of the Council of 13 December 2011 on standards for the qualification of third-country nationals or stateless persons as beneficiaries of international protection, for a uniform status for refugees or for persons eligible for subsidiary protection, and for the content of the protection granted (recast of QD 2004), *Official Journal* L 337, 20/12/2011 p. 9-26.

Council Directive 2004/83/EC of 29 April 2004 on minimum standards for the
> qualification and status of third country nationals or stateless persons as refugees or as persons who otherwise need international protection and the content of the protection granted

Asylum Procedures Directive (APD) 2005
> Council Directive 2005/85/EC of 1 December 2005 on minimum standards on procedures in Member States for granting and withdrawing refugee status, *Official Journal* L 326, 13/12/2005 p. 13-34.

Abbreviations

ACZ	Administrative Court of Zagreb
ABRvS	Court of Appeal in asylum cases (Netherlands)
APD	Council Directive 2005/85/EC of 1 December 2005 establishing minimum standards on procedures in Member States for granting and withdrawing refugee status, or Assessment Procedures Directive
Asylum law	A general term for the law on Refugee status, subsidiary, and Art 3 ECHR protection
BMC	Budapest Municipal Court
CAT	Convention against Torture and Other Cruel, Inhuman or Degrading Treatment or Punishment
CzCC	Czech Constitutional Court
CzRC	Czech Regional Courts, in Prague, Usti nad Labem, Ostrava
CEAS	Common European Asylum System
CJEU	Court of Justice of the European Union
Claimant	All applicants and or appellants for status recognition at all stages.
Dublin Reg.	Council Regulation (EC) 343/2003 of 18 February 2003
EASO	European Asylum Support Office
EC	European Commission
ECHR	European Convention Protection of Human Rights and Fundamental Freedoms 1950
ECJ	European Court of Justice (now usually CJEU)
ECRE	European Council on Refugees and Exiles
ECtHR	European Court of Human Rights
EU	European Union
EU Charter	Charter of Fundamental Rights of the European Union 2000
EWCA	England and Wales Court of Appeal
GC	1951 Convention relating to the Status of Refugees as amended by the 1967 Protocol
GFAC	German Federal Administrative Court
HHC	Hungarian Helsinki Committee
IARLJ	International Association of Refugee Law Judges
IARLJ (EUR)	European Chapter of the IARLJ
ICCPR	International Covenant on Civil and Political Rights
ICESCR	International Covenant on Economic, Cultural and Social Rights
IP	International Protection- includes refugee and/or subsidiary status
LGBTI	Lesbian, Gay, Bi-sexual, Trans-sexual and Inter-sexual
MS	Member State(s) of the European Union
NGO	Non-governmental organisation
QD 2004	Council Directive 2004/83/EC of 29 April 2004 on minimum standards for the qualification and status of third country nationals or stateless persons as refugees or persons who otherwise need international protection and the contents of the protection granted

QD 2011	Council Directive 2011/95/EU of 13 December 2011 on standards for the qualification of third country nationals or stateless persons as beneficiaries of international protection, for a uniform status for refugees or for persons eligible for subsidiary protection, and for the content of the protection granted
QD	Either or both of the above QDs
RSAANZ	Refugee Status Appeals Authority, New Zealand
SACP	Supreme Administrative Court of Poland
SIAC	Special Immigration Appeals Commission UK
TEC	Treaty Establishing the European Community
TFEU	Treaty on the Functioning of the European Union
UK	United Kingdom
UKHL	United Kingdom House of Lords
UKIAT	United Kingdom Immigration Appeal Tribunal
UKSC	United Kingdom Supreme Court
UKUT (IAC)	United Kingdom Upper Tribunal, Immigration and Asylum Chamber
UNHCR	United Nations High Commissioner for Refugees
VCLT	Vienna Convention on the Law of Treaties 1969

Bibliography

Barnes, J. (2007), *A Manual for Refugee Law Judges relating to the European Qualification and Procedures Directives*, Haarlem: IARLJ.

Battjes, H. (2006), *European Asylum Law and International Law*, Leiden (NL): Martinus Nijhoff.

Goodwin-Gill, G.S. and J. McAdam (2007), *The Refugee in International Law*, 3rd edition, Oxford (UK): OUP.

Hailbronner, K. (2010), *EU Immigration and Asylum Law – Commentary on EU regulations and directives*, München (Germ.): Beck.

Hathaway, J. (1991), *The Law of Refugee Status*, Toronto (CND): Butterworths.

Hathaway, J. (2005), *The Rights of Refugees under International Law*, Cambridge (UK): Cambridge UP 2005.

Symes, M. and P. Jorro (2003), *Asylum Law and Practice*, London (UK): LexisNexis.

UNHCR (2011), *Handbook and Guidelines on Procedure and Criteria for Determining Refugee Status*, Geneva: UNHCR.

IARLJ Publications

COI-CG Working Party (2006), 'Judicial Criteria for assessing Country of Origin Information (COI): a Checklist' *IARLJ 7th World Conference - Mexico City (Mexico) 2002*, Haarlem (NL): IARLJ <www.iarlj.org/general/publications>.

Haines, R. (2005), 'The Asylum Process and the Rule of Law: Judicial or Administrative Protection of Asylum-seekers – Content or Form?', *IARLJ 6th World Conference - Stockholm (Sweden) 2002*, Haarlem (NL): IARLJ <www.iarlj.org/general/publications>.

IARLJ (2010), *Guidelines on the Judicial approach to Expert Medical Evidence*, Haarlem (NL): IARLJ <www.iarlj.org/general/publications>.

Sedley, S. (2002), 'Asylum: Can the Judiciary Maintain its Independence?', *IARLJ 5th World Conference - Wellington (New Zealand) 2002*, Haarlem (NL): IARLJ <www.iarlj.org/general/publications>.

0.   Introduction

0.1.   Who is this paper prepared for?

This paper, whilst directed to judges considering refugee and subsidiary protection cases also aims to be instructive and relevant to all decision-makers, counsel and claimants in this unique field of law.

It provides guidance, to judges concerned with the application of EU asylum law, in best practice, criteria and standards for credibility assessment. The guidance is for judges determining both "full merits reviews", and error of law only appeals. The paper will also provide assistance to: government first instance decision makers, claimants, counsel, the UNHCR, European Asylum Support Office (EASO), academics and NGOs working with claimants.

Apologies are made for the extensive use of abbreviations or acronyms (especially to non-English readers). While it is unavoidable in some places, such as citations, we have tried to use only the most common acronyms in the text and to avoid their use to make the paper more readable in places. This is especially the case in the abridged version, which will be translated into French and German.

0.2.   Who prepared this paper and why?

The drafting of this paper was done by the two authors, after extensive consultation and guidance from some 35 highly experienced European judges, from 22 countries.[2] Commentary from the UNHCR, EASO and Hungarian Helsinki Committee (HHC) has greatly assisted the authors, as has advice from psychologists and lexicologists on specialised sections of the paper. It has been prepared under the auspices of the IARLJ (European Chapter), in consultation with UNHCR and HHC, as partners in the European Refugee Fund (ERF) sponsored 'Credo Project'.

The criteria and standards recorded are primarily concerned with credibility is-sues, which may arise in the consideration of refugee and subsidiary protection claims and appeals (together at times termed as IP claims) made under Directive 2004/83/EU (the 2004 QD). It is to be noted that Directive 2011/95/EU (the 2011 QD), in substitution for the 2004 Directive, was passed in December 2011, but will not come fully into operation until 21 December 2013 (see Art 40, 2011 QD). References in the text are, however, generally to the 2004 Directive.[3]

---

2   See page 92.

3   These both relate to minimum standards for the qualification and status of third-country nationals or stateless persons as refugees or persons who otherwise need international protection and the content of the protection granted. Neither Directive applies to Denmark and the later Directive applies to all Member States with the exception of Ireland and the United Kingdom who continue to be bound by the earlier 2004 Directive (see Recitals 50, 51 of 2011 QD). The differences between the two Directives are nevertheless, for our purposes, comparatively minor so that the general thrust of this paper is relevant to all EU Member States with the exception of Denmark.

Detailed analysis by the EC of the application of the QD and Procedures Directive 2005/85/EC (APD), as well as independent assessments by the UNHCR, academics and NGOs, have pointed to the marked differences in the outcome of refugee and subsidiary protection claims between MS throughout the EU and the important part which methods and procedures in credibility assessment play in creating those differences.

Such problems, not only adversely affect obtaining any commonality or harmonisation in assessments throughout the EU but also encourage, so called, 'asylum shopping'. It is hoped the contribution from this guidance paper will enhance the objectives of the IARLJ, and associated to that, the quality of asylum assessment systems and fair and efficient asylum procedures throughout the EU.

A fundamental aim of this paper is to emphasise the importance to judges, and all asylum decision makers, of the use of appropriate criteria and standards of credibility assessment. This ensures that the "accepted past and present facts" about each claimant can be established as an essential first step in the full asylum assessment procedure. The accepted facts, both expressly and impliedly stated, in this context can be conveniently referred to as the claimant's "accepted profile". (The words "accepted profile" used in this paper should not be confused with the terms "profile" or "profiling" commonly used in the criminal law or policing context. Its use here is to cover, holistically, all factors about a claimant accepted by the judge in the context of refugee and other international protection claims only.)

0.3. What is in this paper?

As will be seen from the table of contents, this is the full paper, as published on the IARLJ website. It is sub-divided into six parts.

The authors, in consultation with the IARLJ editorial planning group of experienced European judges, considered that presenting just a set of suggested checklists of credibility assessment criteria and standards *alone*, to judges, new to, or largely unfamiliar with, refugee and subsidiary protection law, without a reasonably substantive background to the unique nature of the subject, its history and the relevant legal framework, was insufficient and fraught with risks. And this is particularly so in this area of law where mistakes in assessment of credibility can have most serious consequences. For this reason the paper required the "scene to be set" and an explanation of the legal and historic background to asylum assessment in the EU and beyond, to accompany the outline of the assessment stages, and the credibility assessment criteria and standards, that are set out in Parts II and III of the paper. Simply stated, the credibility assessment criteria and standards suggested cannot be appropriately used and applied without a reasonably detailed explanation of the relevant international and EU refugee and protection law and its nature.

An abridged version of this paper, which includes most of Parts I, II and III, with hyper links to other parts of the full paper on the IARLJ website, has been submitted by the Association, as its contribution to the Credo Project. This approach allows the core guidance on credibility to be readily accessed, in a shorter document, while directing judges, and other decision makers, to the fuller background as needed. The abridged version will be translated into French and German, as part of the Credo Project. The hyper linked references to parts of this full paper will however only be available in English.

In *Part I* we set out the background to refugee and other protection law by first discussing the unique nature of decision-making in this arcane and highly specialised area of law, before exploring its comparatively recent origins. We then outline the way in which the CEAS is both structured and works in practice.

Part II sets out a structured approach, in chart form, and then with explanation, to judicial determination of appeals or reviews in which the full merits of the claimant's case require consideration.

In *Part III* we set out judicial guidance on criteria and standards for credibility assessment, which are derived from best judicial practice both within the EU and internationally in the application of refugee and other international protection law.

Parts IV, and V then explore in greater detail certain issues, which were briefly introduced in Part I of this paper.

Part VI is a discussion paper only on the highly relevant but vexed issues of burdens and standards of proof that may be applicable in credibility assessment of refugee and subsidiary protection claims.[4]

0.4. What is the meaning of 'credibility' in this context?

0.4.1. *The problem of a duality of usage of the term/word: 'credibility'*[5]

We must recognise contextually, how and when, particularly in English, the term 'credibility' is used and consider the usages, in refugee and other protection claims at all levels of assessment, in the two markedly differing contexts.

In the first context, it is for evaluating 'the credibility of a claimant's evidence, presented as their past and present factual background'. From this it follows that the assessment made by the judge, in this context, must conclude: are the claimant's statements and other evidence as to past events accepted as being believable? Or, put perhaps more simply: what are the "facts as found" by the judge that go to make up the claimant's holistic "accepted profile" that the judge will then use in the prospective risk assessment that follows?

---

4   Those who attended the Madrid workshop, that reviewed this paper in September 2012, agreed that these topics required much more debate and study by the IARLJ (European chapter) and others. A working party within the IARLJ (European chapter) to continue work on credibility assessment, (along with the optional approaches permitted to residual or "benefit" of the doubt issues by Article 4 QD) was established to direct this further study and will publish its findings through the IARLJ.

5   The New Oxford Dictionary meaning is stated as:
    "Credibility: noun; the quality of being trusted and believed in: *the government's loss of credibility*; the quality of being convincing or believable: *the book's anecdotes have scant regard for credibility*."
    "Credible: adjective; able to be believed; convincing: *few people found his story credible; a credible witness*; capable of persuading people that something will happen or be successful: a credible threat."

In the second context, it is often used "loosely" to cover the "credibility of everything related to the *claim* for recognition as a refugee or protected person". In this context the term "credibility" is used as meaning *all* the evidence relevant to the claim for protection status, duly assessed, (including the facts as found that make up the accepted profile of the claimant), does the claimant have a well-founded fear of being persecuted for a GC reason (Article 2 (d) of the QD 2004), if now returned to his or her country of origin. (Or, however, if the facts as found do not support a recognition of refugee status, are there substantial reasons for believing that the claimant would face a real risk of suffering serious harm (Article 2(f) of the QD 2004). Thus in this second context the judge must determine both the past and present facts accepted *and* the future prospective risk of harm.

To avoid any confusion, in this paper we address 'credibility' in the first context above, concerning the credibility of the claimant's past and present factual background.

The use, in lay terms, of the word 'credibility', in these two different contexts, is linguistically valid. However, judges will be aware that Art. 1A(2) of the Refugee Convention does not refer to the credibility of the claim but rather to whether there is a 'well-founded fear of being persecuted'. Thus reliance on the concept of the 'credibility of the claim for recognition as a refugee or a protected person' (or wider meaning) is, in our view, erroneous in law. It is thus strongly recommended that judges and other asylum decision makers should therefore refer to the "validity of the claim of a well-founded fear of being persecuted/persecution" and not use 'credibility' in the secondary wider context.[6]

It is thus important for judges (and all decision makers) to ensure that they clearly understand that the intended meaning can vary depending on its context. From consultation with lexicologist sources it appears these two contextual alternatives, for 'credibility', are common to most European languages. What is needed therefore, in linguistic terms, is "contextual disambiguation" to ensure the concept of "credibility" is used correctly in the two possible contexts.

The experience of reviewing judges in this project shows the misuse of the second wider meaning of the words 'credibility' or 'credible', is more of a problem in some member states than others. This appears to result from some countries having procedural practices that largely overcome the problem or linguistically the difference is more self-apparent. In the several countries, where it is a problem, the contextual differences are often not actually appreciated and the two usages of "credibility" are applied indiscriminately, or in the wrong context. On the other hand in other countries, such as in Switzerland for example, the procedures in the Swiss Asylum Act (s7) make a difference between 'making credible' (*Glaubhaftigkeit*) and 'being credible' (*Glaubwürdigkeit*). The first is the legal test of 'well-founded fear' and the second is the "accepted past and present facts". The result of this ensures the two possible usages of "credibility" are not readily confused and that the steps in the structured approach, set out in Part II, are carried

---

6   Similarly, in the case of subsidiary protection recognition, the proper reference is to the existence of substantial grounds for believing that the claimant has a real risk of suffering the prescribed treatment.

out in a different order (i.e. the risk assessment box first, then believability) than that we suggest. In reality the results should still be the same, although clearly, where there is only a partial acceptance of credibility of past and present core facts the risk assessment may then have to be revisited.

It is largely for this reason we have drawn up the structured chart for decision making (page 123) which breaks the full decision-making process involved in assessing the recognition of refugee or subsidiary protection status into a series of different stages with decision "boxes" as relevant issues arise. Assessing credibility (in its correct contextual meaning) against the backdrop of this structure may greatly assist better understanding of the judicial task, and the making of sustainable credibility conclusions, especially for those who are new to, or have little training in, this arcane area of law.

The contextual confusion is, perhaps unsurprisingly, often held by claimants and their representatives as well. They will often present their claims for recognition on the basis of the claimant's subjective fears and will state that in all their past, present and prospective evidence, and risks on return, they are "wholly credible". However, the judge's task is to consider the evidence on an objective basis at each stage of the decision-making process and to avoid the confusion we explain above.[7]

---

7   Contextual use of the word 'risk': The use of the word 'risk' (as in 'real risk') can also be con-
     textually problematic when (as happens in some jurisdictions, and possibly ECtHR decisions) it
     refers to a standard of proof for acceptance past evidence.(As in Step 2, Issue 1 in the Part II
     chart below). We consider that if a standard of proof is to be used at all, in the acceptance of a
     claimant's evidence of past facts, then referring to a real risk of past events as having occurred
     is contextually confusing. This is because 'risk' is a word more appropriately used in a predic-
     tive assessment, not a past one. (As in Step 4, Issue 2 of the Part II chart). We discuss this issue
     further in Part VI.

1. Part I: Setting the Scene

1.1. The unique character of decision-making in refugee and other international protection claims[8]

Refugee and subsidiary protection law, and related decision making on status recognition, is markedly different from almost all other areas of the domestic law of member states (MS), familiar to lawyers and judges in their respective jurisdictions. Because so much of this now extensive and specialised field of law has only developed in the last 25 years, many lawyers and judges will have had little or no formal training in the field and thus understandably firstly seek to rely on principles of domestic administrative law.

It is important therefore to set out the differences and specific character of refugee and protection law. Unless these, and the combined effects of several of them, are understood the risk of flawed decision making is highly elevated.[9]

We note 11 differential factors. There are three self-evident factors that apply to all cases and then eight other important characteristics that need explanation (which we set out below):

1) One party is a non-national individual claimant while the other is a state;
2) The factual substance of every claim will be difficult to check and thus reference to the country information in other states will be needed;
3) The focus of the case is significantly on the future, not the past.

Those needing explanation are:

4) The core treaties, such as ECHR and GC, are living instruments;
5) The decision-making is international rights-based, not domestic privilege-based;

---

8   This section of the paper reflects this unique character by reference to international law norms. The extent to which construing the EU primary and secondary legislation making up the CEAS may lead to a legally (though generally not practically) distinct application by the CJEU of its rules of interpretation of EU legislation will be considered in the section of this part of the paper dealing with "The legal framework and the CEAS".

9   A paper: "Asylum: Can the Judiciary Maintain its Independence?" by Sir Stephen Sedley, Former Lord Justice of Appeal, England and Wales; which was delivered at the IARLJ Conference 2002, Wellington, New Zealand (see Item 3, at p6) illustrates the differences well where he stated: "Yet this is still not the high point of the problem. I have not reached the critical function of first-instance asylum judges in the majority of the world's developed jurisdictions: the function of fact-finding. (...) I have described this function elsewhere as "not a conventional lawyer's exercise of applying a legal litmus test to ascertained facts; it is a global appraisal of an individual's past and prospective situation in a particular cultural, social, political and legal milieu, judged by a test which, though it has legal and linguistic limits, has a broad humanitarian purpose".
The latter part of this quote is from a UK High Court first instance decision of Sir Stephen that was later approved on appeal in Shah and Islam v Secretary of State for the Home Department [1999] 2 AC 629.

6)   The principles of surrogate protection arise from international treaty obligations;

7)   Refugee and subsidiary protection status are declaratory, not constitutive;

8)   Judicial independence and impartiality can be put under pressure from anti-refugee/migrant or societal pressures;

9)   Many claimants will have vulnerabilities inherent in their situation, thus the psychological and trauma dimensions affecting them must be considered;

10) Claimants will often have difficulties in presenting corroborative evidence and there will unique attention needed in the use and abuse of "supporting" documentation, including web-sourced material; and

11) Cross-cultural awareness and challenges and working through interpreters are the norm.

1.1.1. *The core international treaties and conventions are 'Living Instruments'*

The GC (1951), and the ECHR (1950) are such core documents and like the many related human rights treaties, they are so-called "living instruments". The UNHCR and international law norms posit the interpretation of the GC, as a living instrument, is first and foremost guided by the VCLT (see below) and a dynamic or evolving interpretation in the light of social and political developments together with a liberal interpretation of rights and narrow interpretations of restrictions. This means the interpretation, and indeed whole new fields of coverage under these conventions, are constantly changing and evolving over time to meet new regional and international needs and circumstances. Indeed, many persons currently validly accepted as deserving of protection may never have been envisaged as such when the core Conventions: the GC and the ECHR, were drafted some 65 years ago.

For many judges, not in specialist asylum courts or tribunals cases involving refugee and related protection law, there will be a need for specialist reference to international law and practices. This is unlike most other judicial work where much of the routine statutory legal interpretation, and related judicial decision-making, involves reference to the actual domestic codified law (the "black letter law") and relevant domestic case law, where evolution or change generally only takes place through legislative action.

It is also to be noted that the UNHCR encourages all signatory states to the GC to implement domestic laws and policies that require determination and protection needs to be governed by international law, including relevant rules of treaty interpretation. However for international consistency reference to wider international refugee and protection law is clearly best practice for judges determining such cases.

This essential difference makes working in refugee and other protection law, for counsel, academics and judiciary dynamic, stimulating and never routine. There is thus a positive ability to explore, and often find, totally valid and appropriate human solutions in a changing world.

This is clearly illustrated by reference to the way in which recognition of refugee and protection needs have developed over the past 30 years in the jurisprudence of the ECtHR, and courts around the world determining refugee cases. Solutions for the genuine humanitarian needs of previously disenfranchised vulnerable groups, including women, children, and LGBTI persons, who can now find surrogate protection from persecution or serious maltreatment and discrimination, are graphic illustrations. The law in this field is thus able to adapt, without inappropriate judicial positivism, to meet changing circumstances and without the need for changes to the international treaties and conventions themselves.

1.1.2. *Rights-based, not Privilege-Based Decision-making*

Refugee and subsidiary protection decisions are made in the field of 'rights-based' law and not the domestic "privilege-based" immigration law of member states. Decisions on entitlement to enter and remain, temporarily or permanently, in a member state are made on the basis of domestic immigration laws that set out the requirements to be fulfilled by non-nationals who apply. Each state is entitled to police its own borders and thus grants the privilege to non-nationals to enter and remain in that state. Decisions concerning the recognition of protection rights are, by contrast, derived from the international treaty obligations of the host state which are, in the case of EU member states, reinforced by the requirements of the CEAS (whether, where appropriate, effectively transposed or not into domestic legislation).

In some countries the situation can become confusing for asylum seekers, and judges unfamiliar with this field of law. For example in the UK, many refugee and protection assessments and appeals only arise as a defence raised against an immigration removal directions made by a Border Agency officer who has decided a non-national is either an over-stayer or illegal entrant. The requirement to assess whether the non-national is a refugee or entitled to subsidiary protection thus is not initially set in a claim for international protection recognition but in domestic immigration removal proceedings.

Therefore, in many situations, judges and decision-makers will be required to determine issues of both domestic immigration law and EU asylum law as they relate to the same person.

It is understandable therefore that domestic border control, "privilege-based" immigration law attitudes or perspectives put forward by those validly trying to maintain border control, may but should not be, intermeshed with refugee and protection law issues.

In refugee and subsidiary protection cases, a knowledge and understanding of core international instruments is indispensable even though the ascertainment of recognition entitlement may be addressed through the CEAS.

The specific relevance of the GC and ECHR is, of course recognised in both the TEC and TFEU as well as to the degree to which they have acted as a source of inspiration in the drafting of the secondary EU legislation, which makes the corpus of the CEAS.[10]

---

10   See further the explanation of the application of the VCLT, in the international law context, contained in the paper delivered by Rodger Haines QC at the IARLJ Conference 2005: The Asylum Process and the Rule of Law: "Judicial or Administrative Protection of Asylum-seekers – Content or Form?"

Turning to the GC itself, in its preamble, it relevantly notes:

"*Considering* that the Charter of the United Nations and the Universal Declaration of Human Rights approved on 10 December 1948 by the General Assembly have affirmed the principle that human beings shall enjoy fundamental rights and freedoms without discrimination,

Considering that the United Nations has, on various occasions, manifested its profound concern for refugees and endeavoured to assure refugees the widest possible exercise of these fundamental rights and freedoms, (...)"

These fundamental rights are then identified within the GC itself.[11] The starting point for interpretation of the GC, particularly the "inclusion clause" (Article 1A(2)), is thus found in other international human rights treaties themselves, including the "International Bill of Rights" and the series of conventions and declarations that have flowed from that time. These are considered in more detail in the discussion of the CEAS and EU legal framework in Part IV. The UNHCR also rightly notes that international human rights law, international humanitarian law and international criminal law all inform the interpretation of the GC.

Thus, for example, in every refugee and subsidiary protection claim it is necessary to identify whether the claimant is at risk of "being persecuted"/persecution, or serious harm. The GC however provides no definition of the term "being persecuted". Article 9 of the QD does assist and directs us to "severe violations of basic human rights" and, in particular, to the non-derogable rights in the ECHR. Additionally Article 15 of the QD explains the term "serious harm"'. Thus, to find out what constitutes persecution, or serious maltreatment, we must look for potential breaches of the core international and/or EU human rights instruments and seek the assistance of the QD itself and jurisprudence of EU and domestic courts and tribunals that determine these issues against this international and EU legal framework.

1.1.3. *The Principle of Surrogacy Where There is an Absence of National Protection*

As core knowledge for decision-makers in relation to refugee and other protection issues, it must be understood that these are all driven by the underlying principle set out in the obligations undertaken by signatory states to provide surrogate protection, in the absence of national protection. This principle provides that if the national of another country cannot access "state protection", in their own country of nationality, or habitual residence from being persecuted or severely harmed, then they are entitled to seek and obtain protection from other states. This principle is eloquently stated in the leading Canadian case of *Canada (Attorney-General) v Ward* [1993] 2 SCR689, 709 (SC: Can) which states:

"At the outset, it is useful to explore the rationale underlying the international refugee protection regime, for this permeates the interpretation of the various

---

11   For full discussion and explanation of all the rights within the GC, see J Hathaway, *The Rights of Refugees under International Law* (Cambridge, 2005).

terms requiring examination. International refugee law was formulated to serve as a back-up to the protection one expects from the state of which an individual is a national. It was meant to come into play only in situations where that protection is unavailable, and then only in certain situations. The international community intended that persecuted individuals be required to approach their home state for protection before the responsibility of other states becomes engaged. For this reason, James Hathaway refers to the refugee scheme as "surrogate or substitute protection", activated only upon a failure of national protection: see J Hathaway, *The Law of Refugee Status* (1991), at p135."

1.1.4. *Refugee and Subsidiary Protection Status are Declaratory*

Refugee, and/or subsidiary protection status is declaratory in nature and not constitutive. Under the provisions of the QD, when a claimant, who is fleeing the risk of being persecuted, enters a member state, they must be treated as putative refugees, as set out in the GC, possessing certain rights on arrival or once they come under the control of the receiving country.[12] The declaration, or recognition, of status is therefore made at the time of assessment.

As discussed above domestic immigration law decisions are made on a constitutive basis, whereby an applicant must meet a list of requirements laid down in domestic legislation or rules. The assessment in such a case will be made on the basis of the *information provided at the time of application in accordance with the applicable domestic laws* of evidence and in a manner prescribed by domestic legislation.

The protection and immigration decision-making processes are thus fundamentally different and a failure by decision makers to appreciate the difference often leads to flawed decisions.

1.1.5. *Judicial Independence and Impartiality can be put Under Pressure from Anti-migrant, Anti-refugee Public Perceptions*

Sir Stephen Sedley's comments below, made in his paper: "Asylum: Can the Judiciary Maintain its Independence?" (see Footnote 9) are highly relevant and note another aspect of the unique nature of asylum decision making. He states:

"Asylum law, however, has an aspect which I think makes it unique: the need for it to deal in outcomes which are publicly perceived as having a direct and often unwelcome effect on the lives of the settled population. Asylum judges consequently handle facts and topics which, unlike those addressed by any other branch of the law except crime, are a matter of often passionate daily debate. (...)

What affects judges in such a situation is not a targeted critique of their own role but an ambient pressure to stem the tide, to stop the rot; to reject the stories they hear from asylum-seekers so that they can be sent home. At times this becomes nationality or ethnicity-specific. It does not mean that adjudicators will all lurch in one direction. There is just as much risk that conscientious judges

---

12   See James Hathaway, *The Law of Refugee Status ibid* at p12.

will over-compensate from the pressures they sense around them and that they will succumb to the noise. But the hothouse itself is, I think, peculiar to asylum law adjudication. Probably the nearest we come to it in other fields is in criminal law where, from time, societal pressure to secure a conviction can distort the process of justice; but there it is at least episodic, not a constant daily phenomenon."[13]

Again these comments are applicable not just to the judiciary but also to all first instance and other administrative refugee and protection decision makers.

1.1.6. *The Psychological/trauma Dimension and Recognition of the Special Vulnerabilities that May Arise due to Age, Gender Roles, Sexual Orientation, Social and Educational Backgrounds.*

All judges in refugee and other protection cases, particularly as part of credibility assessments, must recognise that not only are some claimants less able to articulate their story and background than others but also psychological impairment will often affect the evidence and presentation of genuine claimants. Such impairment may arise from past persecution or serious maltreatment and indeed occasionally, through fear of "authority figures", from the IP determination process itself:

"Here, it must be recognised and become a vital p ents that claimants, interviewers and decision-makers at each stage art of the decision-making process in credibility assessm all bring with them their own psychological processes. These then interact, under the overarching context of the social and political milieu. Each of the players brings their own assumptions to the process and perhaps some are held more strongly than we realise. It seems that some assumptions are less correct than others; indeed some are not warranted at all when the empirical evidence is carefully examined."[14]

Refugee and subsidiary protection decision makers should be aware that there is a considerable body of published research material concerning the need to reflect general issues of human fallibility in recall memory, as well as issues directed more specifically to the psychological issues of victims of persecution and the ways in which cultural differences between the claimant and the decision maker need to be taken into account in assessing credibility. Such sources require, of course, the same scrutiny as to their objectivity and sourcing as would apply to any "expert" evidence. As Herlihy and Turner point out in their article:

"An important counter-balance to the reliance on unsupported assumptions in the decision-making is the requirement of caseworkers and immigration judges to record and justify their decisions in writing. However, if decisions are understood within the heuristic model ... which shows how decisions are open to biases and may be based on a lack of understanding of psychological processes, then this risks being an exercise in circularity."

---

13   Sir Stephen Sedley, *ibid at* pp 3 & 4.
14   Jane Herlihy and Stuart W Turner "The Psychology of Seeking Protection" (2009) 21(2) *International Refugee Law Journal* pp171-192 .

These authors suggest that more empirically-based decisions could provide a more effective and defendable process and that:

> "The processes at work in the minds of the claimants, interviewers and decision-makers need to be carefully and systematically identified and understood in this setting. Collaboration across disciplines could ensure that this work is comprehensive and cohesive so that we can be more confident that the best knowledge – empirical, clinical and judicial – is brought into play in what may be life or death decisions."

Guidance should also be made on these issues to the highly reputable *Istanbul Protocol.*[15]

1.1.7. *Documentation and Corroborative Evidence*

As is recognised in Article 4(5) of the QD, in a situation where many claimants are fleeing the risk of being persecuted or severely maltreated, often at the hands of the state, those genuinely in flight may not be able to access full personal documentation: passports, travel documents, membership cards, medical reports etc that would be expected as corroboration in the immigration context.[16] The quality and quantity of supporting corroborative documentation thus needs close assessment.

In the assessment of credibility all documentation presented by an appellant in support will require examination and assessment by the judge. However, in many cases, despite the normal propensity for lawyers, judges and government officials in most domestic law situations to want, and request, corroborative documentation, in this unique field, while noting the guidance of Article 4(5), the credibility of a claimant can, on occasion be more supported by their lack of documentation rather than a voluminous amount of "supporting documentation". Indeed excessive, voluminous or apparently highly incriminating documentation can logically arouse the suspicion of dubious or fraudulent sourcing. Where, however, there is clear evidence that a claimant has deliberately destroyed documents relevant to proof of his claim, including often documents relevant to establishing his country of origin (in course of transit), an explanation of such conduct should always be requested. The explanation may show a lack of credibility or it could in other situations show perhaps, that the claimant was smuggled or trafficked.

We must also *consider the impact of instant electronically sourced material, social media*[17] *("e"-evidence)*. Whilst, as just noted, the unique predicament of those fleeing persecution makes the treatment of corroboration through documentation at significant variance to the domestic rules of evidence in all civil and criminal law cases, we must also recognise the huge impact of "e"-evidence on

---

15 The Manual on the Effective Investigation and Documentation of Torture and Other Cruel, Inhuman or Degrading Treatment or Punishment, 1999, commonly known as The Istanbul Protocol, HR/P/PT/8/Rev.1.

16 See further at para 196 in the UNHCR "Handbook and Guidelines on Procedures and Criteria for Determining Refugee Status" (Geneva, December 2011).

17 E.g. Facebook and Twitter.

refugee and subsidiary protection assessment, including credibility. This should not be underestimated.

Over the past 10-15 years, the ability to obtain almost instant evidence, from virtually every corner of the earth, has meant that such evidence can now impact on COI, used in both credibility and risk assessment, far more dramatically than previously was the case. Thus, often it will now be reasonable for claimants (or assessors/judges) to be able to show very up-to-date electronically sourced material that can, subject to basic fairness principles, be highly determinative of both credibility of past and present facts and prospective risks on return.

1.1.8. *Cross Cultural Awareness and Language Interpretation is the Norm*

By its very nature, refugee and subsidiary protection status determination will, in virtually every case, involve both cross-cultural and language interpretation and translations. This will often also extend to a need to understand subtle cultural, gender, demeanour and linguistic issues. While such issues can arise in domestic law litigation, they are more the exception than the norm.

Quality assessment of all claims and appeals, and in particular credibility, thus depends heavily on having skilful and experienced interpreters, good counsel and informed and experienced judges and decision-makers.

1.1.9. *Summary*

Each of the factors above illustrates the unique and specific character of refugee and subsidiary protection law and decision-making. However, the reality is that in virtually all refugee and subsidiary protection cases many of the above factors will be relevant. It is for these reasons that assessment and ultimate decision-making should always be considered "on the totality of the evidence" or "in the round".

It is against this backdrop that the challenges of fact-finding and prospective assessment of risk in this field should not be under-estimated.

1.2. The legal framework and the CEAS

Having noted the unique and specific character of refugee and protection law, it is now necessary to gain background knowledge of the relevant law in the EU context. While it is not our purpose to carry out a full review of the international and European law relating to issues of refugee and subsidiary protection, a number of essential provisions must be noted. Parts IV and VI consider some of the topics in this section in greater depth.

1.2.1. *A Brief Overview of the Historical Development of Refugee and Subsidiary Protection Law*[18]

History up to end of World War II

Historically, refugees were recognised on the basis that they formed part of groups deprived of protection from their own state. Until the 20th century this was a matter of individual action on the part of nation states. Two well-known historical examples are French Huguenots finding shelter in England and English Catholics finding shelter in France from religiously-based persecution in their respective States during the 16th and 17th centuries.

Following the First World War and mainly under the auspices of the League of Nations, the recognition of refugees began to take on a more international character. Based initially on the need to provide some recognised status for those who, by reason of denial of the protection of their own state, were outside their own country of nationality but unable to settle in another country because no state was prepared to accept legal responsibility for them. The League of Nations provided identity certificates, recognised by contracting states as equivalent to a national passport, both to groups who had been involuntarily deprived of state protection (denaturalised) or who as individuals were denied valid passports by their own state. In 1929 the Advisory Commission for Refugees identified the essential characteristic of persons classed as refugees as being that they "have no regular nationality and are therefore deprived of the normal protection accorded to the regular citizens of a State".

At the same time, however, there were events which caused major population displacement in the European arena. More than a million Russians had fled Russia following the October 1917 Revolution and many Armenians from Turkey fled to avoid persecution during the early 1920's. Similar displacement occurred as a result of events in Germany in the period leading up to the Second World War and these events led for the first time to recognition of refugees being on the *de facto* basis that they were helpless victims of social and political events outside their control which required international intervention because of their loss of protection in their home states.

The international instruments, which recognised the need for such intervention were *ad hoc* provisions brought in response to specific emergency situations affecting groups of persons and so were limited in point of time and geographical area.

Introduction of GC and other international conventions

It was not until the 1951 GC came into force that there was a general recognition that refugee status should be by reference to the individual asylum-seeker's history as it affected him or her. Although it displayed a certain concept of universality in bringing within its protection all those who had been recognised as refugees

---

18   For a full outline of the origins of refugee rights, international alien's law, and the codification of the refugee rights by the League of Negotiations, and then United Nations, see Chapter 2 of J Hathaway, *The Rights of Refugees under International Law, supra.*

under earlier instruments (Article 1A(1)) thus ensuring that the civil rights guaranteed by it applied also to existing refugees, even the GC was, like the earlier instruments, originally subject to temporal and geographical limitations. Article 1A(2) opens with the words "*As a result of events occurring before 1 January 1951 and*" before proceeding with the definition of a refugee with which we are all familiar. Article 1B(1) then goes on to qualify the meaning of that phrase by giving signatory states the option of applying that temporal limit either to "*events occurring in Europe before 1 January 1951*" or "*events occurring in Europe or elsewhere before 1 January 1951*"; a number of signatory states opted for the former and, in some cases, maintained that option for many years after the New York Protocol relating to the Status of Refugees came into force on 4 October 1967.

From 4 October 1967, when removal of the temporal and geographic limitations was generally approved, the GC acquired the universality of the approach. By virtue of the application of the interpretation provisions of the VCLT, including the requirement that regard be paid to subsequent practice, it continues to evolve as a 'living instrument'.

The GC, however, concerns only one specific aspect of human rights law – namely the entitlement of an individual applicant to recognition of refugee status by the receiving State.

At the same time as the process, which led to the making of the 1951 GC was being undertaken, the events of the Second World War and its aftermath inspired a greater general interest in the concept of fundamental human rights which profoundly affected the concept of protection. Indeed, it would not be inaccurate to say that human rights concepts have revolutionised States' laws and their application throughout the world and that this revolution is still forcing change and will continue to do so for the foreseeable future. Not only has it led to substantive changes in procedural law in terms of ensuring the right to a fair trial and an effective remedy, which may in some cases involve the striking down of national laws as being incompatible with fundamental human rights, but it has enhanced the role of the judiciary and in some cases led to confrontation and tension with the national executive governments.

Additionally, for those countries who are signatories to the ECHR, it has resulted in their national laws being subordinated to their obligations under the ECHR and to the acceptance of the ECtHR in Strasbourg as the final arbiter between State and citizen of their respective rights and obligations under that Convention.

These wider changes began with the 1945 Charter of the United Nations and the 1948 Universal Declaration of Human Rights (UDHR) but, although universal in scope, neither of these documents contained any enforcement provisions. The other principal subsequent general human rights instruments are the 1948 Convention on the Prevention and Punishment of Genocide (CPPG), the 1966 International Covenant on Civil and Political Rights (ICCPR) and its optional protocols, the 1966 International Covenant on Economic, Social and Cultural Rights

(ICESCR),[19] the 1969 Convention on the Elimination of all forms of Racial Discrimination (CERD), the 1979 Convention on Elimination of Discrimination against Women (CEDAW), the 1984 Covenant against Torture (CAT) and the 1989 Convention on the Rights of the Child (CRC). Whilst all create obligations on States Parties under international law, they either lack the possibility of complaint by aggrieved individuals or permit such complaint subject to limitations, which significantly reduce the possibility of individual enforcement of their respective provisions. Notwithstanding these difficulties of access, however, the UN Committees concerned with the ICCPR optional protocol, CERD, CEDAW and, in particular, CAT as to the meaning of torture, have all made findings which help to clarify the scope of the respective instruments in IP terms.

The specific regional changes, which affect all EU MS begin with consideration of the effect of the ECHR to which all MS are required to be signatories as a term of their membership of the EU.

The ECHR 1950

The ECHR emanates from the Council of Europe, a wider body than the EU, with 47 members who have ratified the Convention and its Protocols. All 27 EU MS are included in this number. At its inception in 1950, it differed from other international human rights instruments in that it provided for the establishment of the ECtHR but there was initially no unfettered right of individual application for redress to the Court. The ECtHR operated only on a part-time basis in association with the European Commission on Human Rights, another part-time body, which controlled the mechanism of referral to the Court in the case of individual applications. With the coming into force of Protocol 11 on 1 November 1998, the Commission was abolished and the ECtHR became a full-time body to which individuals could apply for redress against any contracting state they claimed to have violated their rights under the ECHR. The jurisdiction of the Court became compulsory where previously it had depended upon the acquiescence of the individual contracting states. This has brought its own problems with a vastly expanded caseload but the ECtHR is, in terms of IP law, unique in providing an international regional court of redress when local remedies in the state concerned have been exhausted. Admission of a reference to it is under the control of the Court alone. The ECHR is the regional counterpart of the ICCPR and protects rights first spelt out in the 1948 Universal Declaration of Rights.

The EU Charter and the Lisbon Treaty

There is one final regional instrument to which we must refer to complete this summary of the development of refugee and subsidiary protection rights – the EU Charter. Since the coming into force of the Lisbon Treaty, the EU Charter provides rights for citizens of MS, the effect and scope of which is a matter of EU Law. Such matters are ultimately for the decision of the CJEU whose decisions bind all MS in relation to this and to other areas of refugee and subsidiary protec-

---

19   The ICCPR, ICESCR and the UDHR are often collectively referred to as the "International Bill of Rights".

tion law which fall within the EU laws relating to the CEAS. In broad terms, the CJEU will have regard to the case-law of the ECtHR where relevant. There is a substantial body of ECtHR jurisprudence which deals with issues which are relevant to refugee and other international protection law.

1.2.2. *The CJEU – Impact on Refugee and Subsidiary Protection Law*

The jurisdiction of the CJEU will overcome one *lacuna* in refugee and subsidiary protection cases where the ECtHR held that it had no jurisdiction to hear complaints. This relates to claims under Article 6 ECHR that a claimant had been denied the right to a fair trial since the Court had held in *Maaouia v France* [33 EHRR 1037 GC] that State decisions concerning *"the entry stay and deportation of aliens do not concern the determination of an applicant's civil rights or obligations"*. No such limitation applies to the similar rights arising under the EU Charter in respect of which the CJEU has jurisdiction.

It must, however, be emphasised that there is one important area where the CJEU diverges from the position under international law norms considered earlier in Part I. This is in the approach to interpretation of relevant instruments. Under international law the interpretation of international treaties and conventions is governed by the VCLT as we have noted above. EU instruments (including not only the EU Treaties and Charter, but also the secondary instruments making up the body of the CEAS) are not international instruments and are not subject to interpretation under the VCLT. Their interpretation is governed by the EU rules of construction applied by the CJEU. These differ in one important respect whereby subsequent agreement on interpretation and subsequent state practice (as in Articles 31(2) and (3) VCLT) have no role in the interpretation of EU legislation by the CJEU. Insofar as the CEAS draws upon and seeks to apply concepts derived from international instruments – and the ECHR and GC are of particular relevance – this difference in interpretative approach has the potential to affect the concept of the international treaties as 'living instruments' for the purpose of interpretation of the meaning of EU instruments which reproduce their terms. The effect of this divergence is arguably, however, more theoretical than real and we consider the issue in greater depth in Part IV of this Paper.'

1.2.3. *The Legal Structure of the CEAS*

The CEAS is one of the most ambitious EU projects and is designed to be assimilated into the national law of MS gradually over a period of years. In Part IV we look in more detail at the structure of the CEAS and, in particular, the QD and the APD which are the two pieces of EU legislation most directly relevant to IP applications.

Nevertheless, it is important to bear in mind that the CEAS is an overall concept not confined to the important element of the qualification for and procedural application of issues of status recognition dealt with by the QD and APD and for a full picture the interaction between the various instruments and policies which it comprises need to be understood.

The EU legislative instruments which make up the CEAS are currently:

- Article 63 TEC (the first primary enabling provision for the CEAS) from which the authority for the provision of minimum standards for the recognition of protection status is derived);
- Directive 2001/55/EC of 20 July 2001 (dealing with minimum standards for temporary protection in the event of mass influx and issues of solidarity consequent on such recognition);
- Directive 2003/9/EC of 27 January 2003 (laying down minimum standards for reception of asylum seekers);
- The 2004 QD (2004/83/EC of 29 April 2004);
- The APD (2005/85/EC of 1 December 2005);20
- Regulation (EC) 343/2000 of 18 February 2003 (the 'Dublin' Regulation) concerned with identifying the MS responsible for examining an asylum application together with its associated Commission Regulation (EC) 1560/2003 of 2 September 2003 laying down detailed rules for its application, and the two Council Regulations (EC) 2725/2000 of 11 December 2000 and (EC) 407/2002 of 28 February 2002 relating to the implementation of 'Eurodac' concerning fingerprinting requirements;
- The 2011 QD (2011/95/EU of 13 December 2011 (which replaces the 2004 QD (with minor amendments) for all Member States except Ireland and the United Kingdom who remain bound by the earlier QD of 29 April 2004. Denmark is not bound by either QD or the APD.[21]

To these must be added by way of primary legislation those Articles of the EU Charter, which have a bearing on protection issues which came into full effect, creating enforceable rights, when the Lisbon Treaty took effect on 1 December 2009. Articles 1, 7, 11, 14-16, 18, 21, 24, 34 and 35 are all of potential relevance (see Recital (16) QD).

In terms of secondary legislation, Directive 2011/51/EU of 11 May 2011 amending Council Directive 2003/109/EC to extend its scope to beneficiaries of international protection is also relevant. It came into effect on 20 May 2011 and extends the scope of long term resident status under Directive 2003/109/ EC on the terms and conditions set out in the later directive to claimants recognised as refugees or persons in need of subsidiary protection where that status proves long-term in nature.

During the first stage of its implementation, under the authority of Article 63 TEC, the concept of the CEAS has been to prescribe 'minimum standards' to be observed by MS in determining international protection claims. But, this has already thrown up problems of differences of approach particularly in procedural terms which have had a substantial impact on uniformity of the essential issue of credibility assessment with which the Credo Project is concerned. Historically, each signatory to the GC has been left free to provide its own internal state mech-

---

20 A recast APD was due to be passed by end 2012 but is still awaited. It contains important clarifications of the APD including, in particular, the meaning of '*effective remedy*' in Article 39.

21 Many of the Articles of the 2011 QD do not, however, come into effect until 21 December 2013. Those which came into effect on 2 January 2012 are Articles 3, 5, 6, 12-15, 17, 18, 21, and 36-42.

anisms for determining recognition of international protection rights arising under both international and national law.

The second stage of the development of the CEAS will be governed by Article 78 TFEU, which came into effect on 1 December 2009. There has to date been no proposal for subsidiary legislation to implement its provisions which introduce the fundamental change from the concept of 'minimum standards' under Article 63 TEC to that of 'uniform status' both for refugee and subsidiary protection status effective throughout the EU coupled with 'common procedures' for determining protection status (Article 78(2) TFEU).

1.2.4. *A Brief Introduction to the QD and the APD*

Both the 2004 and 2011 QD's (which are set out in the Appendices) are regional instruments applicable to MS only, but in the provisions which they make for the recognition of international protection rights of refugees, they are expressly stated to be "*based on the full and inclusive application of the Geneva Convention ... as supplemented by ... the Protocol, ... thus affirming the principle of non-refoulement and ensuring that nobody is sent back to persecution*" (Recital (2) 2004 QD).

Whilst the EU legislation detailed above is the primary source of EU law defining the protection regime applicable under the CEAS, it is derived from the principles relating to international protection under both EU instruments and international treaties and conventions.

Recital 3 of the 2004 QD acknowledges that the GC and its 1967 Protocol provide "*the cornerstone of the international legal regime for the protection of refugees*", but the EC have made clear in many of their explanatory documents relating to the CEAS that the two Directives are also based on the common humanitarian values shared by all MS. The Explanatory Memorandum of 12 September 2001, for example, dealing with the concept of serious harm for the purposes of subsidiary protection, confirms that the QD definition is based on international human rights instruments relevant to subsidiary protection of which Article 3 of the ECHR, Article 3 of CAT and Article 7 of the ICCPR are specifically referred to as having informed the definition adopted. There are also a number of references to the importance of reflecting the jurisprudence of the ECtHR when considering protection applications.

The international treaties and conventions are human rights-based and interpreted in jurisprudence from jurisdictions around the world. They are also the subject of much academic commentary. For refugee law judges, they are relevant sources of law insofar as the European instruments from which they draw their inspiration are, to a large extent, modelled upon these source materials.

The QD also introduced, for the first time, the additional concept of subsidiary protection status which, put simply, extends the concept of international protection to those who do not meet the requirements for recognition of refugee status, but are nevertheless at real risk of suffering serious harm, as defined in the QD, if *refouled*.

As a regional instrument, the QD is concerned only with the protection issues of third country nationals and stateless persons who will be referred to as claimants in this document. Nationals of MS are excluded from its protection, as are those third country nationals and stateless persons who fall within the specific exclusion provisions of the QD (Articles 12 and 17 QD). It may be that those who do not qualify as a claimant under the QD, will be entitled to seek protection from *refoulement* under other international instruments – Article 3 of the ECHR, for example, is absolute in its terms and permits no exclusion from its protection – but that is outside the scope of this introduction which is concerned with outlining the protection rights arising under the CEAS, which will be explored in greater detail in Part IV.

The QD is supplemented by the APD. Although stated to apply only to claims for recognition of refugee status, in practice member states have also applied its provisions to consideration of claims for recognition of subsidiary protection status. It can therefore be treated, for our purposes, as applying equally to both bases of international protection recognised by the QD.

As these requirements are contained in EU Directives, it is the duty of MS to transpose their effect into their national legislation. In so far as they fail to do so, the Directive provisions may have direct effect. This may give rise to issues of law as to whether their provisions are mandatory or merely permissive in considering whether more favourable national standards are compatible with the QD and the concept of a CEAS.

Finally, as already noted, rights arising under the EU Charter must also be taken into account (see Recital (16) of the 2011 QD).

1.2.5. *The Judicial Structure within the EU*

Claims for international protection made under the QD will be decided in the first instance by the MS responsible for determining the claim under the provisions of the CEAS.

MS must ensure that from that decision the applicant has the right to an effective remedy before a court or tribunal (Article 39 APD).

The forum for that effective remedy will be determined by the national law of the member state concerned. In some cases, that national law may provide for a full rehearing of the application; in others, the issue may be limited to the determination of whether any refusal of the claimant's application was in accordance with the law; it may be that both a first instance and appellate jurisdiction will apply. In any event, the national court or tribunal will have the power to refer any issue of law raised by the application to the Court of Justice of the European Union (CJEU) for a preliminary ruling and their decision will be final on the issue referred to them.(See further in the IARLJ(EU) publication "Preliminary references to the Court of Justice of the European Union: a note for judges handling asylum related cases".)

Whatever the structure of the process under the national law, however, the remedy provided must be effective for the preservation of the claimant's right to recognition of international protection status where the evidence supports such a conclusion.

Moreover, the national court or tribunal is adjudicating upon rights which arise under EU legislation, even where that legislation has been transposed into the national law. It must therefore be borne in mind that when the national court is concerned with the enforcement of rights arising under EU law, it may effectively be sitting as a part of the EU judicial system.

Although the role of the national courts of MS is of the first importance, the CEAS is unique in imposing a common EU legislative basis designed to deal with fundamental concepts concerning the recognition of IP rights. Where this raises questions of the effect of rights arising under that legislation, national courts have the right to refer specific questions of interpretation to the CJEU for authoritative determination. The decisions of the CJEU as to the effect of that legislation must then be implemented by the national court concerned but also act as legal precedents which are binding on all MS.

As has already been noted above, the ECtHR, although not an EU court, has been responsible for explaining and developing the legal interpretation of the ECHR whose provisions have partly inspired the QD. The CJEU does not have a body of jurisprudence concerned with the application of refugee and subsidiary protection law because of the recent nature of the CEAS legislation. In general terms, however, the CJEU will have regard to the ECtHR jurisprudence although it is not bound to apply it.

All these issues will be explored in greater depth in Part IV and VI of this Paper.

1.3. The Role of the Judge in Refugee and Subsidiary Protection Cases

For reasons of jurisdiction, the remedy available from the national court may differ, as indicated above. In Part V of this paper, we have analysed the task of the refugee law judge who is required to make a fresh decision based on a full review of the evidence. Whilst many national judges will be operating within limited jurisdictions (confined to judicial review, or "decisions at the margin") the focus of this paper is on a full protection hearing. However this paper will assist substantively those review only judges as well in understanding what should be expected of decision makers who make findings on the protection issues themselves.

We have chosen to analyse a full protection hearing because it is the judicial task which most closely resembles the task which is faced by the initial decision-maker. But there is no exact parallel. Unlike the initial decision-maker, the judge does not start with a 'blank sheet' because it is the duty of the court or tribunal to consider a review or appeal from that initial decision. It therefore follows that the material before the decision-maker, that decision itself, and any input from the failed claimant supporting the review or appeal application, will be before the court from the outset of the reference to it.

The need for a full judicial protection hearing will therefore usually arise under Article 39 of the APD where there is good reason in law why the initial decision cannot stand. Nevertheless, it is important that the initial decision-maker should understand what will be involved in the review or appeal process, because the judicial guidelines set out in Part III below, which the court will apply to its own deliberations, are those that the initial decision-maker will also need to take into account in arriving at his or her initial decision. The task of the court or tribunal may be summarised sequentially as follows:

- to decide whether the claimant is entitled to recognition as a person in need of international protection –
- as at the date of the hearing –
- by reference to the relevant provisions of the QD governing recognition of refugee and subsidiary protection status –
- on the totality of the evidence before the court –
- including that obtained by the court of its own volition –
- considered and assessed objectively –
- so as to establish whether –
- if then immediately returned to his country of origin –
- there is a well-founded fear of the claimant being persecuted (Article 13 refugee status recognition) or –
- if not recognised as a refugee pursuant to Article 13 of the QD –
- whether, if so returned, substantial grounds have been shown for believing there is –
- a real risk that the claimant will suffer serious harm as defined in the QD (Article 18 subsidiary protection status recognition).

We set out further elaboration of each of these points in Part V to this paper.

1.4. The Burden and Standard of Proof in Refugee and Subsidiary Protection Cases

Finally, in this section, it is necessary to consider the question of the burden and standard of proof in the CEAS in refugee and protection cases.

Whilst the concept of burden of proof is one with which all courts in the MS will be familiar, starting from the basic precept that the burden of proving an assertion lies on he who makes it, the concept of the standard of proof in these cases raises greater difficulty. It is a concept with which those familiar with the common law adversarial procedure are familiar but it has traditionally played little or no role in the civilian tradition.

We need only observe in this introduction that it is our view that the jurisprudence of the ECtHR provides appropriate guidance for an understanding of how these concepts require to be applied in the CEAS in international protection cases, as it relates to the risk on return assessment. The standard of proof, in the assessment of the credibility of past and present facts (claimant's personal evidence), is however not so readily ascertainable from ECHR law, as we discuss in Part VI.

These two related issues are explored in greater depth in Part VI.

2. Part II: A Structured Approach
to the Decision-making Process in Refugee and Subsidiary Protection Claims (Part II)

Noting the "protection obligations" states have entered into, pursuant to EU and international law (as described in Part I), and recognising the gravity of the predicament that may face claimants who are in need of international protection, judges must approach all claims with an outlook that gives claimants full individual personal respect; and recognises the seriousness of the task being undertaken.

Judges carrying out full merits reviews in refugee and subsidiary protection cases (especially judges new to, or irregularly involved with, these cases) will be greatly assisted by approaching each case in a systematic, step by step manner. In all cases up to nine steps can be involved. The following one-page chart sets out the steps and issues involved, with brief explanations of tasks to be completed at each stage. This is followed by the expanded explanation of each step.

The core issues to address are: what are the accepted past and present facts found by the judge (or the accepted profile) of the claimant; then what is his/her predicament on return; then should he/she be granted refugee or subsidiary protection status, under the QD. The step-by-step process we set out below is suggested as a way in which confusion can be minimised by making the required findings in the correct order and basing them on the appropriate evidence and information.

2.1. Step 1: Preliminary enquires

As a preliminary step however, in refugee and subsidiary appeals, of claimants with unique profiles, it will prove convenient and pragmatic for the Court to consider:

a. Assuming that the whole factual basis of the refugee or other protection claim is accepted, *without reservation*, do these fully accepted facts establish, as a matter of law and pursuant to the QD, that the claimant has actually *not* made out his or her case and thus *cannot* be recognised either as a refugee or as a person deserving of subsidiary protection? (If so, effectively the appeal may be disposed of at this point. *For example*: if the claim made, and/or prospective fear, is of mere discrimination only, and not of persecution or serious harm, the appeal cannot succeed as the claim, at it highest, does not reach the threshold of acts of persecution or serious harm as defined in Articles 9 and 15 respectively of the 2004 QD. Indeed, occasionally the grounds of appeal, again taken at their highest, may show the claim is manifestly unfounded or clearly abusive and further analysis and time should not be spent on it.)

b. At the other extreme, credibility is not always or necessarily determinative of a refugee or protection claim. Whilst credibility is at the heart of every appeal, it may sometimes occur that, by virtue of the situation in the appellant's country of origin, that he or she can qualify for refugee or subsidiary protection status merely because they are accepted as being of that nationality and are of a particular age, gender or ethnicity – e.g. members of certain minority tribes in Somalia have been in this situation in the past.

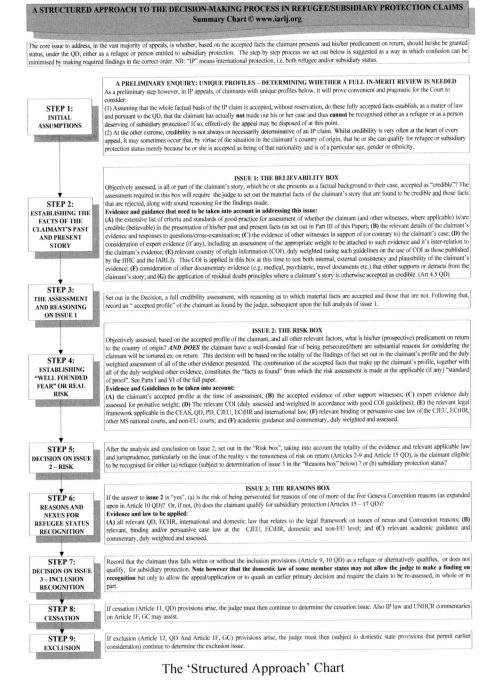

The 'Structured Approach' Chart

2.2. Step 2: Establishing the accepted facts of the claimant's past and present story (The 'believability box')

Issue 1 – Objectively assessed, is all or part of the claimant's story, which he or she presents as a factual background to their case, accepted as "credible"?

The assessment required in this box will require the judge to set out the material facts of the claimant's story that are found or accepted to be credible *and* those facts that are rejected, along with sound reasoning for the findings that are made.

Evidence and guidance that needs to be taken into account in determining this issue are:

a. The extensive list of criteria and standards of good practice for assessment of whether the claimant (and other witnesses, where applicable) is/are credible in the presentation of his/her past and present facts (see § 3);
b. The relevant details of the claimant's evidence, written and oral, and responses to questions and cross-examination;
c. The evidence of other witnesses in support of (or contrary to) the claimant's case;
d. The consideration of expert evidence (if any), including an assessment of the appropriate weight to be attached to such evidence and its inter-relation to the claimant's evidence;
e. Relevant COI duly weighted (using such guidelines on the use of COI as those published by the HHC and the IARLJ). This COI is applied in this step or 'box', at this time, to test the claimant's evidence using the 'basic criteria' from Part III including internal and external consistency; and plausibility of the evidence.
f. Consideration of other documentary evidence (e.g. medical, psychiatric, travel documents) that either supports or detracts from the claimant's story;[22] and
g. The application of residual doubt principles, as envisaged under Article 4 QD (see § 3.7.1.), where a claimant's story is otherwise accepted as credible.

2.3. Step 3: The assessment and reasoning on Issue 1

Set out in the decision, the full credibility assessment findings, including sound reasoning on the material facts that go to the core of the claim. This will include a note of the material past and present facts that are accepted and those not accepted. From that assessment the judge can then set down as a finding the "accepted

---

22 Often it will be impossible to determine the authenticity of a document. Decision-makers should therefore take into account the general credibility of the claimant, and relevant COI on the standards of documentation from the claimant's country of nationality. Decision-makers should, of necessity, be cautious in placing too much reliance on documentation, particularly those that may be forged or readily available from illegal sources and people-smugglers. The appropriate approach is that taken from the UK case of *Tanveer Ahmed* [2002] ImmAR 318 where the Tribunal ruled that the burden of proof is upon the claimant to show that documentary evidence submitted can be relied on. However, it is for the decision-maker to consider whether a document is one upon which reliance should be properly placed after looking at all of the evidence "in the round". See also our comments on the use of web or electronic ("e") documentation in Parts I and III.)

profile" of the claimant. Thus there may be an "accepted profile" that includes: a full acceptance of the entire claimant's evidence, a partial acceptance of some of the evidence and rejection of other evidence, or possibly a full, or near total, rejection of the entire claimant's evidence. It is this "accepted profile" of the claimant that then becomes a core part of the prospective risk assessment that then follows. It should be noted that even if only nationality is accepted the decision should still proceed to the next step of assessing the risk on return.

2.4. Step 4: Establishing 'well-founded fear' or real risk (The 'risk box')

Issue 2 – Objectively assessed, based on the accepted profile of the claimant, and all other relevant factors, what is the (prospective) predicament of the claimant on return to his or her country of nationality or former habitual residence? (NB: the claimant's *subjective* assessment, of their fear on return, will almost always be part of their "story" or claim *but the test for the judge here is an objective test only* and the claimant's subjective evidence or claims are not part of the assessment of what is often called, confusingly perhaps, a "credible claim". Only when the subjective claims or fears are fully in accord with the objective evidence, on assessment by the judge of that evidence, will those subjective elements become part of the "facts as found".)

This step is at the nub of the case. It involves the assessment of the risk to the claimant on return, frequently characterised as a 'real' risk. This equates it with the test applied by the ECtHR in relation to risk of treatment in breach of Article 3 ECHR on return. In refugee recognition claims the risk to be established is a well-founded fear of persecution for a GC reason (Article 2(b) 2004 QD), and in subsidiary protection cases substantial grounds must be shown for believing that the claimant would face a real risk of suffering serious harm as defined in Article 15 2004 QD (Article 2(f)). It is, however, suggested that there is no difference in practice between the levels of risk required under either status.

The conclusions of the judge here will be based on the totality of the findings of fact he or she has set out as the claimant's profile *and* the duly weighted assessment of all of the other evidence noted below. The combination of the accepted facts that make up the claimant's profile, together with all of the duly weighted other evidence constitutes the 'facts as found' upon which the risk assessment is made at the applicable 'standard of proof' (see Part VI for a full discussion on Standard and the Burden of proof issues).

2.4.1. *Evidence to be taken into account in the risk assessment:*

a. The claimant's accepted profile at the time of assessment;
b. The accepted evidence of other support witnesses;
c. Expert evidence duly assessed for probative weight;
d. The relevant COI (duly assessed and weighted in accordance with COI guidelines, such as those of HHC and IARLJ);
e. The relevant legal framework applicable in the QD, APD, CJEU and, ECtHR and international asylum law;

f. Relevant binding or persuasive case law of the CJEU, ECtHR, other member state national courts, and possibly relevant case law from non-EU courts; and
g. Academic guidance and other commentary duly weighted and assessed.[23]

2.5. Step 5: Decision on Issue 2 – Risk

After the analysis and conclusion on Issue 2 set out in Step 4 (The "Risk box" decision – see § 2.4), taking into account the totality of the evidence and relevant applicable law and jurisprudence on the issue of well-founded fear or serious reasons for considering (which is widely accepted as the assessment of *the reality versus the remoteness of risk on return*), the judge must turn their mind to the question of whether the claimant is eligible to be recognised for either:

a. Refugee status (subject to determination of Issue 3 in Step 6 'Reasons and nexus box' – see § 2.6); or
b. Subsidiary protection status?

2.6. Step 6: Convention grounds and nexus for refugee status recognition (The 'reasons box')

Issue 3: If the answer to *Issue 2* is "yes":

a. Is the risk of being persecuted for reasons of one of more of the five GC grounds (as relevantly discussed in Article 10 QD)?Or, if not:
b. Does the claimant qualify for subsidiary protection status (Articles 15 – 17 QD)?

2.6.1. *Evidence and law to be applied:*

a. All relevant QD, EU law, relevant domestic legislation and UNHCR other international guidance that relates to the issues of nexus and Convention reasons;
b. Relevant, binding and/or persuasive case law at the CJEU, ECtHR, domestic and non-EU level; and
c. Relevant academic guidance and commentary duly weighted and assessed.

2.7. Step 7: Decision on inclusion recognition

The conclusion should then record that the claimant falls within or outside of the inclusion provisions, (Articles 2,5, 9, 10 and 13 QD, (with reference to Article 1A(2) GC), as a refugee), or alternatively qualifies, or does not qualify, for subsidiary protection status (Articles 15 and 18 QD). NB: *Note however that the domestic law of some Member States may not allow the judge to make a finding on recognition* but only to allow the appeal or application and/or to quash an earlier

---

23 See for example "The Michigan Guidelines on Well Founded Fear (2004)" Program in Refugee and Asylum Law (2009), <www.refugeecaselaw.org>.

primary decision and require the claim to be re-assessed, in whole or in part at an earlier instance.

2.8. Step 8: Cessation

If cessation (Article 11 QD) provisions arise, the judge must then continue to determine the cessation issue. Also, international jurisprudence and UNHCR commentaries on Article 1C of the GC may assist to give further *guidance* to the judge.

2.9. Step 9: Exclusion

If exclusion (Article 12, QD) provisions arise, the judge must then continue to determine the exclusion issue. Also, international jurisprudence and UNHCR commentaries on Article 1F of the GC may assist to give further guidance to the judge. It must be noted that in some Member States, by virtue of domestic legislation, exclusion issues can or should be addressed before inclusion or real risk issues.

3. Part III: Judicial Guidance
for the Assessment of Credibility under the EU Qualifications Directive
Basic Criteria and Standards of Good Practice

3.1. Introduction

This Guidance has been developed by the European chapter of the IARLJ as a partner with HHC and UNHCR in the "CREDO- improved credibility assessment in EU asylum procedures" project. The Guidance consists of a statement of basic criteria applicable for credibility assessment of past and present evidence presented by claimants and a set of judicial standards for good practice in such assessment.[24] They have been agreed, after an extensive consultative process involving some 35 experienced IARLJ members and other European judges from across almost all member states who participated in this project. There was also input from the European wider judiciary, EASO, UNHCR, HHC and NGOs, academics and experts in this field.

The aim of the IARLJ, and all others involved in the Credo project, has been to promote and attain excellence, not only in the core task of assessing credibility, but also in achieving greater overall consistency, in refugee and subsidiary protection decision making across the EU. This is fully consistent with the objectives of the IARLJ, namely to promote the "rule of law" in refugee and other international protection determination. It is planned, in the near future, that the Guidance and content of this paper be used in judicial training projects across the EU. A working party, within the IARLJ (EU), will continue to update and improve the contents of this paper and related judicial procedures.

These criteria are prepared with the underlying recognition that:

a. It is the duty of claimants[25] to present their own applications for recognition of refugee and or subsidiary protection status and each application is to be assessed on an individual basis (Article 4.1-4.5 QD).
b. The determination of eligibility for protection within the EU is an onerous and specialist task.[26] Whilst the initial source of judicial reference will be the national law of the Member State transposing the applicable EU Directives in the CEAS, it must always be borne in mind that this will be informed by the GC and other European and international human rights conventions

---

24 We have referred in this Guidance to the role and duty of the judge but most of what is contained in this Part is equally applicable to decision-makers at all levels.
25 See discussion on burden of proof in Part VI (§ 6).
26 See Part I (§1).

themselves, together with judicial interpretation by courts over the past sixty years.[27]

c. Because the issues involved (for both claimants and states) are so serious in nature and involve fundamental principles of justice, only the highest standards of fairness are applicable in the determination process. It is this most fundamental premise, inherent in the humanitarian nature of international and EU protection that directly or indirectly underpins this Guidance.

d. The assessment of credibility of past and present facts (evidence) presented by a claimant is a tool used to establish the "accepted profile" of the claimant and to determine their international protection needs. This profile is a vital part of the "material facts" in determining the risk of the claimant being persecuted or suffering serious harm on return. Thus, as shown in Part II ("The structured approach" above), it is necessary to decide Issue 1 before moving on to Issue 2 ("the prospective risk").

e. This Guidance is based on EU administrative law principles, including the right to a fair and public hearing, equality of arms (*audi alteram partem*), proportionality, legal certainty, and the right to an effective remedy. These principles are set out in the core instruments of the EU (including the TFEU and the EU Charter) and the ECHR.[28]

f. The principles contained in this Guidance are derived from EU legislative instruments, the jurisprudence of relevant courts and the experience of the judges who have participated in this project.[29] In addition we have had regard to guidance from the UNHCR Handbook and Guidelines (2011) and leading academic publications.

g. In EU, and wider international law, there are some basic criteria (as set out below), applied in all valid judicial reasoning, to evaluate the "lawfulness" of credibility assessment. These criteria, and the detailed standards of good practice that expand on them, specifically in the assessment of credibility in refugee and subsidiary protection cases, have been developed in asylum law and practice over the past 60 years. The explanatory memoranda of the EC make it clear that EU legislative principles are drawn largely from accepted international practices in the field of asylum and international human rights law and that in many instances the EU legislation is partly declaratory of the best international practice. A failure to apply these criteria and/or meet the

---

27 Certain national legislation of MS seeks to prescribe issues which are to be reflected in the assessment of the claimant's credibility – e.g. s. 8 of the UK Asylum and Immigration (Treatment of Claimants, etc.) Act 2004. Such national legislation cannot be relied upon as a substitute for assessment of credibility being made on an '*individual, objective and impartial*' basis in order to comply with both EU and internationally recognised standards of decision-making – see, e.g., Article 47 EU Charter and Article 8 APD.

28 For further elaboration, see Parts IV to VI.

29 The legislative instruments include both the primary legislation, such as TEC, TFEU and the EU Charter, and secondary legislation comprising regulations and directives concerned with the implementation of the CEAS, with particular reference to the QD and APD. The jurisprudence includes not only that of the CJEU and ECtHR but also that of the national courts of MS and internationally recognised case-law dealing with IP law principles. That hierarchy has been adopted in the sources quoted in the text.

standards, will, on judicial review, lead to consideration of whether an error of law in the decision making has rendered it unsustainable.

h. This Guidance is non-exhaustive. It includes, often with overlap between them, standards of good practice based on fundamental fairness, including procedural requirements and recognition of the specialised needs of vulnerable sub-groups of claimants. For ease of use the standards of good practice are grouped into four sections: those relating to fundamental fairness issues, those of a more procedural nature, those applicable in assessing the claims of vulnerable groups with special needs; and a discussion of how residual doubt, and Article 4 QD issues (or what is also referred to in some jurisdictions as "the benefit of the doubt") should be dealt with.

3.2. Basic criteria applicable for credibility assessment of claimants

Unless there is a conceded or obvious acceptance, *in full,* of a claimant's credibility, the judge independently must carry out the assessment task. This assessment must be approached by the judge impartially and so as to minimise their own inherent subjectivity so far as possible. To ensure objectivity and concentration on the core elements in credibility assessment, the following criteria are seen as judicial best practice. Following these criteria should ensure judges (and all other decision-makers) reach high quality decisions. The credibility findings, in respect of the assessment of the claimant's accepted profile, should explain (as applicable) whether the following criteria are established or not:

a. *Internal consistency*: These are findings on consistencies or discrepancies within the statements and other evidence presented by claimants from their first meetings, applications, and personal interviews and examination at all stages of processing their application/appeal until final disposal.

b. *External consistency*: These are findings on consistencies or discrepancies between the statements of the claimants and all the external objective evidence, including duly weighted COI, expert and any other relevant evidence.

c. *Impossibility*: These are findings, which when set against objective internal or external evidence, show alleged "facts", presented by a claimant, as impossible (or near thereto) of belief. For example: relevant dates, locations, and timings, mathematical, scientific or biological facts.

d. *Plausibility*: These are findings on the plausibility of the claims including explanations by the claimant of alleged past and present "facts", and whether they add to or subtract from acceptance of those facts as being able to be believed. Within this criterion several specific issues may be relevant, such as: a lack of satisfactory or logical detail in explanation, explanations for the use of false or misleading documentation, delays in presentation of claims; and reasons given in previous claims and appeals. Plausibility will, to some extent, often overlap with external consistency findings.[30]

30　See M. Kagan, "Is Truth in the Eye of the Beholder? Objective Credibility Assessment in Refugee Status Determinations" (2003) 17(3) *Georgetown Immigration Law Journal* 367-415. Espe-

→

e. *"In the round"*: Overall credibility conclusions should not be made only on "non-material", partially relevant or perhaps tangential findings only. Thus the substantive findings in the assessment of accepted credibility profiles, including the weight accorded to the above issues, should be made "in the round" based on the totality of the evidence and taking into account that findings on a, b, and c (above) criteria will logically have more weight than those solely relying on "implausibility".[31]

f. *Sufficiency of detail*: With rare exceptions, based on a claimant's incapacity, a claim should be substantively presented and sufficiently detailed, at least in respect of the most material facts of the claim, to show it is not manifestly unfounded.

g. *Timeliness of the claim*: Late submission of statements and late presentation of evidence may negatively affect general credibility, unless valid explanations are provided.[32]

h. *Personal involvement (persönliche Betroffenheit)*: If all the above criteria are met it is still important to ensure the claimant has been personally involved in the "story" or evidence presented (*Realkennzeichen*).

3.3. EU judicial standards of good practice in credibility assessment

Many of the following standards of good practice are often to be found in the Codes of Administrative Procedure in many Member States. Additionally they have been developed by EU and international judges on a wide range of issues that are applicable in credibility assessment. The list that follows is not exhaustive and experienced judges may indeed consider applying many of them "goes without saying". However this list aims to be as extensive as possible, especially to assist and guide those judges, and all others, unfamiliar with this area of law, to carry out the challenging task of credibility assessment, with the assistance of the cumulative experience reflected in these suggested standards.

Also, it must be said that, while appropriate deference to skill and experience will normally be accorded to experienced, first instance decision-makers, or full merits review judges, a material failure to adhere to one or more of these standards will often lead to an error of law conclusion on judicial review. For ease of use they are grouped in the four categories that follow.

---

cially section on plausibility at pp. 390-391where he argues that plausibility "adds very little" to external consistency.

31 See, e.g., *Cruz Varas and Others v Sweden* [1991] 14 EHRR 1; *Vilvarajah v UK* [1991] 14 EHRR 248; *A v SSHD* [2006] EWCA Civ 973; Article 80 Polish Code of Administrative Procedure (CAP); Section 108(1) and (2) German Code of Administrative Court Procedure. .

32 See ECtHR in *B v Sweden* (28 October 2004) *ECtHR* Appl No 16578/03; *Khan v Canada* (15 October 1994) Convention Against Torture Committee CATC No 015/1994; *Kaoki v Sweden* (8 May 1996) No 041/1996.

3.4. (A) Treatment of Substantive Evidence

3.4.1. *A.1 Consistency*

Past or present facts should be presented by claimants in an internally and externally consistent manner.

Explanation: The effect on credibility assessment of inconsistencies and discrepancies in the evidence, taking into account the personal circumstances of the claimant, should be clearly explained to them and they must be given the chance to respond. The responses and explanations given by claimants when challenged on the apparent contradictions must be taken into account.

Examples: Claimant A states he was a member of a named political movement on arrival but in later statements claims this is not the case. No satisfactory explanation is provided when confronted on this.

Claimant B's evidence at all stages is consistent with well-sourced COI from UNHCR reports.

Authorities:
- *R.C. v. Sweden* (2010) ECtHR, Appl No 41827/07;
- Committee Against Torture "General Comment No. 1: Implementation of Article 3 of the Convention in the context of Article 22" A/53/44, annex IX, 21 November 1997;
- United Kingdom: *Y v SSHD* [2006] EWCA Civ 1223;
- Poland: SACP File 11OSK 902/10 (20 April 2011);
- Croatia: *Re. Miroshnikov* (15 June 2012) ACZ No Usl-1287/12;
- Norway: *Case HR-201102133-A* (16 November 2011) Norwegian Supreme Court, 2011/817 (also provides commentary on the burden and standard of proof applicable in international protection cases under the Immigration Act 2008);
- Czech Republic: CzRCP (26 January 2006) File No 48 Az 44/2005; CZRCUnL (12 March 2009), File No 58 Az 26/2008 (Treatment of implausible statements by claimant)
- Netherlands: *Malumba* ABRvS (27 January 2003), No 2002062971, *JV* 2003/103.

3.4.2. *A.2 Plausibility*

The plausibility of factual evidence will be reflected in the assessment of credibility of the claimant's history.

Explanation: These are not ends in themselves. Plausibility may potentially reflect the subjective view of the judge. Awareness of the judge's own personal theories of "truth" and "risk" should be noted by the judge to ensure objectivity is maximised. It is a fundamental characteristic of refugee and subsidiary protection claims that their proper consideration requires that specific conditions applicable in the claimant's country of origin be understood and reflected in the assessment. Rejections of evidence for implausibility must be fully reasoned, including explanations provided by claimants in regard to the potentially implausible parts of their evidence. Decisions based solely on implausibility are likely to be less persuasive than those based on a wider range of basic criteria.

Examples: Claimant A from a country with a poor human rights record but efficient police force claims he escaped from custody to leave the country, whereas all COI indicates there are no records of detainees escaping. No satisfactory explanation was provided and the escape appeared implausible.

Claimant B presents a story that has minor inconsistencies, but, in the round, the core of the evidence is plausible.

Authorities:

* United Kingdom: *XY (Iran) v SSHD* [2008] EWHC Civ 533; *Y v SSHD* [2006] EWCA 1223;
* Poland: SACP (31 August 2011) File No. II OSK 1535/ 10; SACP (20 April 2011) File No II OSK 902/10 and II OSK 903/10;
* Czech Republic: CzRCP (19 August 2004), File No 4 Azs 152/2004;
* New Zealand: *Refugee Appeal No 1/92 Re SA*(30 April 1992).

3.4.3. *A.3 Coherence*

Coherently presented evidence by claimants is prima facie more likely to be accepted as credible.

Explanation: Subject to the personal circumstances and background of the claimant (which could include suffering trauma from past maltreatment), their evidence of past and present facts should be expected to be coherently presented. An incoherent story may reflect a lack of credibility or a poorly "learned account". Similarly to plausibility, coherence of evidence must be assessed against the background presentation of the claimant in national, ethnic and personal terms and claimants must be given the opportunity to explain apparent incoherence in their evidence.

Authorities:

* Article 4(5)c QD and also see "Plausibility" above as these two standards are often considered together.

3.4.4. *A.4: Audi alteram partem or Equality of Arms*

The "other side" must be heard. Potentially negative material evidence, in respect of which a claimant is not afforded the opportunity for explanation or rebuttal, should not be taken into account in assessment of credibility.

Explanation: All claimants must be provided a reasonable opportunity to refute, explain or provide mitigating circumstances in respect of contradictory or confusing evidence that is material and could potentially undermine core elements of their claim.

Examples: Following the conclusion of the interview process, but before the final decision, COI information is received which raises issues as to the credibility of the claimant. The proper course is to provide that evidence to the claimant and to invite comments and if necessary, to resume the interview.

Authorities:

* Germany: GFAC (21 July 2010), 10 C 41.09 – para 3 ff;

- Hungary: BMC (30 September 2010), Decision No24.K.32 957/2009; *SWJ v OIN* (2010) Decision No 17.K.30.302/2010; *SWJ v OIN* (21 April 2011) (NB: since April 2011 the Budapest Municipal Court no longer has exclusive authority in asylum cases);
- Czech Republic: CzRCP (28 July 2009), File No 5 Azs 40/2008; CzRCP (21 December 2004), File No 6 Azs 235/2004; CzRCP (13 March 2009), File No 5 Azs 28/2008, CzRCP (29 October 2003), File No 48 Az 44/2005.

3.4.5. *A.5: Reasons*

Judges must provide substantive, objective and logical reasons, founded in the evidence, for rejecting past or present facts presented by claimants in support of their claim.

Examples: It is self-evident that a decision that fails to record the reasons for rejecting, or accepting a claimant's evidence will be potentially flawed.

Authorities:

- United Kingdom: *Karanakaran v SSHD* [2000] EWCA Civ 11; *Y v SSHD* [2006] EWCA Civ 1688; *Ilkhani v SSHD* [2005] EWCA 1674; *Traore v SSHD* [2006] EWCA Civ 1444;
- Germany: German Code of Administrative Procedure s.108(1); GFAC (17 November 2008), 10 B 10.08 para 2 ff; GFAC (29 June 2010), 10C 10.09-para 20-22; GFAC (22 June 2011), 10 B 12.11para 2 ff.

3.4.6. *A.6: Materiality*

Judges must reach credibility conclusions on facts material to the claimant's case that go to the core of the fundamental issues.

Explanation: This relates to core evidence that the claimant presents as the basis of their well-founded fear of being persecuted on return to their country of nationality (i.e. the findings on Issues 1 and 2 of Part II above). Firstly, while it may appear self–evident, it must be noted that in order to reach conclusions on core facts (particularly in inquisitorial hearings), judges must ensure questions to the claimants are focussed on the material facts of the claim. Some core issues, like those of identity and nationality, will be essential in every case. However even validly reasoned rejections, in respect of only peripheral or minor present or past facts, will not be a substantive basis for the rejection of material past or present facts presented by the claimant. Whilst questions about events outside the core elements of evidence are a proper basis for testing the general consistency of an account, they will not render core testimony incredible unless they undermine central, as opposed to peripheral or incidental, elements of the account.

Authorities:

- United Kingdom: *HH (Iraq) v SSHD* [2006] EWCA Civ 1374; *Ngrincuti v SSHD* [2008]EWHC (Admin) 1952;
- Germany: GFAC (9 May 2003), 1 B 217.02.

3.4.7. *A.7: Speculation*

Judges must not engage in subjective speculation in their reasons for rejecting the credibility of claimants' evidence as to do so would be to rely on unfounded assumptions.

Explanation: This is particularly so where judges or other assessors may put subjective speculative questions regarding potential risks to other persons and the manner in which other people may be expected to react to potential danger. The claimant's unique predicament is to be assessed, not generalised risks or speculative risks to others in the home country.

It is, however, legitimate for judges or decision-makers to draw inferences as to what may happen in the future, from all the evidence, when undertaking the prospective risk assessment (see Major issue 2 (Risk Box) above). Where since arrival of the claimant there have been fundamental and durable changes in the country of origin which render a past fear no longer sustainable, such an inference may clearly be drawn from reliable COI.

Examples: Without obtaining detailed knowledge of the COI situation, the judge finds the evidence is not credible on the basis that he/she does not, on unsubstantiated evidence or personal feelings, believe such behaviour could take place.

Authorities:
- United Kingdom: *Ilkhani v SSHD* [2005] EWCA 1674;
- Germany: GFAC (16 April 1985), 9C 109.84 para 16;
- Czech Republic: CzRCP (13 March 2009), File No 5 Azs 28/2009.

3.4.8. *A.8: Objective approach*

All credibility assessments in refugee and subsidiary protection claims must be undertaken with a balanced and objective approach.

Explanation: This goes to the issue of mind-set or outlook explored in greater detail in Part I above. Thus when considered in the round, decisions and reasoning should not reflect a culture of either disbelief or of naïve acceptance. Simplistic rejection, ill-considered and also naïve acceptance of evidence by judges or decision-makers, without appropriate questioning and reference to objective evidence and COI, will often lead to a flawed assessment of credibility. A balanced approach will include taking into account the accepted background of the claimant's education, social, gender, age and medical status.

Examples: In refugee and subsidiary protection claims, in contrast to the situation which applies in civil *inter partes* litigation, there will only exceptionally be any evidence *directly* relating to matters upon which the credibility of the claimant rests, except possibly by reference to COI evidence, which is necessarily usually of a more general nature. Such evidence may thus either support or undermine the claimant's account of personal experiences. However the judge, in an asylum case, does not have the opportunity to assess and contrast the accounts of opposed parties as to past events, which is often determinative of the credibility assessment in the more familiar pattern of civil litigation.

Authorities:
- Article 4(5)(c) QD;
- United Kingdom: *JK(DRC) v SSHD* [2007] EWCA Civ 831;
- Czech Republic: CzRCP (20 March 2008), File No 47 AZ 28/2008;
- New Zealand: *Refugee Appeal No 70074/96* (17 September 1996).

3.4.9. *A.9: Excessive or unreasonable concentration on details*

Excessive or unreasonable concentration on details may on occasions lead to flawed findings of fact on material issues. Claimants cannot always be expected to have detailed knowledge, exact recall of dates, events, names, officers, or organisations in their evidence.

Explanation: While in most situations claimants should be able to provide coherent details of their background, especially those events that are material to their claim, there are situations where this may not apply.

Examples: Where the evidence related to events which happened many years back, claimants had only minor roles in the events giving rise to the risk of being persecuted; and/or age, gender, or other vulnerabilities are relevant. Embellishments and exaggerations can also have relevance in credibility assessment but they may also be irrelevant in some situations. These are factors that must be assessed in the round.

Authorities:
- Czech Republic: CzRCP (28 July 2009) File No 5 Azs 40/2009.

3.4.10. *A.10: Relevant corroborative documentation (hard copy or web-sourced)*

The credibility of all relevant documentation (not including COI which is discussed below at A.14) should be accepted or rejected on the same basis as oral or written evidence from the claimant.

Explanation: It is for the judge to consider whether the document is one upon which reliance should be properly placed, after considering the evidence in the round as part of the totality of the evidence. Thus no documentation should be considered in isolation from the rest of the claimant's claim. It is not, however, appropriate or sustainable for a decision-maker to attach no weight to a relevant document presented in support of a claim, without giving clear reasons for such a finding. Supporting documents should not be dismissed merely because such documents may be easy to falsify, or that the originals could not be provided by the claimant.

Authorities:
- Article 4.2 and 4.3 (b) QD;
- *Singh and others v Belgium* (2 October 2012), ECtHR, Appl No33210/11;
- United Kingdom: *Tanveer Ahmed* [2002] ImmAR 318;
- Czech Republic: CzRCP (1 April 2008), File No 9 Azs 15/2008.

3.4.11. *A.11: Delayed claims*

A delay in the presentation of a claim should not be treated as a presumption that the whole claim lacks credibility.

Explanation: Claimants should be expected to give good reasons for their delay and failure to do this *may* contribute to a lack of credibility. However, there should be recognition of situations where avoidance of disclosure may have arisen through shame, possibly associated with sexual violence, cultural/wider family and indirect personal "costs" of disclosure.

Example: A Kosovar woman who potentially might lose her children if her husband learnt of her being raped and thus is extremely reluctant to give evidence of the rape and may delay providing such evidence.

Authorities:
- Article 4(5)(d) QD (in contrast to Article 8.1APD);
- *Jabari v Turkey* (11 July 2009), ECtHR, Appl No 40035/98 (Limited to Turkey);
- United Kingdom: *Q v* SSHD [2006] EWCA Civ 351; *Shah v SSHD [2006]* EWCA Civ 674;
- Germany: GFAC (19 October 2001), 1B 24.01, para 6; GFAC (27 March 2000), 9B 518.99- para 21;
- Czech Republic: CzRCP (6 March 2012), File No 3 Azs 6/2011;
- New Zealand: *Refugee Appeal No 2254/94* (21 September 1994).

3.4.12. *A.12: Past persecution*

Judges must make specific findings on evidence of past persecution or serious maltreatment.

Explanation: It is important to make such findings (in Step 2 Part II above). If accepted, this is a serious indication of a claimant's accepted profile and subsequently risk of being persecuted or suffering serious harm on return.

Authorities:
- Article 4(4) QD;
- Germany: GFAC (27 April 2010), 10C 5.09 - para 23; GFAC (27 April 2010), 10 C 4.09 - para 31[33];
- Czech Republic: CzRC (26 March 2008), No 2 Azs 73/2006;
- New Zealand: *Refugee Appeal No 70366* (22 September 1997)(this case provides discussion on comparative jurisdictions).

---

33 With English translation in:
   <http://www.bverwg.bund.de/enid/6116b3c12d03e766a9e86e379ec57539,0/Decisions_in_Asylum_and_Immigration_Law/BVerwG_ss__C_4__9_nh.html>

3.4.13. *A.13: Absence of past persecution*

Judges should not reject the credibility of all past and present facts presented by a claimant because evidence of past persecution has not been provided or is delayed in presentation.

Explanation: As under A.12 above.

Authorities:
* New Zealand; *Refugee Appeal No 300/92* (1 March 1994).

3.4.14. *A.14: Use of COI*

Judges must refer to reliable COI as a vital part of testing the internal and external consistency of a claimant's asserted past and present facts. (Indeed judges should see the obtaining and use of COI as part of "shared burden" approach to credibility assessment.)

Explanation: Reference to COI guidelines, such as those prepared by the UNHCR and the IARLJ (see Attachment 3.2), will assist correct use. It should also be noted that EASO has now commenced issuing COI prepared in accordance with a model methodology to which reference may also be usefully made.[34] The absence of objective COI to support a material fact does not necessarily mean an incident did not occur, or a fact cannot be accepted. This is particularly so with cases involving children, gender and LGBTI claims. Extra vigilance in the assessment of these cases is needed by judges. (See further guidance under C.1 Vulnerable claimants.) However, judges should also be alert to situations where some, less than honest, claimants may "tailor their claims" to be consistent with relevant COI that they consider "assists" their claim.

There are some Member States in which the courts are obligated to make sure that they use the newest available country report of the Foreign Office. Otherwise it as a procedural flaw which normally leads to a reversal of the judgement.

Authorities:
* Article 4(1) *QD*;
* Germany: GFAC (17 December 2007), 10B 92.07;
* United Kingdom: *A v SSHD* [2006] EWCA Civ 973 (Neuberger LJ), *Horvarth v SSHD* [1997] INLR 7; *Ire: Camara v MOJ* [2000] IEHC *1247, Atanasov v Refugee Appeals Tribunal* [2006] IESC 53, *Z v Minister for Justice, Equality and Law Reform [2002]* IESC 14;
* Spain: SC Appeal No 7130/2000(2004);
* Netherlands: Council of State, ABRvS (2005) case no. 200407775/1;
* Belgium: Perm Appeal Bd (2006), case no. 04-3388/ F1755 (2006);
* Slovenia: Admin Ct U 696/2006;
* Hungary: 6K/31468/2005/8;
* Slovakia: 2 Saz/1/2006;
* Lithuania: A6-626-03 and 11112-12-04;

---

34 COI prepared in respect of Afghanistan, July 2012.

- Czech Republic: RC (3 November 2011, File No 2 AZs 28/2011;
- New Zealand: *Refugee* Appeal No 72668/01 [2002] NZAR 649.

3.4.15. *A.15: Expert evidence*

Decision-makers must take note of "expert" evidence and attach appropriate and balanced weight to such evidence.

Explanation: The term "expert" encompasses a wide range of persons with specific knowledge. Sometimes there may be an issue as to whether such persons are in fact "expert" in the legally accepted sense of the word. Where, however, expertise is accepted, the witness is entitled to give "opinion evidence".

'Expert evidence' would include that based on medical, psychiatric and psychological qualifications, as well as COI. All such evidence can be highly determinative of credibility. Expert evidence, which negatively impacts on the claimant's case must always be put to claimants for comment and/or rebuttal. Where necessary and appropriate, judges, recognising in particular that they are not medical or psychiatric experts, must, after balanced and reasoned assessment, ensure that appropriate "deference" or understanding is given to that expertise. Assistance in the use of expert evidence can usefully be obtained from the *IARLJ Publications relating to COI and Expert Medical Evidence* (see Attachment 3.1 and 3.2).

Judges and decision-makers have to come to credibility conclusions by themselves after considering such expert evidence. This will not mean they are obligated to make use of all expert evidence in credibility matters, but reasons should always be given, for not taking such evidence into account. As a rule it is not a legal error of law if the court comes to the conclusion that an expert is not needed to assess the credibility of the claimant and his/her story.

Authorities:
- *Bensaid v UK* (6 February 2001) ECtHR, Appl No 44599/98;
- United Kingdom: *HK v SSHD* [2006] EWCA Civ 1037, *AK (Afghanistan) v SSHD* [2007] EWCA Civ 535;
- Germany: GFAC (17 September 2003), 1 B 471.0; GFAC (11 September 2007), 10C 8.07 – para 13-17;
- Poland: SACP (20 April 2011), File No II 902/10;
- Hungary: *SWJ v OIN* (30 September 2010), BMC Decision No 24.K.32 957/2009;
- *UNHCR Handbook* (2011) at [207] & [208].

3.4.16. *A.16: Findings made in previous claims*

When judges are determining second or subsequent claims from the same claimant, findings from the earlier claim, whether of positive or negative credibility, must be taken into account.

Explanation: The QD and APD (and domestic regulations in many Member States) provide that negative credibility findings from earlier claims can, or must, be adopted by a subsequent decision-maker or indeed, the subsequent decision-maker is bound by earlier findings. The provisions of Article 5 QD (and 5(3) particularly) should be noted in regard to *sur place* claims and potential "bad faith" claims where a claimant "created the circumstances since leaving his country of origin".

Authorities:
• Art 5 QD; Poland: SACP (9 May 2012), File No 1344/11.

3.4.17. *A.17: Corroboration*

Because of the particular nature of refugee and subsidiary protection assessment, there is no specific requirement for corroboration of the claimant's accepted account.

Explanation: In circumstances where there is no reason to doubt the totality of a claimant's evidence of past and present facts, an uncorroborated account can be accepted without further support. Judges and decision-makers may however consider that some facts can be accepted and others require some form of corroboration (where there do not appear to be any particular difficulties in the way of the claimant producing relevant documents or other corroborative evidence). It must also be noted here that the instant availability of web-based COI can, at times, provide corroboration readily, or otherwise, right up to the time of the final determination. Again caution must be exercised to ensure fairness and "equality of arms" in the use of such material.

Authorities:
• United Kingdom: *Traore v SSHD* [2006] EWCA Civ 1444;
• Germany: GFAC (16 April 1985), 9C – 109.84 – para 16;
• *UNHCR Handbook* at [203].
• New Zealand: *Refugee Appeal* No 75962 [2007] NZAR 307.

3.4.18. *A.18: Partly credible claimants*

Rejection of some evidence, material or peripheral, relating to past or present facts will not necessarily lead to a rejection of all of the claimant's evidence.

Explanation: The accepted profile of a claimant, used in "risk/well-founded fear assessment" will consist of *the accepted past and present facts* presented by the claimant. It is important in decision making to explain why the acceptance of some aspects of credibility does not warrant acceptance of the account as a whole, or vice versa. Careful reasoning in relation to material evidence is essential, in which the appropriate weight accorded to different parts of that evidence must be reasoned and assessed. The more peripheral the facts that are not accepted become, the more difficult it will be to justify wholesale rejection of all the claimant's evidence.

Authorities:
• United Kingdom: *Karanakaran v SSHD* [2000] EWCA 11;
• Czech Republic:, RC (18 May 2011), File No 5 Azs 6/2011-49.

3.4.19. *A.19: Treatment of similar claims*

Evidence of either credible or incredible factual findings from similar claims from the same nationality does not imply the subject claimant's evidence is also credible or incredible. Individual assessment is required.

Authorities:
- Article 4(3) QD;
- Czech Republic: RC (6 February 2008), File No 1 Azs 105/2006-59;
- New Zealand: *Refugee Appeal No 71066/98* (16 September 1999) p 10-11.

3.4.20. *A.20: Treatment of substantially different claims*

Evidence from a claimant that is substantially different from that presented in other claims from that nationality does not imply the subject claimant's factual assertions are incredible.

Authorities: Article 4(3) QD.

3.4.21. *A.21: Group-based persecution*

Regardless of A.19 and A.20 it is nevertheless possible, in certain circumstances, for a claimant (whose accepted profile at Step 2 Part II above is established) to succeed merely by virtue of having common characteristics shared by other members of a group.

Example: By virtue of their nationality, sex, age, ethnic or religious identity, or any combination of these at times, based of valid COI, whole groups of people may be recognised as refugees without further facts being accepted by the judge or decision-maker.

Authorities:
- Germany: GFAC (Judgement dated 21 April 2009), 10 C 11.08 (Iraq);
- Czech Republic, RC (30 September 2008), File No 5 Azs 105/2008-70.

3.4.22. *A.22: Treatment of admission of earlier lies, contradictions or inconsistencies*

The effect of earlier lies or inconsistencies, openly admitted and explained, must be explored very carefully as to their impact on credibility.

Explanation: Such evidence may assist positive or negative credibility assessment, particularly taking into account the nature of refugee and subsidiary protection assessment and relevant medical/psychiatric evidence where applicable.

3.4.23. *A.23: "May have happened"*

It is an error of law to make a finding that a fact, or facts, stated by the claimant "may have happened".

Explanation: Merely to say that certain events " may have happened" to a claim-ant (their family, fellow supporters or the like), lacks sufficient clarity to confirm whether the judge or decision-maker means only that there is a possibility the claim made is correct, or perhaps that there is something much stronger in possibility terms. Such a conclusion by a decision-maker is too vague. The task of the decision-maker is to set out the past and present facts from the claimant's evidence that are accepted and those that are not accepted. The accepted facts (the facts as found) make up the profile of the claimant then used as part of the risk/well-founded fear assessment that follows. Thus vague conclusions of what "may have happened", without either accepting or rejecting the evidence/claim made, must be treated as errors of law in the decision-making reasoning process.

Authorities:
- Article 4 (3)(a)-(d) QD;
- Germany: German Code of Administrative Court Procedure, s. 108.

3.4.24. *A. 24: Demeanour*

Caution must always be exercised in using aspects of the claimant's demeanour, and the manner in which a claimant presents his or her evidence, as a basis for not accepting credibility.

Explanation: The basic principle here is that using demeanour as a basis for credibility assessment should be avoided in virtually all situations. If demeanour is used as a negative factor the judge must give sustainable reasons as to why and how the demeanour and presentation of the claimant contributed to the credibility assessment, taking into account relevant capacity, ethnicity, gender and age factors. Additionally it should only be used in a context of evidenced understanding of the relevant culture, and in acknowledgment of culture as a repertoire of possible behaviours which are not binding on any individual. However, it must be recognised that in reality, demeanour can always have some impact in an oral hearing. A major reason for having an "oral hearing" (as happens in most European jurisdictions) is so that judges can "see and hear" the claimant, and witnesses and claimants can see, hear and address the judge(s).

Example: In many cultures, it is a sign of respect not to make eye contact. In Western culture avoiding eye contact is a sign of shame. However, someone from a Western culture trying to combat feelings of shame might decide to use eye contact to indicate defiance of their persecutors.

Authorities:
- United Kingdom: *DP (Israel) v SSHD* [2006] EWCA Civ 1375;
- Kälin, W. (1986), "Troubled Communication: Cross-Cultural Misunderstandings in the Asylum Hearing", 20(2) *International Migration Review* 230-241 (an old, but still relevant article).

3.4.25. *A.25: Behaviour modification as a means of avoiding risks, as indicated by COI*

Explanation: It can be an error of law to conclude that real risks of claimants being persecuted on return may be avoided by them modifying their behaviour. It is vital for judges to make sound findings, on their past and present behaviour, and the depth of their current convictions. As the best indicators of future forms of behaviour (fundamental to the exercise of core human rights) will be found in the past and present behaviour (that is accepted by the judge), sound and well-reasoned findings must be made, and set out as part of the claimant's accepted profile.

This is essentially so when those findings are then used as part of the risk on return assessment, which of necessity must include assumptions on the claimant's future behaviour, especially where that behaviour could involve the exercise, or restraint from exercise, of a core human right.

This is probably the most vexed area of credibility assessment. It typically arises in cases where certain religious, sexual or political beliefs or activities are banned and/or societally or otherwise strongly opposed or punished. The issue of whether a claimant may be held to be capable of avoiding a risk of being perse-cuted, in his or her own country, by refraining from behaviour in ways which are fundamental to the existence of and/or the manifestation of core protected human rights has long been the subject of debate. Recently, there has been growing recognition that the fundamental issue is how the claimant is likely to behave on return to the country of origin. In its landmark ruling in *Germany v Y and Z* (the facts of which are given in the example below), the CJEU held that such consider-ations are irrelevant to the assessment of risk on *refoulement* if, *"it may reasona-bly be thought that ... he will engage in ... practices which will expose him to a risk of persecution"*.

Although the case concerned the exercise of the right of freedom of religion, the principle is arguably of wider application and may extend (as held by the UK Supreme Court in the cases cited below) to cases concerning the right to political opinion and the expression of immutable characteristics arising from membership of a particular social group.

Example: Y and Z are Pakistani nationals and members of the Muslim Ahmadiyya community, which is an Islamic reformist movement. Article 298 C of the Paki-stani Criminal Code provides that members of the Ahmadiyya religious com-munity may face imprisonment of up to three years or a fine if they claim to be Muslim, describe their faith as Islam, preach or propagate their faith or invite oth-ers to accept it. Moreover, under Article 295 C of that Code, any person who de-files the name of the Prophet Mohammed may be punished by death or life im-prisonment and a fine. In the reasoning of the Immigration Judge who assessed the appeal, it was found that on several occasions Y had been beaten in his home vil-lage by a group of people and had stones thrown at him at his community's place of prayer. Those people had also threatened to kill him and reported him to the police for insulting the Prophet Mohammed. Z was also found to have been mis-treated and imprisoned as a result of his religious beliefs. Based upon these essen-tial findings that related to the claimant exercising his core human right to free-dom of religious expression, the Court was then validly able to conclude in the risk assessment that upon return to Pakistan, both Y and Z would continue to en-gage in religious practices, which would expose them to a real risk of persecution.

Authorities:
• Germany: *Germany v Y and Z* (5 September 2012) CJEU, C-71/11 and C-99/11.

This decision highlights the essential need to establish "the applicant's personal circumstances" in the credibility assessment ("Believability box") and the implications such findings have in the risk assessment ("Risk box") that follows. In *Germany v Y and Z* it was held:

1. Articles 9(1)(a) of Council Directive 2004/83/EC of 29 April 2004, on minimum standards for the qualification and status of third country nationals, or Stateless persons as refugees, or as persons who otherwise need international protection, the content of the protection granted must be interpreted as meaning that: not all interference with the right to freedom of religion which infringes Article 10(1) of the Charter of Fundamental Rights of the European Union is capable of constituting an "act of persecution" within the meaning of that provision of the Directive;
   – there may be an act of persecution as a result of interference with the external manifestation of that freedom, and
   – for the purpose of determining whether interference with the right to freedom of religion which infringes Article 10(1) of the Charter of Fundamental Rights of the European Union may constitute an 'act of persecution', the competent authorities must ascertain, in the light of the personal circumstances of the person concerned, whether that person, as a result of exercising that freedom in his country of origin, runs a genuine risk of, *inter alia*, being prosecuted or subject to inhuman or degrading treatment or punishment by one of the actors referred to in Article 6 of Directive 2004/83.
2. Article 2(c) of Directive 2004/83 must be interpreted as meaning that the applicant's fear of being persecuted is well founded if, *in the light of the applicant's personal circumstances*, the competent authorities consider that it may reasonably be thought that, upon his/her return to the country of origin, he/she will engage in religious practices which will expose him/her to a real risk of persecution. *In assessing an application for refugee status on an individual basis, those authorities cannot reasonably expect the applicant to abstain from those religious practices.*

Two recent cases from the United Kingdom courts also give good examples of the essential need to make sound findings on past and present behaviour and "convictions" that go to the expression of core human rights. These are: *HJ (Iran) and HT (Cameroon) v SSHD* [2010] UKSC 31 (relating to membership of a particular social group – homosexuality), which was expanded upon in *RT (Zimbabwe) and Others v SSHD* [2012] UKSC 38 (involving political opinion) and in particular Lord Hope's judgment at paras 18-20.[35]

---

35 See the analysis of Mr Fordham QC that five principal reasons were given by the court. First, the treatment of those who lived openly as homosexuals in Iran and Cameroon constituted being persecuted (para 40-42). Secondly, sexual orientation was a protected characteristic within the category of membership of "a particular social group" (para 42). Thirdly, the underlying rationale of the Convention was that "people should be able to live freely, without fearing that they may suffer harm of the requisite intensity or duration because they are, say, black, or the descendants of some former dictator, or gay" (para 53). See also paras 52, 65, 67 and 78. Fourthly, the necessary modification in order to avoid persecution (carrying on any homosexual
$\rightarrow$

3.5. (B) Procedural Standards

General guidance on procedure.

> **Credibility assessments may be fundamentally flawed where, through faulty or inappropriate procedures, claimants do not have the opportunity to present their claims and supporting evidence fairly and reasonably.**

At the first instance decision stage, the APD contains extensive provisions designed to ensure procedural fairness.

At the appeal or review stage, the requirements are governed by Article 39 APD but, as appears from other parts of this paper, the requirement for granting an 'effective remedy' also requires observance of a number of related concepts for a fair disposal.

Failure to observe procedural fairness requirements, which can lead to errors of law in credibility assessment, also includes the following standards.

3.5.1. *B.1: Interpreters*

> **So far as is reasonably possible, claimants must have access to competent and unbiased interpreters. There must be an ability to communicate effectively.**

This is a major and vexed area of complaint on appeal from primary decision-makers. Whilst caution must be exercised if claimants, or their representatives, do

---

relationships "discreetly") ran contrary to this underlying rationale. It involved surrendering the person's right to live freely and openly in society as who they are, in terms of the protected characteristic, which was the Convention's basic underlying rationale: see per Lord Rodger at paras 75-76, Lord Hope at para 11 and Sir John Dyson SJC at para 110. Fifthly, the modification was a response to the feared persecution "because of these dangers of living openly" (para 40). There was a difference between a case where the individual would live "discreetly" because of "social pressures" (para 61) and the situation where he/she would behave "discreetly" in order to avoid persecution because he/she is gay (para 62). Only the latter would be entitled to refugee protection, assuming, of course, that he/she would suffer persecution if he/she were to live openly as homosexual.

In the course of its reasoning, the court rejected three arguments advanced on behalf of the Secretary of State. The first was that it was necessary for a refugee to be able to characterise living "discreetly" in order to avoid persecution as being itself "persecution". The second was that it was appropriate to see living "discreetly" in such circumstances as analogous to "internal relocation", so that the "unduly harsh" test applied in relation to internal relocation should be applied here too: see per Lord Hope at paras 20 and 21. The third was that the question was whether living "discreetly" was or was not "reasonably tolerable" to the asylum seeker. This was the test enunciated by the Court of Appeal in *HJ (Iran)*.

In reaching his conclusion, Lord Rodger (para 69) followed the reasoning of the majority in the High Court of Australia in *Appellant S395/2002 v Minister of Immigration* (2003) 216 CLR 473. At para 72, he also referred to the approach adopted in New Zealand, particularly in *Refugee Appeal No 74665/03* [2005] INLR 68 where at para 124 the New Zealand Refugee Status Appeals Authority considered that its own approach and that expressed by the majority in *Appellant S395/2002* converged on the same point, "namely that refugee status cannot be denied by requiring of the claimant that he or she avoid being persecuted by forfeiting a fundamental human right".

not raise concerns over interpretation, judges should ensure, so far as is reasonably possible, that claimants have access to competent and unbiased interpreters (particularly in claims involving gender, religious conversion and gender or blood feud violence). In most situations, however, a reviewable error of law will be only be established where incompetence or bias is established.

Examples: There may be circumstances where through claimants speaking rare languages or dialects, able interpreters are simply not available. In such cases fair and pragmatic approaches should be adopted, recognising the constraints. For example, double translation or telephone procedures may be required. There must, however, be a sufficient ability for meaningful communication.

Authorities:
- Article 22 QD; Article 10 and 13(3)(b) APD - a fortiori applies to appeal/review;
- Czech Republic: CC (8 August 2005), File No II. US 186/05 (referring to Art 36 of the EU Charter);
- Poland: SACP (30 October 2008), File No II OSK 1097/07.

3.5.2. *B.2: Legal representation*

Recognising that legal aid/representation is not available in some Member States and/or at all levels of status determination or judicial review, judges should ensure (wherever possible) that claimants have access to competent legal or other suitable representation, with or without legal aid.

Explanation: Unrepresented appellants must be accorded the highest standards of fairness, recognising that whilst the burden to present their case is on the claimant, there is also a shared burden with the decision-maker. This is particularly important for claimants who fall within the vulnerable groups referred to below.

Examples: There is no inherent right to state-funded legal representation at first (state) level – see Article 47 EU Charter and Article 15 APD. Lack of representation of a party shall not affect the duty of the judge to carry out an impartial and objective individual assessment of the evidence.

In situations where this is simply not possible, judges should take a more proactive and involved role to ensure a fair and pragmatic interview and assessment takes place, often by relying more on objective COI, and possibly friends, relatives and supporters of the claimant giving evidence.

Authorities:
- Article 47 EU Charter; Article 15 APD; Article 4(1)-(5),20(1)-(3)QD;
- United Kingdom: *JK(DRC) v SSHD*[2007]EWCA Civ831 - *on competence of counsel;*
- Czech Republic: RC (11 December 2008), File No 9 Azs 64/2008-67;
- UNHCR Handbook (2011) at [196].

3.5.3. *B.3: Effect of time limits*

Unreasonable time limits upon claimants to respond to contradictory or provide fresh evidence of changed circumstances or COI, can breach basic fairness principles, which can render a whole determination/assessment unsustainable.

Authorities:
- *IM v France* (2012) ECtHR, Appl No 9152/09-ECHR 043; *Jabari v Turkey* (2000) ECtHR, Appl No 40035/98(2000).

3.5.4. *B.4: Interview facilities*

A failure to provide a reasonable interview environment can, in some circumstances, breach basic fairness and confidentiality principles amounting to an error of law. However, situations may arise where even in very poor facilities or surroundings a fair hearing has still taken place (e.g. such as, through necessity, within a prison).

Examples: Where a government, tribunal, judge or individual decision-maker fails to provide, where reasonably possible, a conducive physical environment and/ or facilities wherein interviews and/or appeal hearings can be conducted with claimants (including the provision of specialist facilities for children, vulnerable claimants and, where available, the requested gender of judge and/or interpreter).

Authorities:
- Article 4 and Art 13 QD

3.5.5. *B.5: Bias, incompetence and conflict of interest*

Procedural and substantive issues will involve the application of the maxim that manifestly justice must be seen to be done, and where any of these issues do arise potentially any findings on credibility, and indeed all other issues, will prima facie be wrong in law.

Explanation: Such issues should not arise in a well-administered system as they will breach ECHR principles and/or Administrative law codes and principles in Members States.

Authorities:
- Czech Republic: RC (26 July 2006), File No 3 Azs 35/2006.

3.6. (C) Treatment of Vulnerable Claimants

3.6.1. *General guidance on vulnerable claimants*

One general standard of good judicial practice only is provided here, rather than setting a list of separate standards for every known type of vulnerability or sensitivity. This is done as, not only would it be impossible for such a list to be exhaustive, but also it is frequently the case that the vulnerability of individual claimants may have a number of overlapping causes. It is the totality of the claimants' physical and psychological predicament that must be taken into account in the assessment of their evidence.

In adversarial jurisdictions, because of the need to recognise vulnerabilities and their impact on the giving of evidence, its nature and coherence, as well as in the credibility assessment, a more "interventionist" (or shared burden) approach by the judge is often allowed or even encouraged by the highest courts. If it is used, however, it must be used carefully, with the knowledge and co-operation of counsel and/ or the claimant.

Vulnerable or sensitive individuals may be more easily influenced by the way information and choices are presented, leading to a tendency to guess an answer rather than say "I don't know". Apparently contradictory answers may indicate a lack of understanding of a question or a wish to provide answers when in fact the memory of the event is impaired, whether due to psychological difficulties or normal memory decay.

Gaps in knowledge may not of themselves undermine credibility as in many cultures detailed political, religious, military or social matters may not be disclosed by men to women, children, or other vulnerable individuals.

Vulnerable and sensitive witnesses may not be forthcoming with information if appropriate interviewing and questioning techniques are not utilised.

COI may not be readily available to support claims from vulnerable and other minority groups. Their experiences of political or other activity may not be direct and thus not readily corroborated through documentation.

Background reports frequently lack sufficiently detailed reportage and analysis of the position and status of women, children and other vulnerable individuals other than in general societal form. Thus, in such circumstance, the judge will need to ensure that more detailed information is obtained from the claimant and other sources of direct testimony during the hearing.

3.6.2. *C.1: Vulnerable claimants*

In the assessment of the credibility of the evidence from a vulnerable or sensitive claimant, a failure to take into account appropriately their specific vulnerabilities can lead to an error of law.

Explanation: The need for refugee or subsidiary international protection by vulnerable people is at the heart of the humanitarian nature of international protection determination assessment. The predicament of particularly vulnerable or sensitive claimants requires careful understanding and reflection in the credibility assessment (Article 13.3 APD).

Although some individuals are by definition vulnerable or sensitive (for example: children, victims of trafficking, individuals who suffer from psychiatric illnesses or who have sustained serious harm, torture, sexual and gender based violence, and some women), others can be less easily identifiable.

Factors to be taken into account in assessing the level of vulnerability, the degree to which an individual is affected and the impact on assessment of credibility include:

- Mental health problems
- Social or learning difficulties
- Sexual orientation (the LGBTI claimants)
- Ethnic, social and cultural background
- Domestic, education and employment circumstances
- Physical impairment or disability.

Examples: The experiences of women (and other vulnerable and sensitive individuals) often differ significantly from those of the generality of male claimants because for instance, political protest, activism, and resistance may be manifested in different ways.

Awareness of the marginalisation of the experiences of women and other vulnerable and sensitive claimants in the interpretation of the EU and International Conventions must be reflected in the assessment of credibility. For example, expression of political opinion may not be manifested through conventional means, such as involvement in political parties, but may take less conventional forms of expression such as refusal to abide by discriminatory laws or to follow prescribed codes of conduct. Unless it is appreciated that such conduct may either be a manifestation of political opinion or be perceived as such, it may be incorrectly categorised as personal and private conduct. The judge should bear in mind in assessing the accepted profile of claimants that acts suppressing vulnerable claimants in their country of origin may be based on political opinion in its widest sense, and this may be relevant when later assessing the nexus for GC reasons.

Although the primary responsibility for identification of vulnerability lies with the claimant, the judge should be vigilant to recognise that such issues may follow from the nature of the totality of the claimant's personal profile. Vulnerability and its effect on assessment of credibility must be recognised and reflected in the assessment.

Consideration should be given to holding the hearing in private to avoid overt or covert intimidation. Improper or aggressive cross examination should be curtailed to avoid harassment, intimidation or humiliation. Questions asked should be open and appropriate to the age, maturity, gender, level of understanding, personal circumstances and attributes of the witness.

Children often do not provide as much detail as adults in recalling experiences and may manifest their fears differently from adults. In addition, some forms of disability and trauma may cause or result in impaired memory, and the manner in which evidence is given may be affected by mental, psychological or emotional trauma or disability. Torture and other persecutory treatment can produce profound shame and this shame response may be a significant obstacle to disclosure. The special needs of *unaccompanied minors* must be particularly taken into account and it is important that they have appropriate representation to assist in giving their evidence. (See Article 17 APD). A modified, less restrictive approach than with adults, having careful regard to all the objective evidence available, should be adopted in assessing the credibility of children, particularly younger ones. (See: UNHCR Handbook (2011) at [217]).

Family dependants of a claimant, it is important not to assume that vulnerable and sensitive claimants have only derivative claims. Indeed, such claimants, based on their own separate evidence, may have substantially different or even stronger claims. For example, a wife whose husband lodges a politically based claim may have a separate claim based on domestic violence, family honour or potential serious harm based on local customs or norms that she may face on return.

Where a claim was initially made as a dependant or the person was treated as a dependant, a subsequent later claim may be as a result of the person never receiving adequate personal legal advice and, in such cases, an adverse inference may not be appropriate.

The presence of family members in any interview or hearing may be a help or sometimes an obstacle to disclosure of information. Enquiries as to whether family members should attend the interview or not will often be a judgement call based on the best interests of the claimant.

Authorities:
- United Kingdom: *Malabav* SSHD [2006] EWCA Civ 820-Blake J; *AA Vulnerable female-Article 3) Ethiopia CG* [2004] UKIAT 00184; *FS (Camps - Vulnerable Group-Women) Sierra Leone CG* [2002] UKIAT 05588;
- Czech Republic, RC (31 August 2011) File No 1 As 16/2011-98.

3.7. (D) Residual doubts and Article 4 QD

3.7.1. *Reisdual Doubts*

Where residual doubts are held by judges in the assessment of the claimant's facts and circumstances due to unsupported evidence, it will be, prima facie, an error of law not to adopt, at least, the minimum provisions of Article 4 QD.

In Member States which consider that it is the duty of the claimants to submit all elements needed to substantiate their applications (as expressed in Article 4.1 (first sentence), and 4.5 QD), judges who have residual doubts as to credibility (arising where claimant's statements are not supported by documentary or other evidence), must resolve such doubt by applying, at a minimum, Article 4.1 (second sentence), the provisions of Article 4.2 –4.4, and in particular 4.5 (a)-(e).

However, in other Member States where the UNHCR Handbook [195]-[205] "shared duty" and "benefit of the doubt" principles (or principles of a like nature) are adopted domestically, judges, noting also the terms of Article 3 QD, should apply these principles (in lieu of Article 4.1 (first sentence), and 4.5 QD).

Explanation: Consideration of the possibly confusing "optional" approaches and an explanation of the background, drafting history and how Article 4 and related provisions in the APD impact on the issue of residual doubts in credibility assessments of claimants, is set out in Professor Hailbronner's text, *EU Immigration and Asylum Law – Commentary –* 2010, pp 1025 – 1032.

Before looking at the optional minimum standard approach set out in Article 4.1 (first sentence), and the other permissible and well recognised approach found in international refugee and subsidiary protection law,, it is necessary to set out all the relevant provisions of Article 4 and the detail of the "shared burden" and "benefit of the doubt" approach suggested by the UNHCR.[36] Articles 4.1, 4.2 and 4.5 QD provide (in both the 2004 and 2011 versions) (with emphasis added):

4.1 Member states may consider it the duty of the applicant to submit as soon as possible all elements needed to substantiate the application for international protection. In cooperation with the applicant it is the duty of the Member state to assess the relevant elements of the application.

4.2 The elements referred to in paragraph 1 consist of the applicant's statements and all documentation at the applicant's disposal regarding the applicant's age, background, including that of relevant relatives, identity, nationality(ies), country(ies) and place(s) of residence, previous asylum applications, travel routes, identity and travel documents and reason for applying for international protection.

4.5 Where Member States apply the principle according to which it is the duty of the applicant to substantiate the application for international protection and where aspects of the applicant's statements are not supported by documentary or other evidence, those aspects shall not need confirmation when the following conditions are met:

The applicant has made a genuine effort to substantiate his application;

a) All relevant elements at the applicant's disposal have been submitted, and a satisfactory explanation has been given regarding any lack of other relevant elements;

b) The applicant's statements are found to be coherent and plausible and do not run counter to available specific and general information relevant to the applicant's case;

c) The applicant has applied for international protection at the earliest possible time, unless the applicant can demonstrate good reason for not having done so; and

d) The general credibility of the applicant has been established.

In must be noted from the Article 4.1 provisions that other permissible approaches to the consideration of "all relevant elements of an application" are envisaged. Presumably, as the QD provides minimum standards, any other standard adopted by Member States must be of a "more favourable" nature. Researching the general approach on this issue, in several Member States and internationally, shows that the alternative practice emanates from the provisions of the *UNHCR Handbook* (1979), at [195]-[205]. This states that while the burden of proof (or duty on the claimant) to establish their case, lies with the claimant, there is a shared duty be-

---

36   The IARLJ judges and others who participated in the Madrid workshop (September 2012), on this paper, debated the dilemma of the two optional approaches and resolved that this issue was one that needed much more consideration and research by the IARLJ (Europe) Working party, which will continue work on Credibility assessment issues. However it may be of some reassurance to note that, from their anecdotal views and wide experience, the general consensus was that, in practice, if all the other criteria and standards set out in the paper are applied, similar outcomes resulted from the application of either option.

tween the claimant and the state examiner (judge or decision-maker) to evaluate all the relevant facts. Paragraphs [195]- [197] state:

"195. The relevant facts of the individual case will have to be furnished in the first place by the applicant himself. It will then be up to the person charged with determining his status (the examiner) to assess the validity of any evidence and the credibility of the applicant's statements.

196. It is a general legal principle that the burden of proof lies on the person submitting a claim. Often, however, an applicant may not be able to support his statements by documentary or other proof, and cases in which an applicant can provide evidence of all his statements will be the exception rather than the rule. In most cases a person fleeing from persecution will have arrived with the barest necessities and very frequently even without personal documents. Thus, while the burden of proof in principle rests on the applicant, the duty to ascertain and evaluate all the relevant facts is shared between the applicant and the examiner. Indeed, in some cases, it may be for the examiner to use all the means at his disposal to produce the necessary evidence in support of the application. Even such independent research may not, however, always be successful and there may also be statements that are not susceptible of proof. In such cases, if the applicant's account appears credible, he should, unless there are good reasons to the contrary, be given the benefit of the doubt.

197. The requirement of evidence should thus not be too strictly applied in view of the difficulty of proof inherent in the special situation in which an applicant for refugee status finds himself.

Allowance for such possible lack of evidence does not, however, mean that unsupported statements must necessarily be accepted as true if they are inconsistent with the general account put forward by the applicant."

As noted by UNHCR, [shared] research may not always be successful or statements may not be susceptible of proof. In such cases, the claimant should be given the "benefit of the doubt" provided that otherwise the claimant's account appears credible or there are persuasive contrary reasons. The UNHCR Handbook refers, at paras [203]-[204], to "the benefit of the doubt" being given to the claimant, explaining that this does not mean there should be an unqualified acceptance of uncorroborated claims because of these difficulties. Paragraph [204] states:

"The benefit of the doubt should, however, only be given when all available evidence has been obtained and checked and when the examiner is satisfied as to the applicant's general credibility. The applicant's statements must be coherent and plausible, and must not run counter to generally known facts."

At the European jurisprudential level there has to date been no commentary on this issue by the CJEU. However the ECtHR has recently confirmed the application of the benefit of the doubt principle in: *JH v UK Application* (20 March 2012) Appl no. 48839/09. At [52] the ECtHR states:

"*52. The assessment of the existence of a real risk must necessarily be a rigorous one (see Chahal v. the United Kingdom, judgment of 15 November 1996, Reports 1996-V, § 96; and Saadi v. Italy, cited above, § 128). It is in principle for the applicant to adduce evidence capable of proving that there are substantial grounds for believing that, if the measure complained of were to be implemented, he would be exposed to a real risk of being subjected to treatment contrary to Article 3 (see N. v. Finland, no. 38885/02, § 167, 26 July 2005). The Court acknowledges that, owing to the special situation in which asylum seekers often find themselves, it is frequently necessary to give them the benefit of the doubt when it comes to assessing the credibility of their statements and the documents submitted in support thereof. However, when information is presented which gives strong reasons to question the veracity of an asylum seeker's submissions, the individual must provide a satisfactory explanation for the alleged discrepancies (see, among other authorities, N. v. Sweden, no. 23505/09, § 53, 20 July 2010 and Collins and Akasiebie v. Sweden (dec.), no. 23944/05, 8 March 2007)."*

3.7.2. The term "Benefit of the doubt" in different legal contexts

It must be observed also that the phrase "benefit of the doubt" is used, in the asylum context, in a different sense from its more familiar application in criminal proceedings.

In the criminal context it reflects that the burden is on the prosecution (state) to demonstrate that, on the totality of the evidence before the court, there is no residual doubt, which a reasonable person might entertain as to the guilt of the accused. Where such a doubt exists it must be resolved in favour of the accused and the charge against him/her be dismissed. It reflects the fact that the duty on the prosecution is "to prove the defendant's guilt beyond a reasonable doubt".

In refugee and subsidiary protection claims the term's application, as we have noted, is wholly different in nature. First, the primary burden of proof rests on the claimant who is asserting the 'facts' on which he or she relies to support his/her claim. Secondly, it is in the nature of refugee claims, for all the reasons which have been explained above, that a claimant may not be able to 'prove' his or her claims by reference to corroborative evidence, because of the circumstances of his/her departure, the need to maintain the confidentiality of his/her claim, or because of other factors which impair the claimant's ability to give evidence (see the treatment of the evidence of vulnerable claimants discussed at C.1 above).

In Germany and Austria for example, the "benefit of the doubt" principle is a concept in criminal law only, but unfamiliar in refugee and subsidiary protection law. They follow the approach of Article 4.1 and 4.5 QD.

Authorities:
- Article 4 QD; *JH v UK* (20 March 2012) ECtHR Appl no. 48839/09; *Saadi v Italy* (28 February 2008) ECtHR Appeal no. 37201/06; *Karanakaran v SSHD* (2000) 3 All ER 449);
- UNHCR Handbook at pp. 195-204;
- Hailbronner, EU Immigration and Asylum Law – Commentary – 2010, pp 1025-1038;
- Noll G., *"Salvation by the Grace of State? Explaining Credibility Assessment in the Asylum Procedure"* in: G. Noll (ed.), *Proof, Evidentiary Assessment and Credibility in Asylum Procedures* (Martinus Nijhoff Publishers), 197-214.

4.   Part IV: The Operation of the APD and QD in the CEAS

4.1.   Introduction

Part I of this paper introduced the legal framework of international refugee and protection law and the CEAS.

Part IV will consider the CEAS generally and the operation of the QD and the APD within it in more detail. It begins by exploring the origins and nature of the CEAS and its relationship to international human rights law. Then the strengths and weaknesses of the two directives with which the judiciary of the Member States is primarily concerned – namely the QD and the APD will be addressed. These are huge topics in their own right and therefore more detailed consideration and reference sources in the text to this paper are supplemented by the footnotes. But, in general terms, the UNHCR has published detailed (but non-binding) papers on all major issues arising under the GC and more generally its views on human rights issues which do not fall strictly within the ambit of the Convention. They are readily accessible on the internet.[37]

4.2.   The Legal Basis of the CEAS

Until 1 December 2009 the legal basis of the CEAS was largely derived from Article 63 of the Consolidated Version of the Treaty Establishing the European Community (TEC) incorporated under the Amsterdam Treaty of 2 October 1997, which came into force on 1 May 1999. It is pursuant to the authority of Article 63 TEC that the initial secondary legislation comprising the corpus of the CEAS was passed into EU law. Since 1 December 2009 the relevant provisions concerning the continued development of the CEAS are derived from Article 78 TFEC and the EU Charter as primary sources of EU law. The main shift in emphasis is from the application of 'minimum standards' as exemplified in the 2004 QD and APD (Article 63 TEC), to 'uniform status' for those recognised in need of protection under the 2011 QD following 'common procedures' to ascertain such status (Article 78 TFEC). The most important Directive since the TFEC came into force is the 2011 QD but, for practical purposes, this has made only minor amendments to the 2004 QD and, most importantly, has retained the Article 3 minimum standards

---

37   Those interested in further reading through academic writings, may find the following of interest: (a) Guy S. Goodwin-Gill and Jane McAdam: *The Refugee in International Law*, 3rd Edition (2007); (b) James C. Hathaway: *The Law of Refugee Status* (1991); (c) Hemme Battjes: *European Asylum Law and International Law* (2006) and (d) Kay Hailbronner (Editor): *EU Immigration and Asylum Law* (2010). The last two are the only major works concerned solely with detailed consideration of EU legislation from which the CEAS is derived, including extensive analysis of the then relevant directives.

concept in identical terms. Questions of 'uniform statuses' are primarily those relating to civic rights following IP status recognition.

The CEAS is not confined to issues of recognition of international protection needs with which the judiciary are primarily concerned. Its scope is much wider. It extends to immigration policy generally (Article 63(3) and (4) TEC).

4.2.1. *Article 63(1) TEC*

Article 63(1) is directly concerned with refugee issues. It provides as follows:

> The Council, acting in accordance with the procedure referred to in Article 67, shall, within a period of five years after the entry into force of the Treaty of Amsterdam, adopt:

> 1.   Measures on asylum, in accordance with the Geneva Convention of 28 July 1951 and the Protocol of 31 January 1967 relating to the status of refugees and other relevant treaties, within the following areas:
> (a)   criteria and mechanisms for determining which Member State is responsible for considering an application for asylum submitted by a national of a third country in one of the Member States,
> (b)   minimum standards on the reception of asylum seekers in Member States,
> (c)   minimum standards with respect to the qualification of nationals of third countries as refugees,
> (d)   minimum standards on procedures in Member States for granting or withdrawing refugee status.

Note that the GC is specifically referred to but that there is also a general reference to *'other relevant treaties'* in the introductory wording of sub-article 1. Note also the reference to *'minimum standards'* in sub-paragraphs (c) and (d) which are directly concerned with the derivative QD and APD.

4.2.2. *Article 63(2) (a) TEC*

Article 63(2)(a) is concerned both with refugees and 'displaced persons':

> 2.   measures on refugees and displaced persons within the following areas:
> (a)   minimum standards for giving temporary protection to displaced persons from third countries who cannot return to their country of origin and for persons who otherwise need international protection.

Note again the reference to *'minimum standards'*.

4.2.3. *Article 63(3)(a) TEC*

Finally, Sub-article 3(a) bears on the provisions relating to those in need of international protection:

> 3.   measures on immigration policy within the following areas:
> (a)   conditions of entry and residence, and standards on procedures for the issue by Member States of long-term visas and residence permits, including those for the purpose of family reunion.

4.2.4. *The scope of Article 63*

Arriving at the precise scope of Article 63 is not easy save for the obvious require-ment as to a minimum standards approach and the clear reference to international treaties relative to asylum issues. Hemme Battjes[38] carefully analyses these pro-visions and concludes:

> "*Contrary to the first impression that Article 63 TEC might give, Community powers on asylum are not restricted to the areas listed in Article 63(1) and (2). Article 63(3)(a) attributes to the Community the competence to issue measures on entry, residence and procedures for third country nationals, including asy-lum beneficiaries, asylum seekers and persons in need of temporary or subsidi-ary protection, addressed under paragraphs (1) and (2) of Article 63 TEC.*
>
> *Article 63(1) and (2) serve to carve out the obligations for the Community to adopt measures on the areas mentioned there within five years, to exempt Arti-cle 63(1)(a) measures from the limitation to minimum harmonisation applying to Article 63(3)(a), and, arguably, to state with emphasis the requirement of accordance with international asylum law of the issues listed in Article 63(1).*"

4.3. The scope of the CEAS

With the exception of the Charter of Fundamental Rights of the European Union, 2000 (2007/C303/01), which will be considered later, EU legislation im-plementing the CEAS was, until the enactment of the 2011 QD on 13 December 2011 based on the provisions of Article 63 TEC, with the *'minimum standards'* approach firmly entrenched in the QD and the APD.

It was clear, however, since the Tampere Conference of October 1999 that im-plementation of Article 63 TEC was a first and transient stage towards the full concept of the CEAS.

The Conclusions of the Presidency at that Conference deal with this issue. They record that the CEAS was to include, in the short term, a clear and workable determination of the state responsible for the examination of an asylum applica-tion, common standards for a fair and efficient asylum procedure, common mini-mum conditions of reception of asylum seekers and the approximation of rules on the recognition and content of refugee status. These were to be supplemented with measures on subsidiary forms of protection offering an appropriate status to any person in need of such protection. Up to that point, these were matters within the TEC competence. In addition, the Conclusions made clear, however, that, in the longer term, community rules should lead to a common asylum procedure and a uniform status for those who are granted asylum valid throughout the Union. This second stage of the development of the CEAS from 'minimum standards' to 'uni-form status' is reflected in Article 78 of the TFEU (Treaty on the Functioning of the European Union) commonly referred to as the Lisbon Treaty, which came into force on 1 December 2009. Finally, the European Council in Tampere urged the

---

38   *Op. cit.* at Chapter 3.

Council to step up its efforts to reach agreement on the issue of temporary protection for displaced persons on the basis of solidarity between Member States.

4.4.   The principle of freedom of movement within the EU

Freedom of movement of workers and their dependants has been a pillar of the European Union since its original inception in March 1957 as the European Economic Community, and subsequently as the European Community.

In principle it has long been accepted that such freedom of movement should extend to those third country nationals and stateless persons lawfully resident in a Member State provided that certain conditions are fulfilled. Their position was regularised in the Directive on EU long-term resident status (2003/109/EC), which did not, however, then extend to those enjoying long-term refugee or subsidiary protection status. That Directive has now been amended by Directive 2011/51/EU of 11 May 2011 'amending Council Directive 2003/109/EC to extend its scope to beneficiaries of international protection'. The new Directive binds all MS except for Denmark, Ireland and the United Kingdom. The position of those beneficiaries of international protection who otherwise meet the requirements for issue of a long-term residence permit to a third country national is differentiated from those of such other third country nationals only by a requirement that the certificate contains a statement that residence is based on the recognition of protection status by the relevant MS, including the date of such recognition, and that cessation of international protection status may lead to the withdrawal of the long-term residence certificate.

The common requirements for issue of a long-term residence certificate are, in summary: legal and continuous residence for five years; the ability to maintain oneself and family without recourse to social assistance; sickness insurance covering all risks; fulfilment of any integration conditions of the MS; and lack of any threat to public policy or public security of the MS.

There are special provisions for calculating the length of residence of beneficiaries of IP.

4.4.1. *Article 63(4) TEC*

In this connection Article 63.4 TEC provided for:

> 4. measures defining the rights and conditions under which nationals of third countries who are legally resident in a Member State may reside in other Member States.

The earlier provisions of Article 63 TEC were concerned with issues relating to the reception and recognition of protection status. Once a claimant is recognised as in need of international protection, he will become lawfully resident in the Member State concerned so long as that recognition continues. It is clear that the development of the CEAS envisaged that third country nationals enjoying long-term protection status should be in a similar position to other lawfully resident third country nationals.

We would suggest that Article 63.4 TEC always had a central importance in the scheme of the CEAS, which needs to cover not only the application of consistent criteria for qualification for protection and the procedure to be followed when dealing with claims, but also to take into account the long-term effect of recognition having regard to the principle of freedom of movement with the EU.

It is not suggested that freedom of movement was the sole factor driving the CEAS but its importance as a pillar of EU philosophy is not to be underestimated.

Further, it makes clear that the CEAS is and has always been conceived as a regional instrument taking into account the interests of the Member States that, under the principle of solidarity, will share the burden of receiving asylum claimants, as well as the ultimate rights of freedom of movement of those who become effectively permanently established in the EU as persons in need of long-term protection. It is for this reason that the CEAS will require in the long term uniform standards of qualification and procedure in protection claims.

4.4.2. *The restriction to the 'worthy' applicant*

Once this is accepted, the purpose of the restriction of status under the QD to 'worthy' applicants by the application of the exclusion provisions of Articles 12 and 17 QD – which has attracted so much criticism – becomes apparent. A Member State which receives a claim for status from, e.g., someone with a terrorist background may be unable to remove him because to do so would be in violation of its treaty obligations under Article 3 of the ECHR, but such a claimant would have been excluded from protection status under Article 1 F, GC, the concept of which is extended by the QD also to subsidiary protection status. It would be unacceptable that the principle of freedom of movement within the EU should be capable of extending to such a claimant, notwithstanding that the receiving Member State may be unable to remove him from its territory.

Further, it explains the emphasis which the QD puts on cessation of status because of changed circumstances (Articles 11 and 16 QD) – an issue with which judges may become more concerned in the future because it is one of the decisions against which an effective remedy must be provided (Article 39.1(e) APD).

4.5. The first stage of the CEAS

In addition to the QD and APD with which we are concerned, there are a number of EU instruments and policies which are concerned with the first stage of the development of the CEAS.[39] These include:

a) the Decision (2000/596/EC) establishing the European Refugee Fund;
b) the Regulation (2725/2000/EC) concerning the establishment of 'Eurodac' for the comparison of fingerprints;

---

39 Although judges dealing with IP claims are primarily concerned with the QD and APD, it is important to bear in mind that the instruments implementing the CEAS form a coherent body of EU law in which the concepts in one instrument inform similar concepts in others. For a comprehensive approach to EU immigration and asylum law, further reference should be made to the commentary edited by Kay Hailbronner *op cit.*

c) the Directive (2001/55/EC) laying down minimum standards for giving temporary protection in the event of a mass influx of displaced persons;

d) the Reception Conditions Directive (2003/9/EC) guaranteeing minimum standards for the reception of asylum seekers, including housing, education and health;

e) the Dublin Regulation (2003/343/EC), establishing criteria and mechanisms for determining the Member State responsible for examining an asylum application lodged in one of the Member States by a third country national;

f) the Hague Programme.

g) Directive 2008/115/EC concerning common standards and procedures for returning illegally staying third country nationals; and

h) Directive 2011/51/EU concerning the extension of long-term residence certificates to beneficiaries of IP.

The coming into force of the APD completed the first phase of the CEAS.

4.6. An overview of the QD and the APD

The three Directives are:

a) Council Directive 2004/83/EC of 29 April 2004 (the 2004 QD, which came into force on 10 October 2006) on minimum standards for the qualification and status of third country nationals or stateless persons as refugees or as persons who otherwise need international protection and the content of the protection granted;

b) Council Directive 2011/95/EU of 13 December 2011 (the 2011 QD, which came into force on 10 January 2012)[40] on standards for the qualification of third country nationals or stateless persons as beneficiaries of international protection, for a uniform status for refugees or for persons eligible for subsidiary protection, and for the content of the protection granted; and

c) Council Directive 2005/85/EC of 1 December 2005 (the APD, which came into force on 1 December 2007) on minimum standards on procedures in Member States for granting or withdrawing refugee status.

The Directive referred to under (b) above is the first instrument to be passed since the coming into force of Article 78 TFEU. It should be noted that in its title the wording has changed partially to reflect the differences between the 'minimum standards' approach of Article 63 TEC and the 'uniform status' approach of Article 78 TFEU. But, so far as standards for qualification for status recognition are concerned, the change is simply to omit the word 'minimum' and the qualifying 'uniform' applies only once status as 'a beneficiary of international protection' has been recognised under Chapters I to VI of the 2011 QD. The preamble now contains specific reference to the TFEU, instead of the TEC as was the case with the

---

40 As previously noted, a number of the Articles of the 2011 APD do not take effect until 21 December 2013 and these include all those in which there are amendments to the 2004 QD. Those Articles which have immediate effect are Articles 3, 5, 6, 12-15, 17, 18, 21 and 36-42.

2004 QD. We shall consider the differences between the two QD's later but Recital 1 of the 2011 QD makes it clear that it is a recast of the 2004 QD.

The actual changes to the standards for qualification for IP recognition are limited and, in broad terms, the two QD's can be considered together. One major difference, however, which may have implications for future concepts of solidarity between Member States, is that not only does Denmark continue not to be bound by the QD but that the 2011 QD is not binding on Eire or the United Kingdom either although they continue to be bound by the 2004 QD.

We shall seek to deal with certain issues in more depth later but it is helpful at this point to give an overview of the most important features of the Directives.

1. The Directives apply only to third country nationals or stateless persons – not to citizens of Member States – so that they lack the universality of the GC and ECHR.
2. The 2004 QD introduced minimum standards allowing (Article 3) Member States to operate more favourable standards *'in so far as those standards are compatible with this Directive'* – there has been much controversy as to the effect of this provision.

    As already noted, the 2011 QD has omitted the word 'minimum' so that the reference is simply to 'standards' but has retained Article 3 in the same form as appeared in the 2004 QD. It remains to be seen whether, when the second stage of the CEAS proceeds with the full implementation of Article 78 TFEU, the requirement will be for 'uniform standards' for qualification for IP recognition as opposed to that recognition, following the application of 'common procedures', resulting in a 'uniform status'. The latter would appear to accord with the specific wording of Article 78. It may, therefore, be that the problem caused by the *'minimum standards'* concept of Article 63 TEC will effectively remain if the effect of Article 3 QD is preserved.
3. The primary objective of the 2004 QD was twofold:
a) to provide common criteria in order to identify those who should be recognised as being in need of international protection either as refugees under the GC or under international human rights norms as defined in Article 15 of the Qualification Directive (subsidiary protection status) – Chapters I to VI of the QD; and
b) to ensure a minimum level of benefits for those so recognised in all MS (Recital (6) and Chapter VII).

    These remain the objectives of the 2011 QD (Recital (12)) where there are some amendments to issues relating to qualification for protection status (which will be reflected in the text), but the main body of amendments is in Chapter VII concerned with the content of international protection. In this respect there is substantial progress towards a uniform status as the title of the Directive implies.
4. A secondary and closely linked motive is to reduce 'asylum shopping' by applicants since the application of common criteria will render this pointless (Recital (7) of the 2004 QD and (13) of the 2011 QD).
5. The need for protection follows from recognition of an existing status either of refugee or *'person eligible for subsidiary protection'* – the second category

comprises those who, although not qualifying as refugees, can show substantial grounds for believing they would face *'a real risk of suffering serious harm'* in their country of origin.

The degree of uniformity of status aimed for in the second phase of the CEAS is emphasised by recipients of either form of protection being now defined as 'beneficiaries of international protection' (Article 1).

In both QD's the principal Articles dealing with assessment of applications for international protection (Articles 4 to 8) are contained in Chapter II. In the later Directive, Article 7 (Actors of protection) and Article 8 (Internal protection) contain important additions clarifying these concepts. It is doubtful if they have changed the position which would apply under IP law but they have clarified doubts raised by the wording of the former provisions as to their intended meaning for the purposes of the CEAS. They are applicable to recognition of all beneficiaries of international protection.

Issues specific to qualification for refugee status are set out in Articles 9 to 12 in Chapter III and those specific to qualification for subsidiary protection in Chapter V at Articles 15 to 17.

In the 2011 Directive, Articles 9 and 10 contain additions again aimed at clarifying the meaning of the corresponding Articles in the 2004 QD but Articles 11 and 16 dealing with cessation of protection status, introduce an important exception to cessation of status arising from a change of circumstances in the country of origin. Where a beneficiary is 'able to invoke compelling reasons arising out of previous' persecution or serious harm 'for refusing to avail himself or herself of the protection' of the country of origin, such changed circumstances shall not lead to revocation of status.[41]

6. *'Refugee'* has the same meaning as in the GC but, as noted above, various articles of the QD make provisions as to relevant criteria for recognition which settle differences of approach towards interpretation of that Convention which had previously existed between Member States. The most extreme example is acceptance that non-state actors can be actors of persecution – a view which had been rejected in the past by France and Germany who only recognised persecution if it emanated from the State, albeit they might have granted discretionary protection in cases where the persecution feared was from non-State actors.

7. *'Serious harm'*[42] in subsidiary protection status is defined in Article 15 QD as liability to suffer the death penalty or execution;[43] torture or inhuman or

---

41   This applies the position long advocated by UNHCR – see paragraph 136 UNHCR Handbook on Procedures and Criteria for Determining Refugee Status – which had in practice been applied by some Member States for many years.

42   The Explanatory Memorandum of 12.9.2001 states that the definition is based on international human rights instruments relevant to subsidiary protection. The most relevant of them were Article 3 of the ECHR, Article 3 of the UN Convention against Torture and other Cruel, Inhuman or Degrading Treatment, and Article 7 of the International Covenant on Civil and Political Rights.

43   This reflects Article 2.2 of the European Charter which provides that no-one shall be condemned to the death penalty or executed.

degrading treatment or punishment *in the country of origin* [emphasis added];[44] and *'serious and individual threat to a civilian's life or person by reason of indiscriminate violence in situations of international or internal armed conflict'*.[45]

8. Subsidiary protection status is a formalisation for the first time of what has in the past generally been dealt with by way of discretionary complementary protection with one important difference – the concept of exclusion from subsidiary protection on a basis similar to that applying under the GC has been introduced.

9. Much more emphasis has been placed on cessation and disqualification from protection in both categories of status, including posing a threat to internal security or commission of serious crimes – notwithstanding that under the absolute terms of Article 3 ECHR the person concerned may not be removable.

10. The APD lays down minimum standards of procedure to be adopted *in asylum applications* [emphasis added][46] including the right to interview, a right of appeal from or review of the initial decision, requirements as to the qualifications of decision-makers and the circumstances in which accelerated procedures (mainly deemed 'safe country of origin' cases) and inadmissibility of claims may be provided for in the Member States' individual transposing legislation.[47]

11. Member States are to report back to the Commission on the functioning of the Directives on a comparatively short timescale.[48]

---

44   This partially reflects the provisions of Article 3 of the ECHR: but, there are important differences.

45   This is the most controversial provision and the one which has in practice caused most difficulty in interpretation. There is now a body of CJEU and national jurisprudence starting with the judgment of the ECJ, as it then was, in *Elgafaji and another v Staatssecretaris van Justitie* ECJ Case C-465/07 which demands detailed analysis beyond the scope of this paper.

46   This causes a serious asymmetry between the two Directives. In practice, however, all Member States save one apply the APD to both asylum and subsidiary protection decisions.

47   The delay between the coming into force of the two Directives was largely attributable to difficulties in framing the provisions of the APD. Member States apply fundamentally different procedures in their courts. Most European States follow an inquisitorial procedure whereas Common Law jurisdictions like the United Kingdom follow an adversarial procedure. In contrast to the civilian systems, where administrative law is a long-standing concept, it has developed only comparatively recently in countries such as the United Kingdom adopting the adversarial approach. Such development has in part stemmed from issues arising in asylum and immigration jurisprudence where the State is a constant party to litigation involving issues which are not *inter partes* but require a judgment as to the credibility of the claimant on facts which in personal terms are outside the knowledge of the respondent State. In the result procedures adopted in the specialist asylum and immigration tribunals in the United Kingdom have tended to be rather more interventionist. Nevertheless, it is likely that the difference between the inquisitorial and adversarial systems adopted by Member States will continue to throw up procedural difficulties, which may ultimately have to be resolved by a common procedural system at a later stage in the harmonisation process as foreshadowed in Recital 3 APD.

There is a current proposal for a recast APD before the European parliament, which is intended to be enacted during 2012 but there remain some controversial issues so that it is impossible to reflect its proposals in this paper.

48   The advantage of the Directive mechanism, although appropriate under the principle of proportionality, is that transposition of the QD and APD by Member States has quickly thrown up

→

12. The general thrust of the provisions of the 2004 QD and the APD demonstrates the ultimate intention that those recognised as in need of protection status on a long-term basis should have freedom of movement within the EU in the same way as its citizens and lawfully resident long-term third country nationals now enjoy. This has now been effected by Directive 2011/51/EU of 11 May 2011 (see above).

4.7. The CEAS and International Human Rights Law

The CEAS cannot be seen in isolation from the body of international instruments regulating the concept of international surrogate protection for those for whom their national state (or in the case of stateless persons, their country of habitual residence) fails to provide adequate protection having regard to international law norms. The principal United Nations international instruments are, in date order:

- Charter of the United Nations, 1945
- Universal Declaration of Human Rights, 1948
- Convention on the Prevention and Punishment of the Crime of Genocide, 1948
- The Geneva Convention relating to the Status of Refugees, 1951 and the New York Protocol, 1967 (the GC)
- International Covenant on Civil and Political Rights, 1966 (the ICCPR)
- Optional Protocols to the International Covenant on Civil and Political Rights, 1966 (the ICESCRY)
- International Covenant on Economic, Social, and Cultural Rights, 1966
- Convention on Elimination of Discrimination Against Women, 1979 (CEDAW)
- Convention against Torture, 1984 (CAT)
- Convention on the Rights of the Child, 1989

The principal European regional instruments are:

- The European Convention on Human Rights, 1950 (ECHR)
- The European Union Charter of Fundamental Human Rights, 2000 (the EU Charter)

For present purposes, there are three instruments to which specific reference is required These are the GC; the ECHR; and the EU Charter.

4.7.1. *The GC*

As already noted, it is only the GC which is referred to by name in the EU treaties and legislation concerned with the CEAS. The reference in Article 63(1) TEC to *'other relevant treaties'*, although none are specified, signifies that the corpus of

---

problem areas in the harmonisation of law and procedure under the CEAS. This will facilitate identification of problem areas in the second phase of the CEAS. The current proposals for amendment of the APD, for example, are based on the Commission Report on its application COM(2010) 465 final.

international instruments relative to asylum issues are relevant to at least the refugee aspect of the CEAS.

Further, the GC is the touchstone from which the QD derives its qualifications for refugee status but it does not directly inform the provisions of the APD because the GC is silent on such matters and UNHCR, the body charged with its administration, has always left questions of procedure relating to recognition of refugee status to be dealt with in accordance with the laws and practices of the signatory states.[49] For practical purposes the QD largely transposes relevant provisions of the GC into EU Law.

The QD (recital 2, 2004 QD and recital 4, 2011 QD) records that the establishment of the CEAS is *'based on the full and inclusive application of the Geneva Convention'* and Recital 3 notes that it provides *'the cornerstone of the international legal regime for the protection of refugees'*.

4.7.2. The ECHR

The ECHR was adopted by the Council of Europe in 1950. The Council of Europe currently comprises 47 signatory states (some of which have their territory outside Europe) and the Council and its institutions are wholly distinct from the EU although there are areas of co-operation between them including the international enforcement of justice and human rights. Under the terms of the TFEU it is provided that the EU will become a signatory member of the Council of Europe as are all its current Member States. Any breaches of human rights claimed by the newly created Citizens of the EU will then be justiciable in the European Court of Human Rights (ECtHR) in the same way as already applies to Member States. The ECtHR is unique in the range of recourse it gives to those who claim their human rights have been breached in violation of an international treaty obligation by a signatory state.

Since the ECtHR is not an EU institution, it has no jurisdiction in relation to litigation arising under any EU legislation in respect of which the ultimate recourse is to the CJEU in Luxembourg. Nevertheless, since all EU MS are bound by the jurisprudence of the ECtHR, the CJEU generally follows and applies that jurisprudence when relevant to issues before it.[50]

In so far as litigation before the CJEU concerning subsidiary protection raises issues in respect of which there is relevant ECtHR case law, it is likely to be ap-

---

49 The Executive Committee of the UNHCR made recommendations in October 1997 as to the basic requirements, which should be met by national procedures. Although generally observed, they have no binding force but their thrust is generally reflected in the provisions of the APD. They are set out at paragraph 192 of the UNHCR Handbook *op. cit.*

50 Hemme Battjes in his seminal work *op. cit.* notes at para 125: "The [CJEU] persistently emphasises that the Community is not bound by the [ECHR] and other relevant treaties: it does not apply their provisions, but rather 'draws inspiration' from them when formulating 'principle', not rules of Community law concerning human rights. … But paraphrases of this test by the [CJEU] itself … suggest that there is little difference between applications of principles of Community law and application of the corresponding international law norms. … As far as is relevant for asylum, application of general principles of Community law in practice leads to results equivalent to application of the concerned human rights law provisions."

plied by the CJEU. When the EU becomes a signatory to the ECHR, then the relevance of ECtHR jurisprudence will increase.

Article 3 ECHR is part of the inspiration for the status of subsidiary protection as defined in Article 15 QD by reference to Article 2(f) and (g) QD 2011.[51]

4.7.3. *The impact of International Human Rights Law on the CEAS*

There is no question that the CEAS draws its inspiration from the international treaties and conventions which have been noted above with particular reference to the GC and the ECHR, but the issue with which we are concerned here is the level of impact which such international instruments have upon the application of the EU primary and secondary legislative instruments relevant to the CEAS. In particular, the recognition of international protection status under the QD is regulated by the terms of the QD and the adoption of the procedures prescribed in the APD. Those Directives are part of European law and as such are to be interpreted in accordance with the canons of construction which apply to all European legislation. They are not international instruments and the provisions of the VCLT do not apply to their interpretation which is, as with all EU law, a matter for the CJEU under applicable EU interpretation law.

In broad terms the VCLT provides that international instruments are to be interpreted in good faith, by reference both to the instrument's wording and its object and purpose, and to have regard to subsequent practice (VCLT Articles 31 to 33). So far as EU legislation is concerned, however, the CJEU is the supreme authority on all matters concerning both primary and secondary EU law. As Hemme Battjes puts it in European Asylum Law and International Law (*op. cit.*) at Chapter 1.5.5 paragraph 78:

> "This entails interpretation as to the literal meaning, read in the context and, emphatically, to the purpose. The context encompasses the preamble as well as documents or instruments explicitly referred to. ... The method of interpretation ... deviates in some important respects from the rules laid down in Article 31 [VCLT]. Agreements reached or instruments adopted in connection with the conclusion of the Treaty or the adoption of Community legislation, subsequent agreements on interpretation and subsequent state practice ... are denied any role."

This raises two important issues in relation to the construction of the CEAS legislative instruments. First, to what extent are the provisions of international protection law instruments to be taken into account in the interpretation of the provisions of the CEAS legislation? Secondly, how far is the interpretation of international instruments, which has been developed under the VCLT by reference to agreements on interpretation and state practice, which are subsequent to the en-

---

51 Neither the ECHR nor any other international instrument (except the GC) is referred to in the QD but in its Explanatory Memorandum to the proposal for the QD, the EC stated that the most pertinent of the international instruments on which subsidiary protection was based were Article 3 ECHR, Article 3 of the Convention against Torture, and Article 7 of the International Covenant on Civil and Political Rights.

actment of the international instrument and CEAS legislation under consideration, relevant to interpretation of the CEAS legislation concerned? As to the first issue, recognition of international protection status under the QD is regulated by reference to the terms of the QD, and not by direct application of international instruments, save insofar as they are specifically incorporated by its terms. The second issue, which goes directly to the concept of international protection law instruments as 'living' instruments whose meaning is capable of being influenced by subsequent practice, has not to date required specific consideration by the CJEU.

In general terms, academic opinion on these points appears to reflect that these issues are more theoretical than real for practical purposes. They are the subject of very full analysis by Hemme Battjes (*op. cit.*). His conclusions may be summarised as follows:

- International law norms may affect EU asylum law either as: international customary law, as sources of inspiration for general principles of Community Law, and by virtue of reference in primary and secondary Community Law (Battjes, para 139).
- On the first point, the Community is bound to observe international custom (*Poulsen* – ECJ Case C-286/90 at para 9) so that the customary prohibition of *refoulement* works in its capacity as international law (para 107).
- On the second, all international asylum law can serve as a basis for the CJEU established practice of testing "acting within the sphere of Community Law by reference to human rights concepts derived from international law as an application of general principles of Community Law"(para 126) – the customary expression of this principle by the Court is as follows: *"... fundamental rights form an integral part of the general principles of law observance of which the Court ensures. For that purpose, the Court draws inspiration from the constitutional traditions common to the Member States and from the guidance supplied by international treaties for the protection of human rights on which Member States have collaborated or to which they are signatories. The ECHR has special significance in that respect."* (*Roquette Freres* ECJ 22 October 2002, c-94/00, [1991] ECR p 09011).
- Additionally, there are some specific references to international treaties in both primary and secondary Community Law, e.g: Article 6(2) TFEU requires the Community to "respect fundamental rights, as guaranteed by" the ECHR; Article 63(1) TEC requiring the Community to adopt "measures on asylum, in accordance with the [GC] and other relevant treaties" in four specified areas only one of which relates directly to the requirements of the GC, viz "minimum standards with respect to the qualification of nationals of third countries as refugees"; and Article 78 TFEU – "The Union shall develop a common policy on asylum, subsidiary protection and temporary protection with a view to offering appropriate status to any third-country national requiring international protection and ensuring compliance with the principle of *non-refoulement*. This policy must be in accordance with the [GC] and other relevant treaties." [Additionally, there are relevant references in both the EU Charter (Article 18 – Right to asylum; Article 52.3 (rights corresponding to rights guaranteed by the ECHR are to have at

least the same meaning and scope); and Article 53 (level of protection by reference to international law and international agreements to which the EU or all MS are party); in the QD (Recital (3) refers to the CEAS being '*based on the full and inclusive application of the [GC]*' and recital (4) affirms that the GC provides '*the cornerstone of the international legal regime for the protection of refugees*'; Recitals (21)-(22) all refer to the relevance of application of the GC in relation to refugee status; Article 9.1, in defining the elements of acts of persecution requires '*the rights from which derogation cannot be made under Article 15(2) [ECHR]*' to be taken into account; and also in the recitals to the APD and in Article 21 dealing with the role of the UNHCR in the asylum process.

It should also be borne in mind that that MS are required to transpose the provisions of EU Directives into their national law. In so far as the provisions of the QD and APD then become part of national law of MS, it will also be relevant for judges to consider the rules of interpretation of their own law in relation to those transcribed provisions. In this connection any national law requirements for MS legislation to be construed in accordance with the provisions of international treaties and conventions of which the MS is a signatory will also be relevant to the interpretation of the transposed CEAS Directive provisions.

The above comments are concerned with the appropriate approach to interpretation of provisions of the EU instruments. The issue of the over-arching effect of international instruments in relation to issues of protection which fall outside the CEAS is considered separately below.

4.7.4. *The EU Charter*

The EU Charter was formally incorporated into primary EU law on 1 December 2009 following the ratification of the Lisbon Treaty and is on the same level as treaty law. The directives and regulations which make up the CEAS must be interpreted in accordance with the Charter.

Previously, however, it had limited effect as it was not then an instrument of the EU but rather a Charter 'solemnly proclaimed' by the European Parliament, the Council and the Commission.

The degree to which the Charter now provides rights enforceable by individuals is not straightforward. There is a distinction between articles which guarantee an individual right and articles which contain principles which are not directly enforceable. The Commentary edited by Kay Hailbronner (*op cit.*) explains the point as follows:

> According to art. 52 para. 5, the provisions of the Charter which contain principles may be implemented by legislative acts of the Union and by acts of Member States implementing Union law. However, those provisions may be applied in court only with regard to the interpretation of such acts and in deciding on the legality of such acts. The provision, thus, excludes that individual rights may be directly deduced from such principles. The Charter, however, leaves open to what extent the provisions in the Charter guarantee rights or contain only 'principles'. In some cases it is quite clear from the wording that a provision guarantees an individual right such as the rights guaranteed in Title I until

Title III.[52] In any case, principles as well as individual rights are not only relevant for the interpretation of secondary EU law but also a binding yardstick for the judicial control of measures of the Union and the Member States in implementing EU legislation.[53]

The 2011 QD provides for the relevant provisions of the Charter to be implemented when applying the 2011 QD - Recital (16) reads:

This Directive respects the fundamental rights and observes the principles recognised in particular by the [European Charter]. In particular this Directive seeks to ensure full respect for human dignity and the right to asylum of applicants for asylum and their accompanying family members and to promote the application of Articles 1, 7, 11, 14, 15, 16, 18, 21, 24, 34 and 35 of that Charter, and should therefore be implemented accordingly.

Of these Articles, the most relevant to IP recognition issues are:

- Article 1 providing that 'human dignity is inviolable ... and must be protected and respected';
- Article 7 concerning the right to respect for private and family life;
- Article 18 guaranteeing the right to asylum with due respect to the GC and in accordance with the TFEU;
- Article 21 prohibiting discrimination based on any ground such as '*sex, race, colour, ethnic or social origin, genetic features, language, religion or belief, political or any other opinion, membership of a national minority, property, birth, disability, age or sexual orientation*'; and
- Article 24 concerning the rights of the child.

Additionally, the following Articles may give rise to EU rights which are relevant:

- Article 4 (prohibition of torture and inhuman or degrading treatment or punishment);
- Article 5 (prohibition of slavery and forced labour);
- Article 19 (protection from removal, expulsion or extradition '*to a State where there is a serious risk that he or she would be subjected to the death penalty, torture or other inhuman or degrading treatment or punishment*';
- Article 47 which provides:
- *Everyone whose rights and freedoms guaranteed by the law of the Union are violated has the right to an effective remedy before a tribunal in compliance with the conditions laid down in this Article.*
- *Everyone is entitled to a fair and public hearing within a reasonable time by an independent and impartial tribunal previously established by law. Everyone shall have the possibility of being advised, defended and represented.*
- Legal aid shall be made available to those who lack sufficient resources in so far as such aid is necessary to ensure effective access to justice.

52 These Titles comprise Articles 1 to 26 of the Charter.
53 The extract is from Chapter I of the Commentary which is an introduction into EU immigration and asylum law setting out a helpful summary of the general principles involved.

Even where the provisions of the Charter create individually enforceable rights, however, the question arises whether their procedural effect is different from existing binding IP law norms so that they may be no more than declaratory of the existing position. This is arguably the case with, for example, Article 19 which may simply be declaratory of the effect of Article 3 ECHR as explained in the relevant ECtHR jurisprudence. Similarly, in the case of Article 18, no obligation to grant asylum is imposed and the right to make the claim for IP recognition already exists under the QDs and national law recognising binding obligations under international instruments.

Finally, Article 47 has procedural implications where a Charter right is guaranteed so as to give rise to individual remedy.[54] This is arguably the case with the rights in the first two sentences of Article 47 but the wording of the remainder of the Article suggests that those parts may be statements of principles only. But, again, it is doubtful whether the first two rights are more than declaratory of the fundamental principles upon which MS judicial systems already operate, quite apart from the detailed provisions of the APD which is, with one exception, applied by all MS to the consideration of both refugee and subsidiary protection claims and their appeal or review requiring the provision of an effective remedy (Article 39 APD).

Even before 1 December 2009, Article 47 (right to fair trial) had at first instance been referred to as a reaffirmation of a general principle of Community law and some domestic courts had referred to Charter articles when identifying obligations under international law – Article 19 prohibiting refoulement is a further example. But, there are already ways in which international law norms may have effect independently of EU legislation as already noted.

It should be noted that the Czech Republic, Poland and the United Kingdom, have a limited derogation from the Charter under the Lisbon Treaty and the TFEC but the CJEU have now held that this does not affect the rights of individuals arising under the provisions of the Charter.

4.7.5. *The over-arching effect of existing treaty obligations of Member States*

All Member States are signatories to at least the GC and ECHR, and will remain bound by the provisions of those instruments additionally to the obligations and duties imposed on them by the EU legislative measures which underpin the concept of the CEAS.

This is important because, as already noted, the QD lacks the universality of the GC and the absolute nature of Article 3 ECHR in the following important respects:

    (a) it applies only to third country nationals or stateless persons and not to citizens of MS both in regard to refugee status and subsidiary protection status

---

54   See also paragraph 76 *infra* making clear that the exclusion of Article 6 ECHR remedies in relation to asylum and immigration issues in the ECtHR does not apply in proceedings before the CJEU.

(Article 2(e) and (g) 2011QD repeating earlier provisions of the 2004 QD), and then only to serious harm feared in the country of origin;

(b) claimants whose removal would be in breach of Article 3 ECHR (where their own past conduct is irrelevant to their right under Article 3), will not be eligible for subsidiary protection status under the QD if their past conduct merits exclusion from protection under Article 17 QD.

(c) Article 12 makes similar provision for exclusion from refugee status largely in line with the existing exclusion provisions contained in Articles 1.D, E and F of the GC, but with some amplification of the GC exclusion grounds in Articles 12.1.(b) and 12.2(b) and (c).

The CEAS is intended to create a general framework under which applications made within a MS should be initially considered and determined including provision for appeal against or review of the first instance decision before a court or tribunal which shall provide an effective remedy to the claimant (Article 39.1 APD). Although the provisions of the APD are currently mandatory only in respect of appeal or review of decisions denying refugee status, in practice all but one of the MS have accepted that the APD applies equally to subsidiary protection status recognition.

Where a claimant does not qualify for international protection under the QD, it may still be necessary to consider his position under the provisions of specific relevant international instruments binding on the MS.[55] In addition to the GC and the ECHR (bearing also in mind that there are a number of qualified articles falling entirely outside the provisions of the QD), other potentially relevant international instruments include the CAT, 1984 (note the prohibition of *refoulement* under Article 3); the obligations of the state under the Convention on the Rights of the Child, 1989 (in particular Article 22 concerning child asylum applicants whether accompanied or unaccompanied); and the ICCPR (particularly Articles 6 and 7).[56]

The most familiar example is where the claimant cannot succeed under the QD or GC because his own past conduct excludes him from such protection. Apart from any issue as to whether the claimant has a freestanding right under Article 19.2 of the EU Charter on the basis that removal would expose him to torture or inhuman or degrading treatment or punishment, he would still be entitled to claim that under Article 3 ECHR his removal would be in breach of his human rights and unlawful.

---

55 This is clearly recognized in terms in the CEAS because the APD makes specific provision in Article 3.4 that 'Member States may decide to apply this Directive to procedures for deciding on applications for any kind of international protection.' It is, of course very much in the interests of Member States to have a 'one-stop' procedure in protection cases.

56 See Goodwin-Gill and McAdam 'The Refugee in International Law' at Chapter 8 para 2.1 for a summary of its effect.

4.8. The second stage of the CEAS

As we have seen in the reference to the Conclusions of the Presidency following the Tampere Conference, the first phase was always seen as a transitory stage in the development of the CEAS.

4.8.1. *The EC Green Paper of October 2008*

The EC's view of the important objectives to be achieved by the second phase of the CEAS are set out in the Commission's Green Paper published in 2008 following extensive consultation:

> "A genuinely coherent, comprehensive and integrated CEAS should:

> ensure *access to those in need of protection*: asylum in the EU must remain accessible. Legitimate measures introduced to curb irregular migration and protect external borders should avoid preventing refugees' access to protection in the EU while ensuring a respect for fundamental rights of all migrants. This equally translates into efforts to facilitate access to protection outside the territory of the EU;

> provide for a single, *common procedure* for reasons of efficiency, speed, quality and fairness of the decisions;

> establish *uniform statuses* for asylum and for subsidiary protection, which shares most rights and obligations, whilst allowing for justified differences in treatment;

> incorporate *gender* considerations and take into account the special needs of *vulnerable groups*;

> increase *practical cooperation* in order to develop, inter alia, common training, as well as jointly assessing Country of Origin Information and organising support for Member States experiencing particular pressures;

> determine *responsibility and support solidarity*: the CEAS must include rules on the determination of the Member State responsible for examining an asylum application and provide for genuine *solidarity* mechanisms, both within the EU and with third countries;

> ensure *coherence with other policies* that have an impact on international protection, notably: border control, the fight against illegal immigration and return policies."

Again, these objectives emphasise the broad remit of the CEAS but, they also have a direct and important bearing on IP law and practice – the two areas with which we are concerned. The Green Paper recognises the problems in implementation of the 2004 QD and APD which have arisen in practice:

> "Member States are nowadays bound by an important asylum acquis. However, large discrepancies between asylum decisions (even within similar caseloads) still exist. This is due on the one hand to the low standards of harmonisation of the current legislation, and on the other hand, to different practices in national

administrations. It is therefore necessary to accompany legal harmonisation with effective practical cooperation.

One of the main goals of practical cooperation is to improve convergence in asylum decision-making by Member States, within the EU legislative framework. A substantial number of practical cooperation activities have already been undertaken in recent years. The replies to the Green Paper showed wide support for enhancing practical cooperation activities and for the idea of creating a dedicated structure to support and coordinate such activities in the form of a European Asylum Support Office (EASO) for Asylum."

These shortcomings are considered specifically in relation to the implementation at that point in time of the QD and APD, where the Green Paper has this to say as to future developments:

"3.2. The Asylum Procedures Directive (APD)[57]

Diverse procedural arrangements and qualified safeguards produce different results when applying common criteria for the identification of persons genuinely in need of international protection. This can damage the very objective of ensuring access to protection under equivalent conditions across the EU. In addition, both the Hague Programme and the TFEU call for the establishment of a common asylum procedure. This requires a fundamentally higher level of alignment between Member States' asylum procedures, as confirmed by the Green Paper consultation.

In order to achieve this goal, the amendments to the [APD] (to be proposed in 2009) will primarily aim at:

- setting up of a single, common asylum procedure leaving no space for the proliferation of disparate procedural arrangements in Member States, thus providing for a comprehensive examination of protection needs under both the Geneva Convention and the EU's subsidiary protection regime;

- establishing obligatory procedural safeguards as well as common notions and devices, which will consolidate the asylum process and ensure equal access to procedures throughout the Union;

- accommodating particular situations of mixed arrivals, including where persons seeking international protection are present at the external borders of the EU; and

- enhancing gender equality in the asylum process and provide for additional safeguards for vulnerable applicants.

---

57   It is interesting that the Green Paper puts amendments to the APD before those proposed to the QD, and that they are so very much more fundamental in nature, perhaps reinforcing the reasoning in footnote 12 above. It is also noteworthy that the thrust of the proposed amendments appears to go primarily to first instance procedures and that there is no specific reference to amendment of Article 39 APD although the relevant recast article includes important provisions clarifying the meaning of effective judicial remedy.

3.3. The [2004] Qualification Directive (QD)

The QD has secured a minimum alignment on both the criteria for granting international protection and the content of protection statuses across the EU. The positive impact of the Directive has been evident in many Member States. However, data show that the recognition of protection needs of applicants from the same countries of origin still varies significantly from one Member State to another. To some extent, this phenomenon is rooted in the wording of certain provisions of the QD.

In order to ensure a truly common interpretative approach and to achieve the objective of introducing uniform statuses (as required by The Hague Programme and the TFEU) the Commission will propose, in the course of 2009, to:

– amend the criteria for qualifying for international protection. To this effect, it may be necessary inter alia to clarify further the eligibility conditions for subsidiary protection, to define with more precision when non-state parties may be considered as actors of protection, or when a person may be considered as not in need of international protection if he stays in a certain part of his country of origin; and

– reconsider the level of rights and benefits to be secured for beneficiaries of subsidiary protection, in order to enhance their access to social and economic entitlements which are crucial for their successful integration, whilst ensuring respect for the principle of family unity across the EU.

In addition, the possibility of establishing an effective transfer of protection mechanism will be explored, either as part of the amendment to the QD or as a separate instrument.

Finally, a study will be launched on the possible alignment of national types of protection status which do not currently fall under the EU's regime of international protection."

4.8.2. The relevance of Article 78 TFEU to development of the CEAS

These changes were put forward on the basis of the changed emphasis in asylum and immigration policy which would follow adoption of Article 78 of the Treaty on the Functioning of the European Union (TFEU), commonly referred to as the Lisbon Treaty. As noted above, the TFEU came into force on 1 December 2009. It provides for development of a common policy on asylum, subsidiary protection and temporary protection at Article 78:

"1. The Union shall develop a common policy on asylum, subsidiary protection and temporary protection with a view to offering appropriate status to any third-country national requiring international protection and ensuring compliance with the principle of non-refoulement. This policy must be in accordance with the Geneva Convention of 28 July 1951 and the Protocol of 31 January 1967 relating to the status of refugees, and other relevant treaties.

2. For the purposes of paragraph 1, the European Parliament and the Council, acting in accordance with the ordinary legislative procedure, shall adopt measures for a common European asylum system comprising:

(a) a uniform status of asylum for nationals of third countries, valid throughout the Union;

(b) a uniform status of subsidiary protection for nationals of third countries who, without obtaining European asylum, are in need of international protection; …

(d) Common procedures for the granting and withdrawing of uniform asylum or subsidiary protection status; …"

Note that this is in contrast to the provisions of Article 63 TEC which referred to the establishment of minimum standards in respect of qualification of third country nationals for refugee or subsidiary protection status and minimum standards on procedures for determining the issue of refugee status recognition.

The importance of the long-term harmonisation of protection law and procedures under the CEAS has been made clear since the commencement of its implementation. The shortfalls in the first stage implementation have been clearly identified. So far as the qualification for protection status is concerned, these have been partly addressed by the 2011 QD.

There are currently proposals for a recast APD which would go some way further to providing for common procedures but it is beyond the scope of this paper to deal in detail with issues which must await a future directive save to say that it is in this field that the greatest problems of harmonisation of state practices remain to be resolved.

4.9.   Specific Issues under the QD and APD

We turn now to the second subject of this Part, namely to comment upon the strengths and weaknesses of the 2011 QD and the APD with particular reference to the issues which primarily concern the discharge of the judicial function of appeal or review under Article 39.1 APD.

In this part we shall seek to deal principally with the following specific topics:

1) Article 39.1 APD and the meaning of *'effective remedy'*;
2) the distinction between the mandatory and permissive provisions in the Directives;
3) the "new" regime of 'subsidiary protection' introduced by the QD; and
4) the essential simplicity , contrary to appearances, of the APD provisions.

Issues relating to burden and standard of proof are dealt with separately in Part VI. But, first, we consider in broad terms the strengths and weaknesses of the two Directives.

4.9.1. *The strengths and weaknesses of the QD and APD*

The application of the minimum standard approach pursuant to Article 63 TEC may be seen as a fundamental, although perhaps politically necessary, weakness in both Directives. Whilst the use of such an approach is well known in EU legislation, the method of application in these Directives differed from the normal usage in which a specific unqualified saving for existing higher standards than those imposed by the EU legislation normally appears.

The relevant provision (Article 3 QD and Article 5 APD) is couched in identical terms:

> 'Member States may introduce or retain more favourable standards for determining who qualifies as a refugee or as a person eligible for subsidiary protection, and for determining the content of international protection, *in so far as those standards are compatible with this Directive.*' [Emphasis added]

It is the qualifying words at the end of the Articles which raise issues as to the extent to which it is open to MS to apply more favourable standards in the recognition of protection status under the QD. The preponderance of the academic view, supported by UNHCR, is that there is no restriction on more favourable standards, as this is not incompatible with the purpose of imposing a minimum standard. On this argument MS have an unfettered discretion to apply any more favourable standard they wish to apply to recognition of status under the QD.

That argument, however, effectively treats the qualifying phrase as meaningless. It is clearly at variance with the intentions of the EC as expressed in 14348/02 JUR 449 Asile 67 of 15 November 2002.[58] Whilst those views are not, of course, binding in terms of interpretation, the academic views give no weight to the overall scheme of the first phase of CEAS which is in part based on the need to prevent 'asylum-shopping' (Recital (7) of the 2004 QD and Recital (13) of the

---

58   Para 5 notes that although the Amsterdam Treaty term 'minimum standards' does not preclude Member States from maintaining or introducing more favourable standards for persons within the scope of the acts in question, *'in order not to annihilate the objective of harmonization, this possibility cannot be unlimited'* and emphasises the need for such standards to be compatible with the QD. Para 7 notes that a number of provisions (including the definition Article and Articles related to it) *'...are fundamental not only for the directive in question, but also have a bearing on other areas, such as the notion of refugee status ...'* so that *'any deviation in national law from* [those provisions] *would be incompatible with the objective of harmonizing the contents of those notions, unless the definition itself allows for the inclusion or exclusion of a certain group of persons as part of a wider category'*. Para 8 states: *'The use of the words "shall" or "may" constituted only a rough indicator as to whether or not a provision is intended to allow Member States to retain or adopt more favourable provisions'*. It is pointed out that the use of the word *'may'* in what is now Article 8(1) and (2) (*sur place* claims) *'does not indicate that those provisions are optional: it follows from their context that they define specific facets of the notions "well-founded fear of being persecuted" and "real risk of suffering serious harm" which are part of the definitions in Article 2(c) and (e) from which, as stated before, no derogation is possible'*. The advice then points out that, contextually, the use of the word *'shall'* in Chapter VII of the QD (content of international protection) is concerned with the objective of laying down minimum standards which must be implemented, while leaving it open to Member States to grant more favourable treatment of those recognized as entitled to international protection.

2011 QD) and included the proposal to extend provision of certificates of long residence to those in receipt of long-term protection now achieved, and the issue of burden-sharing under the principle of solidarity. All those aspects underline the importance of reasonable uniformity in the application of the QD by Member States, particularly in relation to those requirements of status recognition which are couched in mandatory terms.[59]

In its second phase, the provisions of Article 78 TFEU underline the intention to move to a basis of uniformity of status in relation to both refugee and subsidiary protection status, with the differences in the practical consequences of recognition being increasingly eroded from that which applied under the 2004 QD. This is already apparent in the provisions of the 2011 QD.

The arguments are complex.[60] But there can be little doubt that the tensions between the opposing views will become more critical as the CEAS develops towards the concept of uniform status with common procedures. It appears that to date most MS have in practice tended to adopt a restrictive view of their powers under Article 3. Moreover, Recitals (8) to (10) of the 2011 QD are explicit in the intention of confirming the principles underlying the 2004 QD as well as seeking to achieve 'a higher level of approximation of the rules on the recognition and content of international protection'.

A second weakness is the provision under Chapter VII QD 2004 for application of differing levels of the content of protection consequent on the recognition of refugee status on the one hand and subsidiary protection status on the other. It is difficult to see on what basis there should be such a distinction between those recognised as in need of international protection (see Recital 6 2004 QD) but the differences have already been eroded in important respects in the provisions of Chapter VII of the 2011 QD.

The third weakness is the restriction of the mandatory application of the APD to refugees, its application to those seeking other kinds of international protection (including subsidiary protection) being permissive (Article 3.4 APD) unless MS employed a joint first instance determining procedure when the requirements of the APD must be observed (Article 3.3 APD). This creates an asymmetry between the two Directives which are in all other respects complementary. This is compounded by the extent to which MS may deviate from the basic principles and guarantees of Chapter II APD in the circumstances provided in Chapter III, primarily aimed at curtailment of the basic processing of claims.

All these issues are, of course, to be addressed in the second phase of implementation of the CEAS and it appears that to date they have caused few problems in practice save for the extent to which some MS appear to have disposed of

---

59 Support for this view may be obtained from the judgment in *Germany v B and D* [2010 CJEU C-57/09 and C-101/09] where the Court interpreted Directive 2004/83 as meaning that Member States may grant a right of asylum under their national law to a person who is excluded from refugee status pursuant to one of the exclusion clauses laid down in that Directive, provided that that other kind of protection does not entail a risk of confusion with refugee status within the meaning of the Directive.

60 The arguments are more fully set out in the Commentary edited by Kay Hailbronner *op cit.* Chapter IV.3 at pp. 1021-3.

claims by giving subsidiary protection status rather than carrying out a full process designed first to determine the claim for refugee status recognition.[61]

There is, however, a very positive side to the Directives and the EC is to be congratulated on having been able to achieve the degree of unanimity which it did in the face of real political concerns on the part of many MS.

First, the supremacy of the GC as the primary source of international refugee law is maintained, subject to the glosses in Articles 4 to 10 QD which generally seek to incorporate the effect of international jurisprudence on questions of application of the Convention which have, in the past, raised difficulties.

Secondly, it has been recognised that the international protection needs arising from threat of serious harm as defined in Article 15 QD should also attract a specific protection regime by way of subsidiary protection rather than those who meet the requirements for such protection simply being able to avoid *refoulement* and otherwise to rely on such civic rights as the receiving state was prepared to give them.

Finally, and arguably the most significant innovation since it is not based on existing treaty obligations, the APD prescribes a code of principles and guarantees to be observed in determining an application for recognition as a refugee, including a mandatory requirement for provision of an effective judicial remedy by way of appeal or review.[62]

4.9.2. *Article 39.1 APD and the meaning of 'effective remedy'*

Article 39.1 APD provides, with deceptive simplicity, that:

'Member States shall ensure that applicants for asylum have the right to an effective remedy before a court or tribunal ...'[63]

---

61   UNHCR in its Annotated Comments on the EC Council Directive 2004/83/EC of April 2004 (January 2005) notes, the need to consider refugee eligibility before subsidiary protection is implied by: (i) R3 which states that the Refugee Convention provides the "cornerstone of the international legal regime for the protection of refugees"; (ii) the use of the word "subsidiary"; (iii) the definition in A2 (e) ("'person eligible for subsidiary protection' means a third country national or a stateless person who does not qualify as a refugee but in respect of whom ..."); (iv) the internal ordering throughout the Directive which deals with refugee eligibility first; and (v) the wording of R24 which defines subsidiary protection as "complementary and additional to" refugee protection."

62   The degree of controversy raised by procedural issues is apparent from the substantial number of 'exceptional' procedures and the fact that its adoption was delayed. Nevertheless, the standard procedure, which will apply in the vast majority of cases, lays down a significant code of principles to be observed by first instance decision makers.

63   It should be noted that if the recast APD is enacted in its present form, there will be an important addition in Article 41 (the recast Article 39) with implications for the current practice of some MS. The proposed Article 41.3 provides: '*Member States shall ensure that the effective remedy referred to in paragraph 1 provides for a full examination of both facts and point of law, including an ex nunc examination of the international protection needs pursuant to Directive [....;../EC] [the Qualification Directive], at least in appeal procedures before a court or tribunal of first instance.*

It then goes on to list the decisions in respect of which this right exists. The list effectively comprises all first instance decisions concerned with the recognition of refugee status, including withdrawal of recognized status.

The meaning of *'the right to an effective remedy'* is not defined in the APD but it is a term of art in international law. It appears in numerous international treaties and conventions including the ICCPR (Article 2), the ECHR (Article 13) and the EU Charter of Fundamental Rights (Article 47). Under these instruments local remedies must be exhausted prior to seeking the assistance of the relevant treaty body.

H. Battjes (*op cit.*) provides a helpful overview and analysis of the relevant standards of international law and EC law in appeal procedures as well as the specific provisions of Article 39 of the Procedures Directive at Chapter 6.3. Whilst the full text of this chapter can be read with advantage, we set out by way of footnote his conclusions at paragraph 420 in relation to the general international and EC law obligations binding on Member States.[64]

In so far as ECtHR has pronounced on the scope of enquiry appropriate to provide an effective remedy, it is potentially very wide-ranging. In *Jabari v Turkey* Case 40035/98, where there had been a complete denial of any substantive consideration of the claim on purely procedural grounds, the language used in the judgment is in similar terms to other cases dealing with issues of effective remedy and it is clear that the Court chose to put their position in broad terms because of the gravity of risk in *refoulement* of a claimant who has not had his or her claim adequately considered.[65] In its more recent judgement (January 2007) in the *Case*

---

64 'The Member States must provide for an effective remedy against a decision to expel if the alien can present an 'arguable claim' that expulsion will result in ill-treatment (Articles 13 ECHR and 2(3) CCPR). A claim is arguable for the purposes of Article 13 ECHR if the claimant runs prima facie a real risk of ill-treatment upon expulsion. The remedy must satisfy several conditions. The 'authority', that is to offer the remedy must perform an independent and rigorous scrutiny (article 13 ECHR). This implies that it can do findings of fact for itself, and that the review of the decision to expel is not limited to issues of law (Article 13 and 3ECHR). The principle of equality of arms applies, and the applicant should be offered sufficient time and facilities to prepare the case (Article 34 read in conjunction with 13 ECHR). The authority must have the power to suspend expulsion of those who have an arguable claim that expulsion will result in ill-treatment (article 13 ECHR). Arguably, states cannot expel an alien who appealed to article 3 ECHR, without allowing him to apply for leave to remain to this authority, as it is this authority who decides on the arguability of the claim. If the alien claims to be a refugee, he cannot be expelled until the authority has decided upon the case unless it is beyond reasonable doubt that he is not a refugee (article 33 ECHR).

International law has served as a source of inspiration for the general principles of Community law concerning appeal proceedings, as well as for Article 47 Charter. But these principles, and this Charter provision offer in several respects more extensive protection. To begin with, they require an effective remedy if the right guaranteed by Community law is affected (the 'arguable claim' requirement does not apply). Moreover, the obligations laid down in article 6 ECHR apply to all Community rights (thus not only to 'civil rights and obligations or criminal charges') - including administrative proceedings, such as asylum procedures. It follows that under Community law, the effective remedy must be offered before a court or tribunal, and legal aid must be available.'

65 At paragraph 50 the Court said: 'In the Court's opinion, given the irreversible nature of the harm that might occur if the risk of torture or ill-treatment alleged materialised and the importance which it attaches to Article 3, the notion of an effective remedy under Article 13 re-

→

of Salah Sheekh v The Netherlands [Application No 1948/04] the Court rejected a claim that there had been a breach of Article 13 ECHR but nevertheless proceeded to carry out a full factual review of the Article 3 claim as at the date of the hearing and to find that expulsion would be in breach of the claimant's Article 3 rights.[66]

It is important also to emphasise that the CJEU has not accepted the limitation which the ECtHR placed upon the extent of its jurisdiction by classifying asylum and immigration claims as claims to which Article 6 ECHR did not apply. The effect of bringing the issue of effective protection onto a Community law base is, therefore, to increase the scope of the protection offered to claimants to include Article 6 ECHR rights.

Although the APD is binding only in respect of refugee claims, a 2008 ECRE Study[67] found that all reference countries employed a sequential procedure to deal with Subsidiary Protection issues following the conclusion of the asylum claim process. The EC has stated that all Member States, with one exception, apply Article 3.3 APD.

In any event, prior to the enactment of the EU Charter as part of EU primary law from 1 December 2009, there was an argument that a claimant seeking the right under the QD to recognition as a person entitled to subsidiary protection status will be entitled to an effective remedy against any executive decision denying such recognition irrespective of the terms of the APD and the way in which

---

quires independent and rigorous scrutiny of a claim that there exist substantial grounds for fearing a real risk of treatment contrary to Article 3 and the possibility of suspending the implementation of the measure impugned. Since the Ankara Administrative Court failed in the circumstances to provide any of these safeguards, the Court is led to conclude that the judicial review proceedings relied on by the Government did not satisfy the requirements of Article 13.'

66   At paragraph 136 the Court expressed its duty in Article 3 cases in the following terms: 'The establishment of any responsibility of the expelling State under Article 3 inevitably involves an assessment of conditions in the requesting country against the standards of Article 3 of the Convention (see *Mamatkulov and Askarov v. Turkey* [GC], nos. 46827/99 and 46951/99, ECHR 2005-I, § 67). In determining whether it has been shown that the applicant runs a real risk, if expelled, of suffering treatment proscribed by Article 3, the Court will assess the issue in the light of all the material placed before it, or, if necessary, material obtained proprio motu, in particular where the applicant – or a third party within the meaning of Article 36 of the Convention – provides reasoned grounds which cast doubt on the accuracy of the information relied on by the respondent Government. In respect of materials obtained proprio motu, the Court considers that, given the absolute nature of the protection afforded by Article 3, it must be satisfied that the assessment made by the authorities of the Contracting State is adequate and sufficiently supported by domestic materials as well as by materials originating from other, reliable and objective sources, such as, for instance, other Contracting or non-Contracting States, agencies of the United Nations and reputable non-governmental organisations. In its supervisory task under Article 19 of the Convention, it would be too narrow an approach under Article 3 in cases concerning aliens facing expulsion or extradition if the Court, as an international human rights court, were only to take into account materials made available by the domestic authorities of the Contracting State concerned without comparing these with materials from other, reliable and objective sources. This further implies that, in assessing an alleged risk of treatment contrary to Article 3 in respect of aliens facing expulsion or extradition, a full and ex nunc assessment is called for as the situation in a country of destination may change in the course of time.'

67   'The Impact of the EU Qualification Directive on International Protection' published in October 2008 following a survey of the practices of nineteen Member States.

such claims were required to be dealt with under Member States' transposing legislation.[68]

4.9.3. *The competence of the national court*

The competence of the national court is a matter which will be regulated by national law. It may be that the jurisdiction of particular courts or tribunals will be so limited that they will not have the ability to provide an effective remedy in the terms set out unless and until the recast Article 41.3 takes effect when the recast APD becomes law (see footnote 54 above). In those circumstances, the claimant may ultimately have to look to the ECtHR or to the CJEU for his remedy. But, even where the power of the relevant national court of tribunal is limited to review of the lawfulness of a first instance decision, there are important areas of enquiry based on the provisions of the QD and APD which we suggest cannot be excluded from its competence.

The issues addressed in Chapter II QD and, particularly, the elements of assessment set out in Article 4.3 QD must demonstrably have been considered by reference to a written decision (Article 9.1 APD), properly reasoned both as to facts and law (Article 9.2 APD), following a personal interview (Article 12 APD), with the benefit of the guarantees contained in Article 10 APD. Moreover, the decision-maker must be a person *'who has the appropriate knowledge or receives the necessary training in the field of asylum and refugee matters'* (Recital 10 and Articles 8.2 (determining authority personnel) and 4.3 APD (other authorised decision makers)). Where there has been a failure to comply with these standards and requirements in the first instance decision-making process, it will not be a lawful disposal of the claimant's application.

4.9.4. *The distinction between the mandatory and permissive provisions of the QD and APD*

From a judicial viewpoint, the importance of this distinction will arise when it is argued that the transposing legislation of the MS has failed properly to give effect to the primacy of the mandatory provisions of the QD. The argument is closely

---

68 In her Research Paper No.134 of November 2006 for UNHCR (The European asylum procedures directive in legal context) Cathryn Costello sets out the basis of such argument:
Under the EC general principles, the right to effective judicial protection is well established. Moreover, it applies in all instances where EC rights are at stake, and so is of broader scope than article 13 ECHR. As the ECJ stated in the seminal Johnston case, "Community law requires effective judicial scrutiny of the decisions of national authorities taken pursuant to the applicable provisions of Community law." Thus, it applies not only in the context of internal market guarantees, but also when third country nationals have rights under EC law. Even if national law purports to oust strict judicial review, these national provisions are simply ineffective in the EC law context. The right to effective judicial protection has taken shape in order to vindicate individual rights accorded by EC law. This is reflected in Johnston, where the ECJ held that the right to effective judicial protection precluded the acceptance of an official certificate as conclusive evidence, in that case to justify derogation from the principle of equal treatment for men and women. Instead, judicial review had to be available to scrutinise official claims in each individual case.

linked with the controversy relating to *'more favourable standards'* (Article 3 QD). This may, therefore, be a transient issue which will be resolved in phase two of the CEAS by the application of the *'uniform status'* '(provided that such status applies to the substantive provisions relating to recognition as being in need of international protection and not merely to the civil status consequences of such recognition)and *'common procedure'* criteria.

For the time being, however, the Commission view is that mandatory provisions must be transposed intact into national law in order to comply with EC Law. As regards the permissive provisions, MS have an area of discretion in terms of their incorporation into the transposing national law, although some provide that, if incorporated, certain elements will then become mandatory.

Reference has already been made[69] to the Council's Legal Services Opinion 14348/02 of 15 November 2002 dealing with issues arising from what was then Article 4 in the proposed Directive and is now Article 3. It is perhaps helpful to note here that the advice given was that any deviation from the definitions laid down in Article 2 of the Qualification Directive (the definition section) would be incompatible with the intended harmonisation.[70] The same advice applied to what are now Articles 6 (actors of persecution or serious harm), 7 (actors of protection), 9 (acts of persecution), 11 (cessation), 12 (exclusion), 13 (granting of refugee status), 15 (serious harm), 16 (cessation), and 17(1) and (2) (exclusion).[71]

4.9.5. The "new" regime of 'subsidiary protection' introduced by the QD

Before the QD came into force, all MS had policies in force to deal with claimants who could not meet the requirements of the GC, but who, nevertheless, could not be sent back to their own countries without breach of the receiving state's obligations under other international instruments. The most important of these was Article 3 ECHR and, subject to attempts to apply special measures in relation to those who posed a security risk to the receiving state, there was generally little to dif-

---

69 Paragraph 63 above.

70 'unless the definition itself allows for the inclusion or exclusion of a certain group of persons as part of a wider category'.

71 The effect of the Opinion was summarised by Jane McAdam (*Complementary Protection in International Refugee Law*, OUP 2007): 'This background document sets out three main general principles governing the scope and application of Article 3: First, deviations in national law from definitions set out in A2 and related articles 6, 7, 9, 11, 12, 13, 15, 16, 17(1) and (2) would be incompatible with harmonisation unless the definition itself permits the inclusion or exclusion of a particular group of persons as part of a wider category. Secondly, 'shall' or 'may' roughly indicate whether or not a provision allows Member States to adopt or retain more favourable standards. Where 'may' defines the 'normative intensity' of a provision, it normally indicates that the provision is optional. In articles 5(1) and (2), 'may' does not mean that those provisions are optional but rather defines specific aspects of the notions 'well-founded fear of being persecuted' and 'real risk of suffering serious harm'. Since these form part of the definitions in A2, no derogation from them is possible. Most of the provisions of the Directive use the term 'shall', yet from their context it is apparent that they leave it open for Member States to grant more favourable treatment, since their objective is simply to set out minimum standards'. Finally, provisions that incorporate the term 'in particular' indicate that elements of the provision are not exhaustive, thus allowing Member States to take into account additional aspects in their national laws.'

ferentiate them in practice from recognised refugees. There was, however, no enforceable instrument providing for their rights during their enforced stay in their countries of refuge.

In broad terms, the QD now provides such persons with a specific status and the content of their protection regime is set out in Chapter VII QD. The EU is unique in having afforded a formal status to those who comply with the requirements leading to subsidiary protection, and this is a major step forward in terms of international protection rights.

It should be remembered, however, that this new status does not correspond with those who are otherwise irremovable by the State. It applies only to third country nationals and stateless persons. It is further restricted to the 'worthy' claimant by the application of exclusion provisions similar to (but not identical with) those applicable to refugees. Article 17 QD is more widely drawn than Article 12 QD (exclusion provisions relating to refugees).[72]

4.9.6. *The essential simplicity (contrary to appearances) of the APD provisions*

The provisions of the APD require careful analysis but they have become complex because of the number of exceptional procedures, which MS have sought to build onto the standard procedure which will apply in the decision process applicable to the vast majority of claims.

The three principal areas of complexity of procedure arise in the following circumstances: first, some MS have different procedures depending on whether the asylum application is being treated as a port application or as an in-country application; secondly, all MS see the need to apply accelerated and/or curtailed procedures in certain classes of application,[73] particularly where they consider the claimant to be from what they regard as a safe country of origin; finally, there is a further category of claims which they seek to treat as inadmissible, primarily where the claimant is regarded as entering from what is regarded as a safe third country.

Whether the classification of claims in this way, and the consequent application of different sets of procedure rules, really achieves the objectives of efficiency and time-saving which legislators attribute to them, is, perhaps, a moot point. The need to provide an effective remedy, by way of appeal or review is not thereby obviated. Refugee law judges may well be more adept at selecting those appeals which may usefully be the subject of fast tracking or joint listing with other similar claims for speedy disposal than legislators appreciate.

The safe third country concept is particularly confusing since there are a number of overlapping concepts in this respect.

---

72 See the analysis of the differences in the commentary on these articles in Kay Hailbronner *op. cit.*, Chapter IV.

73 In the UK, for example, there has on average been one new Act annually for the last ten years in which procedural issues have figured prominently. On one occasion there was even a proposal for ouster of the jurisdiction of the superior courts although it did not survive beyond the initial draft stage.

The first category of safe third countries falls outside the scope of the APD. It comprises those countries in which the selection of the State appropriate to deal with the asylum application is ascertained by application of the Dublin Regulation, 343/2003/EC. It includes all MS (which are not, of course, strictly third countries for normal definition purposes under the Directives) as well as certain third countries who have by agreement acceded to the Dublin Regulation, namely Iceland, Norway, and Switzerland. The Dublin Regulation makes detailed provision for identification of the appropriate State to deal with the asylum application and includes its own permissive provision for appeal or review against such a decision.

The second category consists of countries identified as safe third countries where the application may be treated as inadmissible under Article 25.2(b) or (c). This concept is dealt with in Articles 26 and 27 of the Directive. It applies without geographical limitation in respect of countries where the claimant has been recognised as a refugee or otherwise enjoys sufficient protection provided that the country concerned will readmit the claimant and meets the requirements of Article 27. These include not only requirements as to the nature of the protection afforded by the country concerned, but also require there to be a connection between the claimant and that third country which makes it reasonable for him to re-enter that third country.

The third category consists of countries which meet the requirements of Article 36[74] for classification as European safe third countries. Subject to transitional provisions, they must either be approved accession countries or included in a list adopted by the Council. There is currently no approved list under Article 36. There is some doubt as to whether there are any other European countries who would qualify for inclusion on such a list.[75] Until, however, there is a Council approved list, the transitional provisions will continue to apply. Where the claimant is from a country to which Article 36 applies, his application may be subject to no or to a curtailed examination process.

Subject to these matters, however, the provisions as to the carrying out of the standard process of evaluation of claims which will apply in the majority of cases is really straightforward and appropriately comprehensive, both as to the qualifications of the personnel concerned and the nature of the enquiry which is to be made before reaching a written reasoned decision.

Article 4.1 requires there to be a single determining authority in each Member State to carry out the prescribed examination and make the first instance decision on it, with particular reference to the requirements of Articles 8.2 and 9. In this respect the most important provisions of the later Articles are that the decision is to

---

74 But see *European Parliament v Council of the EU* ECR [2008] I-3189 where the ECJ annulled Articles 29.1 and 2 and Article 36.3 as granting a legislative power exceeding its authority.

75 Iceland, Norway and Switzerland would all have been obvious candidates but, since they are already full participants in the Dublin Regulation, there is little point in their being placed on the list. European States which are non-EU Member States but are on the Council of Europe have ratified the ECHR and so are potential candidates for inclusion: but, there may in some cases be concerns about their observation of human rights norms which would make inclusion problematic.

be taken *'individually, objectively and impartially'* by personnel who *'have the knowledge with respect to relevant standards applicable in the field of asylum and refugee law'* and on the basis of *'precise and up-to-date information ... as to the general situation'* prevailing in the country of origin of the claimant. These are the procedural requirements appropriate to ensure the carrying out of an assessment in accordance with the provisions of Chapter II of the QD.

The basic principles and guarantees in the asylum process appear at Articles 6 to 22 of Chapter II of the APD.

These provisions are at the core of the Directive. They establish the minimum requirements of the asylum process at first instance in applications requiring full consideration under Article 23 of Chapter II, as well as on appeal or review under Article 39, Chapter V of the Directive. They are also highly relevant in the case of the exceptional procedures because they provide the benchmark from which specific derogation is then made.

The various Articles cover the following issues: access to the procedure (Article 6); the suspensive effect of making the application (Article 7); the duties of the MS in carrying out the examination of the claim (Article 8) and the matters to be dealt with in the first instance decision (Article 9); the procedural guarantees to be given to applicants (Article 10) and their obligations (Article 11); detailed provisions in relation to the personal interview to which the claimant is entitled (Articles 12, 13 and 14); the right to legal assistance and representation (Article 15) and its scope (Article 16); special provisions in relation to dealing with applications by unaccompanied minors (Article 17); the prohibition of detention on the sole ground that the claimant is applying for asylum and the right of judicial review of any such detention (Article 18); procedures on withdrawal (Article 19) and abandonment (Article 20) of the application; the role of the UNHCR (Article 21); and, finally, provisions as to the duty of confidentiality to the claimant (Article 22).[76]

Chapter II of the APD provides a straightforward but comprehensive process, the proper application of which will ensure a full and fair assessment of the claim. The basic procedure, unlike the glosses on it, is essentially simple and straightforward of application.

4.10. Conclusion

The provisions of the QDs and the APD represent a major step in the progress towards the CEAS.

This is so particularly in the case of the QD where many points of difference have been addressed. If the more conservative interpretation of Article 3 as to the limitation on the provision of more generous standards is correct, the harmonisation of the application of the law relating to the recognition of the need for international protection will have been achieved in substantial measure.

Whilst the APD inevitably raises many areas of difference and potential difficulty, the core provisions relating to the requirements for processing the majority

---

76   The IARLJ Manual *op. cit.* contains a full analysis of the APD at Chapter 4.

of applications have set high standards for the determining authorities in all MS and formalised important safeguards for asylum claimants. It is particularly in the case of the APD that the transposing legislation and the degree to which MS choose to rely on their pre-December 2005 procedures, will clarify the scope of the task which remains in order to achieve a common procedure throughout the EU.

As we have seen, the EC is clear on many of the areas which now need to be addressed to move forward the concept of the CEAS into its second phase, but the judiciary has a significant role to play in the implementation of the Directives and in pointing the way to realisation of the goal of the CEAS.

They will initially be responsible for providing claimants with an effective remedy against executive decisions in accordance with the requirements of existing Strasbourg jurisprudence. Their judicial independence is preserved by the requirements of objectivity, impartiality and individual consideration of asylum claims which are required under the APD. Upon their willingness to share the jurisprudence of other MS and to seek greater harmony of application of that jurisprudence much of the future of the CEAS will depend.

5. Part V: The role of the national judge within the CEAS

5.1. Introduction

In Part I we set out an analysis of the role of the judge in a full merits hearing of an IP claim[77] as follows:

- to decide whether the claimant is entitled to recognition as a person in need of international protection –
- as at the date of the hearing –
- by reference to the relevant provisions of the QD governing recognition of refugee and subsidiary protection status –
- on the totality of the evidence before the court –
- including that obtained by the court of its own volition (subject to procedural safeguards)–
- considered and assessed objectively –
- so as to establish whether –
- if then immediately returned to his country of origin –
- there is a well-founded fear of the claimant being persecuted (Article 13 refugee status recognition) or –
- if not recognised as a refugee pursuant to Article 13 of the QD –
- whether, if so returned, substantial grounds have been shown for believing there is –
- a real risk that the claimant will suffer serious harm as defined in the QD (Article 18 subsidiary protection status recognition).

In this Part we consider these sequential steps in detail. They are relevant to all judges concerned with IP claims whether on a full protection hearing or on cassation or judicial review because an important element of the analysis is to identify where errors of law may occur.

5.2. The entitlement to recognition as a person in need of international protection

IP cases differ fundamentally from cases concerning the right of a non-national to enter and remain in another country (immigration cases).

In immigration cases, whether the non-national is entitled to enter and remain in the country concerned, for how long and under what conditions, are real matters for the national law of each state to determine subject to any overarching provisions of EU Law concerning the right of freedom of movement within the EU.

---

77 If Article 41.3 of the recast APD is enacted in its presently proposed form, the holding of such a hearing as part of providing an effective remedy will become obligatory in MS.

The non-national has no "right" (privilege) of entry or stay, save in so far as he can bring himself within the rules and regulations of the receiving state as to the treatment of aliens.

In contrast, in cases where recognition of IP status is sought, the claimant is exercising a right to seek the protection of the receiving country under either the provisions of international treaties and conventions to which the state is a signatory or under the provisions of EU Law. The receiving state cannot restrict or qualify those provisions by its national laws save insofar as may be permitted by the relevant instruments of IP law.

The rationale of the international protection status regime is that where his or her own state effectively denies him or her that degree of protection to which all its citizens are entitled, the claimant is entitled to seek international surrogate protection. If the requirements of the QD and/or other binding instruments of international protection law are met, then the claimant is entitled to recognition of protection status.

5.3. As at the date of the hearing

In the vast majority of civil and criminal cases which come before the national courts, the issues for resolution will be the ascertainment of past relevant facts and the application of the national law to those facts. In many cases the decision as to what constitute those past relevant facts – that is the scope of the area of inquiry – is a matter for the parties to decide rather than for the court, even where the hearing is inquisitorial in nature.

IP cases are fundamentally different, particularly in relation to evidentiary standards applicable. Although past events will usually, although not always, be of relevance in ascertaining the basis on which a claimant seeks recognition of his or her need for protection, the essential issue for determination by the court is whether on the totality of the evidence before it, the claimant has a currently well-founded fear of persecution (refugee status) or a real risk of being subjected to serious harm (subsidiary protection status).

In other words, the fundamental duty of the court in protection cases is to make an assessment concerning prospective risk, based on the assumption of immediate *refoulement* of the claimant, in which past history plays a significant part, but not always a decisive one,[78] in carrying out that assessment.

Because of the very serious consequences of returning a claimant to a country where such treatment may be suffered, IP claims demand the utmost scrutiny.

5.4. By reference to the relevant provisions of the QD

Under the CEAS, whether a claimant is entitled to protection status is determined by reference to the provisions of the QD. Since the QD, being a Directive, is required to be transposed into its national law by each MS, the primary recourse will be to the relevant provisions of the national law. Insofar, however, as the national

---

78   In *sur place* claims it may have no or very little relevance at all.

law has failed properly to transpose the mandatory requirements of the QD, the court may have to take into account those provisions by direct reference to the QD.

The two forms of protection provided for in the QD are mutually exclusive and, as already noted, the appropriate order of consideration is first whether refugee status should be recognised but, if not, whether the right to subsidiary protection status is made out.

If the claimant does not succeed under the provisions of the CEAS, that may not, however, be the end of the matter. Where the court finds that the claimant is excluded from protection under either Article 12 or 17 QD, it may be necessary to consider whether return would nevertheless be in breach of the claimant's human rights under the European Convention on Human Right (ECHR), to which all MS must be signatories.[79] In particular, Article 3 of the ECHR is cast in absolute terms and a claimant cannot be disqualified from its protection, however he may have behaved in the past. Although such a finding would not grant the claimant any positive status, it would render his removal unlawful.

Finally, it must be noted that even where the MS fails to take the point, it remains the duty of the court to take into account all relevant requirements of the QD in determining status recognition, including the exclusion provisions referred to above.

5.5. On the totality of the evidence before the court

This may seem obvious, but it is surprising how many decision-makers fall into the error of considering the evidence on a piece-meal basis and, once having rejected one part of the evidence, use that rejection as a basis for rejecting subsequent parts of the evidence on a cumulative basis. To do so is a fundamental error of law and will vitiate any decision based upon such reasoning. To take an obvious example of such a 'compartmentalising' approach, it would be a clear error for a judge to reject the evidence of a medical report on the ground that he did not believe the claimant to be personally credible where the report addressed issues of credibility.

Chapter II QD sets out the broad basis for assessment of facts and circumstances (Article 4) and Articles 5 to 8 go on to deal with the approach to specific issues which have been the subject of differences of approach internationally (*sur place* claims, who are actors of persecution and serious harm and who are actors of protection, and internal protection issues) broadly applying the current international consensus as the basis applicable under the CEAS.

Evidence as to the situation in the country of origin, both during the period of the claimant's narrative leading to his departure and up to the time of assessment of his claim, is highly relevant to the assessment of the general credibility or believability of the claimant's personal history. Post-departure evidence may, for

---

79   Reference to ECHR rights will depend on whether the national court has jurisdiction under its national law to consider such issues on a 'one-stop' basis (as, for example, in the UK) or whether a separate process for claims to relief under the CEAS is prescribed.

example, serve to confirm a general situation which may have been developing at the time the claimant left. The current country of origin evidence is, of course, also of considerable importance in assessing the other context we have noted, i.e. establishment of the credibility of the prospective risk on which recognition of protection status depends.

It has often been said that although it is, on general principles, for the claimant to establish his case, the process of assessment of a claim to international protection involves a shared burden between the state and the claimant. This is now enshrined in Article 8.2 APD which, after providing that MS shall ensure that "applications are examined and decisions are taken individually, objectively and impartially", goes on to provide that it is also the MS's duty to ensure that:

> "precise and up-to-date information is obtained from various sources, such as the United Nations High Commissioner for Refugees (UNHCR), as to the general situation prevailing in the countries of origin of applicants for asylum and, where necessary, in countries through which they have transited, and that such information is made available to the personnel responsible for examining applications and taking decisions."

Since the APD requires that all decisions are given in writing and that, where the claim is rejected, "*the reasons in fact and in law are stated in the decision*" (Article 9.2 APD), the court will have before it details of the evidence which has been taken into account by the initial decision-maker, including any documents and statements submitted by the claimant and a record of interviews carried out.

5.6. Including that obtained by the Court of its own volition

The court's duty being to determine eligibility as at the date of its own decision, it is not, however, limited to the evidence which was before the initial decision-maker. It can and should consider not only evidence which should, under the shared burden, have been taken into account in the making of the original decision, but also later evidence relevant to issues of current risk on *refoulement*.

Nor is the court confined to the evidence brought before it by the claimant and the State. Refugee Law Judges frequently acquire considerable expertise in relation to the situation in countries with which they are regularly required to deal and are aware of evidence as to the situation in the country of origin which may be highly pertinent to their decision. Provided that this is made freely available to both parties and that they have the opportunity to comment on its relevance to the issues before the court, there is no reason why the court should not introduce evidence of its own motion pursuant to its duty of giving the utmost scrutiny to the claim before it.

5.7. Considered and assessed objectively

It has been noted above that the initial decision-maker is required to consider the application and take the decision "*individually, objectively and impartially*" and, of course, the court must apply equally high standards in its deliberations. Nor can it be doubted that its decision must be in writing and set out the reasons in facts and in law in support of its decision.

The claimant's personal subjective fear of return, insofar as it has any relevance, is adequately demonstrated by the fact that a claim for international protection has been made.

Consideration of a claimant's personal history is, of course, highly relevant to the court's task because it can be decisive as to whether the claimant has a sufficient personal profile which, taken together with the country of origin and other relevant evidence, could lead to the finding that there is a real risk of persecution or serious harm if the claimant is *refouled*.

Even in a full protection hearing, however, where the court will have to make factual findings, it must always be borne in mind that the court's ultimate function is not simply as a fact-finding tribunal, but as the assessor of prospective risk on the hypothesis of a current return to the country of origin. For this reason, there may be cases where, despite rejection of important elements of a claimant's personal credibility, he or she nevertheless belongs to a class within their country that is at real risk of persecution or serious harm on the totality of the evidence. If so, he or she will be entitled to recognition as in need of international protection.

In considering the claimant's personal history, there are three matters, which the Court will bear in mind:

First, it frequently happens that a claimant has left his country of origin in haste or clandestinely in circumstances, which would have made it difficult for him to bring supporting documentary evidence with him. Where the state or its organs are the claimed agents of persecution, it will usually be impossible to obtain confirmation of claims made from that country's official records because the details of the application are confidential to the claimant and there is a risk that approach to the authorities would reveal that he is seeking international protection; this might jeopardise the physical integrity of the claimant and/or his dependants and other family members remaining in that country (see specifically the embargo on seeking to collect such information in Article 22 APD). In any event, there is evidence before the court of such matters because they form part of the claimant's testimony and it is an error of law to reject credibility simply on the basis of lack of corroborative evidence of the claims made.

For these reasons, it has long been recognised that there are likely to be often important elements of the claimant's personal history which depend on his personal testimony alone. The proper approach to assessment of evidence in such cases is clearly set out at Article 4.5 QD.

Second, the use of the term "objective assessment" serves as a warning to the court that in immigration cases generally and in international protection cases in particular, great care must be exercised to avoid a subjective approach on the part of the court. The court will be asked to assess events which have happened in countries with which it is not familiar and must, for example, avoid falling into the trap of disbelieving claims because they reflect conduct which is outside the experience of the court and could not have occurred in the host country. It is wrong, in principle, to dismiss part of a claim because the judge does not believe that people behave in such a way – he/she must be alert to the fact that much of what he hears will, thankfully, be entirely outside his personal experience yet may be prevalent in the country of origin.

In making that objective assessment, the court must give due weight to specific matters which may, unless reflected in the objective reasoning, distort the true effect of the evidence concerned.

It is in this sense that the personal circumstances and background of the claimant need to be taken into account. Nationality, ethnicity, age, gender and psychological state are all relevant and need to be reflected, but these considerations do not make a claimant's account 'subjective', save in the sense that such an account will necessarily be affected by those personal circumstances and background which may lead to a danger of misunderstanding the evidence unless it can be seen as a reflection of the claimant's experience.[80]

For example, in countries where ill-treatment in police custody is routine, and there is a claimed history of past arrests and detentions, a claimant may assume that the fact of some ill-treatment whenever detained is a 'given' and only deal with the more serious assaults in evidence. Where the background evidence confirms the generality of such generalised police behaviour, it would be wrong to disbelieve any claimed occasions of detention where a specific claim of ill-treatment was not made simply for that reason. Similarly, there are many reasons for late claims to ill-treatment which may stem from the current psychological issues of the claimant, particularly in cases of sexual abuse where they feel a sense of shame.

It must be stressed that the objective approach applies to all the evidence – that of the claimant, country of origin evidence, medical evidence and any further material before the court. Any or all of that evidence may be subjective to some degree – COI reports are, for example, written from the point of view of the producer of the report and may reflect national or organisational prejudices or perceptions which are not objectively justified, as may also be the case with specific expert and medical reports. It is the task of the decision-maker to evaluate the objectivity of the evidence and the weight, which is therefore to be accorded to it.

Third, there are circumstances that do truly reflect the need for an understanding of the subjective vulnerability of a clamant. These may, for example, arise from mental or physical impairment, age, maturity or gender issues specific to the individual claimant. The principle is that such considerations may render a claimant particularly vulnerable and that the objective assessment of whether the

---

80 An experienced art historian cautioned that history is often conceived as a series of recorded events driven by dry, rational motives and continued: "it is forgotten that events are frequently determined by weird and wonderful beliefs and that to understand the past we have to seriously the strange imaginings of its participants. We cannot make sense of the terrible witch hunts of early modern Europe, for instance, without understanding that, among pre-Enlightenment peasantry and intelligentsia alike, many of the folkloric horrors with which we amuse ourselves at Halloween were thought to be real. ... history is not just about facts; it is also about beliefs. To understand the past we have to enter into other people's minds – minds generally very different from our own." (Thomas de Wesselow – The Sign – 2012). We suggest that this analogy, suitably translated, is equally applicable to credibility assessment in IP cases. See also http://en.wikipedia.org/wiki/The Great Cat Massacre - by Robert Darnton.

prospective treatment amounts to persecution or serious harm must take such specific issues into account.

Finally, it must again be stressed that the objective assessment of current risk must be made on the totality of the evidence before the court.

5.8.   If then immediately returned to the country of origin

As has already been made clear, the court must approach its assessment of risk of harm on the assumption that the claimant will be subject to immediate return to his country of origin. Initial consideration may focus on the position in the claimant's home area in the country of origin – what has sometimes been described as the 'parachute-drop' assumption. This concept does not, however, preclude the necessity of also considering whether at the point of entry or in the journey to his home area, the claimant may also be at real risk of proscribed treatment. It must be borne in mind that, however the claimant may have left his own country, any forced return by the *refouling* state will be made with the full knowledge of the state organs of the country of origin, whose co-operation in readmitting the claimant is a necessary part of the return mechanism. The assessment of risk on return must be made on the assumption that in most cases the claimant's return will be known to the state authorities at all points from actual re-entry until arrival in his home area.

5.9.   Well-founded fear/real risk of "being persecuted"

The QD definition of 'refugee' at Article 2(c) QD closely follows that contained in the GC in requiring a 'well-founded fear of being persecuted' for one or more HC reasons, coupled with an inability or an unwillingness to return to the country of origin. EU and international jurisprudence has strongly established that such a 'well-founded fear' opening is demonstrated by what has been variously described as the existence of a 'real risk', 'reasonable chance', 'reasonable likelihood', 'real chance' or 'serious possibility' of the relevant harm eventuating.

It is noteworthy that the QD adopts the 'real risk' test for recognition of subsidiary protection status where the definition clause specifies the test as 'substantial grounds for believing that [the claimant] ... would face a real risk of suffering serious harm as defined in Article 15' (Article 2(f) QD).

Although the GC does not define 'persecution', Article 9 of the QD gives extensive non-exclusive guidance as to the meaning of persecution, which is derived generally from international instruments and jurisprudence on the issue.

It is also a requirement of the QD that there must be (*'for reasons of"*) a nexus between the prospective persecution and one of the five GC reasons and Article 10 QD similar guidance on this aspect.

5.10.   If not recognised as a refugee

The appropriate order in which the court should consider the claim for international protection is first whether the claimant qualifies for recognition as a refugee and, if he does not, next whether he is a person entitled to subsidiary protection status.

5.11. Real risk of serious harm

The level of risk to be demonstrated by the claimant on the totality of the evidence before the court has already been noted above.

This formulation applies the same level of risk as is required to establish a breach of Article 3 of the ECHR and there is substantial jurisprudence of the European Court of Human Rights as to its meaning in this respect.

The difference in the wording in the QD as to the relevant risk to be demonstrated in international protection cases has resulted in differences of academic opinion: some commentators have suggested that the level of risk to be demonstrated in subsidiary protection status cases is higher than is required to establish refugee status recognition; others that it is lower; and yet others that there is no difference between the relevant level of risk in the two protection categories. Although the CJEU has not yet been called to adjudicate on this issue, there is no logical reason to suppose that the level of risk differs between the two forms of international protection provided for in the QD. Both are examples of persons in need of international protection and the Preamble to the QD specifically notes at Recital (24) that "subsidiary protection should be complementary and additional to the refugee protection enshrined in the Geneva Convention". There are, of course, compelling reasons in practical terms for applying the same test in the assessment of the right to recognition of being in need of international protection.

Serious harm is defined by Article 15 QD. Broadly speaking, the type of harm specified under Article 15(b) is that which would, but for the absence of a Geneva Convention reason, usually qualify the claimant for recognition of refugee status. The serious harm envisaged under Article 15(a) is potentially wider than that applicable under the Geneva Convention since the real risk of suffering the death penalty or execution will always amount to serious harm. Article 15(c) covers a type of harm, which would rarely amount to persecution under the Geneva Convention and raises issue of law which have already been the subject of extensive reference before the CJEU as to the proper interpretation of its scope. The substantive provisions of the QD therefore clearly demonstrate that subsidiary protection status is both complementary and additional to refugee status.

6. Part VI: Discussion paper
on the burden and standard of proof in refugee and subsidiary protection claims and appeals in the EU

6.1. Introduction and Overview

Until this point in other parts of this paper we have been concerned primarily with considering issues of credibility assessment in relation to the first stage of ascertaining the claimant's profile. In this Discussion paper, however, it will be necessary also to consider issues going to the ascertainment of real risk of proscribed treatment, the second stage in the assessment of entitlement to recognition of refugee or subsidiary protection status.

The reason for this arises partly from the fact that judges do not always clearly distinguish between the nature of the assessment within each of these two stages, and partly because in many jurisdictions there has been an approach of deference on the part of judges to the factual findings made by the State initial decision-maker, even in cases where the judge may have the jurisdiction to carry out a full review of both facts and law. This deference extends in most appeals to the international courts and bodies concerned with reviewing first instance decisions. The combination of these two elements has resulted in many of the pronouncements as to judicial assessment being effectively restricted to the second stage of assessing future risk.[81] As we shall see, in reviewing the approach of the European Courts and international committees later in this Paper, where such tribunals have carried out factual reviews it has been on a case by case basis making it more difficult to extract general principles as to what will trigger a factual reassessment of the first stage claimant's past and present profile assessment.

What does seem clear is that of late judges are becoming more willing to revisit the first stage (past and present) factual assessment. It may well be that this is a consequence of the way in which an emphasis on human rights law is gaining ground against past habits and jurisdictional limits which preserved a deference to the factual findings of the State decision-makers. Such a change of approach will, of course, become a legally binding requirement if and when the recast APD, Article 46.3 (replacing the current Article 39 APD concerned with provision of an effective judicial remedy) becomes part of EU law.

Since personal credibility assessment is at the heart of the decision-maker's task, and adverse credibility findings will in most cases lead to a rejection of the protection claim, it is of vital importance to the development of the CEAS that the same principles for assessment should be applied by all MS. At present, as we shall see, that is certainly not the case.

---

81 The jurisprudence of the CJEU and the ECtHR appears to establish that in relation to prospective risk on refoulement the question is whether on the totality of the evidence a 'real risk' is established but it is difficult to draw any conclusions as to what standard these courts apply to the initial profile assessment.

The root of the problem may lie in the different legal traditions of MS. While reference to both the burden, and to a lesser extent standard, of proof is common to most judicial systems their meaning varies between states and systems. However, it must be remembered that these concepts are no more than tools employed by judges to assist them in assessing the 'believability' of the evidence before them.

In systems based on the more adversarial Common Law, the concept of the standard of proof produces a range of defined levels of assessing the probability of the accepted truth of the factual evidence which differs according to the nature of the litigation. Failure to apply these normative standards properly will result in the findings being unsustainable as a matter of law. In many continental systems, based on Civil Law concepts, however, the 'standard of proof' is not so objectively, or perhaps scientifically, defined by the judge. We would suggest that what is common in the field of asylum law to both these concepts is that the decision maker is considering the 'believability', or 'acceptance', of the claimant's factual evidence.

Rather than allowing the differences of approach to the concept of standard of proof to cloud the issue of credibility assessment, we suggest that there is already much common ground between the national courts of MS, in the use of the concept of burden of proof, which has developed in asylum law. Both systems now include the concept of a 'shared burden' of proof, and particularly in the asylum law of the ECtHR, of the application of 'the benefit of the doubt' (or like relaxation of evidentiary standards) to those areas of the evidence which are not provable other than by the claimant's assertions. In addition, as noted in Part III of this paper, the UNHCR Handbook has provided guidance to the assessment of credibility and acceptance of past and present facts which are, to a substantial degree, reflected not only in much EU and MS jurisprudence but also in legislative provisions – see, for example, Article 4 of the 2004 QD.

We would further suggest that appropriate application of the criteria and standards contained in Part III of this paper will go far to ensure high quality and consistency across the EU in credibility assessment and the practical application of these concepts of proof in the full asylum assessment process.

6.2. The burden of proof

The concept of the burden of proof is the less controversial. In broad terms most legal systems (and the UNHCR) place the onus of establishing the facts on the party who asserts them. But, as we have already seen, asylum claims demand a different approach from that which generally applies in both the criminal and civil laws of each State.

In the criminal process, the State asserts that on the factual basis put forward the defendant has acted in breach of the criminal law. The defendant is free to put forward such evidence as will controvert the factual basis on which the State relies. In *inter partes* civil litigation, each party will have the opportunity of putting its evidence as to the issues for determination. In each case, the court is concerned to reach a decision on the basis of past facts and their effect upon the application of the law to the issues before it.

In all types of asylum claims, however, the ascertainment of past, and present, facts (or accepted profile) of the claimant is only the first part of the total determination process. The judge must then assess, noting that accepted profile, and all other evidence relevant to the current situation, whether the claimant is at a real risk of being persecuted on return, as would entitle recognition of international protection.

It is that first part (step) of the assessment process this paper has been concerned. As we have noted, even in this stage, there are important differences from the standard litigation process.

Firstly, the only party with direct knowledge of what has happened in the past will be the claimant and, possibly, any personal witnesses he or she may have. The State (or respondent) party will have no direct knowledge of the matters which form the core elements of the claimant's account of past treatment. In that sense, the burden of proof does lie on the claimant and it will be for the State party assessor or counsel, to make clear what of the claimant's account is accepted and what is disputed. It is, however, only exceptionally that the State party will be able to bring any direct personally related evidence to challenge that account and, in so far as it is disputed, will have to rely on such discrepancies and implausibility as can be shown to exist in the disputed past factual claims.

Secondly, it has long been recognised that for all the reasons which have been explained previously in this paper, claimants may be subject to handicaps in proving their past history. Whilst the GC makes no provision regarding the procedural aspects of the processing of the asylum claim by the receiving State, leaving such issues to be determined under the law of each signatory State, the UNHCR Handbook (1979-2011) sets out general guidance, as to establishing the factual basis of the claim, which has found general acceptance.

6.3. The effect of EU legislation

In the EU, however as partly explained in Part III, D1 of this paper, both the QD and APD include some provisions which go to the issue of burden of proof. The most important of these is Article 4 QD.[82] This provides as follows:

> 1. Member States may consider it the duty of the applicant to submit as soon as possible all the elements needed to substantiate the application for international protection. In cooperation with the applicant, it is the duty of the Member State to assess the relevant elements of the application.
>
> 2. The elements referred to in paragraph 1 consist of the applicant's statements and all the documentation at the applicant's disposal regarding the applicant's age, background, including that of relevant relatives, identity, nationality(ies), country(ies) and place(s) of previous residence, previous asylum applications, travel routes, travel documents and the reasons for applying for international protection.

---

82 Although the 2011 QD does not come into force until 22 December 2013 in respect of certain of its Articles, Article 4 is drawn in identical terms in both the 2004 and 2011 QD and will apply under the earlier QD until it takes effect pursuant to the later QD on that date.

3. The assessment of an application for international protection is to be carried out on an individual basis and includes taking into account:

(a) all relevant facts as they relate to the country of origin at the time of taking a decision on the application, including laws and regulations of the country of origin and the manner in which they are applied;

(b) the relevant statements and documentation presented by the applicant including information on whether the applicant has been or may be subject to persecution or serious harm;

(c) the individual position and personal circumstances of the applicant, including factors such as background, gender and age, so as to assess whether, on the basis of the applicant's personal circumstances, the acts to which the applicant has been or could be exposed would amount to persecution or serious harm;

(d) whether the applicant's activities since leaving the country of origin were engaged in for the sole or main purpose of creating the necessary conditions for applying for international protection, so as to assess whether those activities would expose the applicant to persecution or serious harm if returned to that country;

(e) whether the applicant could reasonably be expected to avail himself or herself of the protection of another country where he or she could assert citizenship.

4. The fact that an applicant has already been subject to persecution or serious harm, or to direct threats of such persecution or such harm, is a serious indication of the applicant's well-founded fear of persecution or real risk of suffering serious harm, unless there are good reasons to consider that such persecution or serious harm will not be repeated.

5. Where Member States apply the principle according to which it is the duty of the applicant to substantiate the application for international protection and where aspects of the applicant's statements are not supported by documentary or other evidence, those aspects shall not need confirmation when the following conditions are met:

(a) the applicant has made a genuine effort to substantiate his application;

(b) all relevant elements at the applicant's disposal have been submitted, and a satisfactory explanation has been given regarding any lack of other relevant elements;

(c) the applicant's statements are found to be coherent and plausible and do not run counter to available specific and general information relevant to the applicant's case;

(d) the applicant has applied for international protection at the earliest possible time, unless the applicant can demonstrate good reason for not having done so; and

(e) the general credibility of the applicant has been established.

It will be immediately apparent that this Article includes a number of provisions of a procedural nature.[83] It contains nothing which goes directly to issues of standard of proof but does have important implications for the burden of proof.

A question of major importance is how Article 4.1 is to be construed. Beyond the analysis in Part III, it is now important to look in some further depth. It will be noted that it contains two sentences which arguably contain opposing requirements. The first sentence is permissive ('*may*') and applies in circumstances where the procedures of the MS require a claimant to 'submit as soon as possible *all elements* needed to substantiate' the claimant's application (emphasis added). The second sentence is mandatory ('*it is the duty*') and requires the MS '*in co-operation with the applicant ... to assess the relevant elements of the application*'.

If the MS applies under its national law the requirement specified in the first sentence of Article 4.1, then it must also apply the provisions of Article 4.5 concerning the lack of need for further confirmation to establish the credibility of such '*aspects of the applicant's statements [as] are not supported by documentary or other evidence*' in circumstances where the claimant meets all the requirements of Article 4.5. (a) to (e). These requirements form an exhaustive list and each must be satisfied for the claimant to have the benefit of that lack of need for confirmation. This gives partial statutory effect in those circumstances to the concept of the application of the 'benefit of the doubt' to which the UNHCR Handbook refers at paragraphs 203 and 204. Article 4.5, however, applies only '*where Member States apply the principle according to which it is the duty of the applicant to substantiate the application*' – that is where the MS exercises its option to rely on the first sentence of Article 4.1 either specifically or because this principle forms part of its national law concerning evidential requirements.

The first sentence of Article 4.1 refers to all 'elements' needed to substantiate the application. The second sentence also refers to 'elements' but, in this case those which are relevant to the application. Article 4.2 then defines what is meant by the term 'elements'. These are all concerned with the personal history of the claimant (and any 'relevant relatives') both in the country of origin and en route to the MS responsible for determining the application. They include the claimant's statements and all documentation pertinent to that personal history and, finally, '*the reasons for applying for international protection*' – a phrase which it is suggested falls to be construed *ejusdem generis* with the preceding definitive list of 'elements'.

The 'relaxation' of the burden of proof imposed by Article 4.5 relates only to those aspects of the claimant's statements which are not supported by documentary or other evidence, and are therefore primarily concerned with questions

---

83 The drafting history shows that certain parts of this Article were originally intended to be contained in the PD and that there were substantial modifications in the course of agreeing the final form. Some indication of the difficulties that this caused is given by the reference in Article 4.1 (first sentence) to submission of all elements '*as soon as possible*' which contrasts with the provision of Article 4.5(e) that the application should be made '*at the earliest possible time, unless the applicant can demonstrate good reason for not having done so*'. This is in line with the provisions of Article 8.1 PD requiring MS to ensure that applications for asylum are not rejected '*on the sole ground that they have not been made as soon as possible*'.

of his or her 'profile'. Since the first sentence presupposes a national evidential requirement that puts the entire burden of proof on the claimant, the question arises as to what extent the second sentence will, in those circumstances, have any application so as to introduce the issue of shared responsibility advocated by UNHCR or whether that is an alternative mandatory provision which applies only where the MS does not impose the burden of proof on the claimant specified in the first sentence under its national laws.

There is academic opinion that on its proper interpretation the second sentence of Article 4.1 limits that shared responsibility to 'a mere examination of the elements provided by the claimant'[84] where the first sentence applies. It must, however, be doubted if so restrictive an interpretation is sustainable. Whilst it is correct that such a requirement may limit the areas of co-operative assessment to the 'elements' which it is the duty of the claimant to provide, a proper assessment of those elements will require consideration of relevant COI. In this respect, applying the principle of the equality of arms, the MS is likely to have the ability to access COI evidence which might not readily be available to the claimant. This is reinforced by the provisions of Article 4.5(c) which require not only that the claimant's statements are found '*coherent and plausible*' but that they do not run counter to '*available specific and general information relevant to the applicant's case*'. It would seem clear that the element of cooperation in assessment remains relevant to all matters upon which the claimant relies at the stage of personal credibility which do not directly arise from the 'elements'. This would include reference to relevant COI evidence within the knowledge of the State party. Moreover, where those elements take the form of documents, the MS will need to say whether they are accepted or rejected and, if the latter, state clearly the grounds on which such rejection is based (Article 9.2 PD).

In circumstances where the MS does not rely on the first sentence to Article 4.1 QD, so that the provisions of Article 4.5 do not apply, how is the burden of proof under the QD affected? It would seem that there is no burden of proof on the claimant *stricto sensu* although he or she will retain the basic obligation to furnish the facts in support of the claim together with all such relevant documentation ('elements') as is available together with an explanation for the lack of any apparently relevant documents. The QD does not require the MS to investigate the claim but the MS may, as part of the cooperative/shared approach, seek evidence to support the claim. Where this is not available, or there are statements not susceptible of proof, application of the UNHCR guidance on 'shared burden' and 'benefit of the doubt', to the extent required by asylum law, has generally been followed and has in fact become adopted as standard practice in some MS, for many years. This approach includes the application of the principle of the 'benefit of the doubt' in respect of elements not susceptible of proof after such a cooperative approach. Strict compliance with all the requirements of Article 4.5(a)-(e) would not, in such circumstances, be a pre-requisite of acceptance of credibility but, to the extent that they follow accepted internationally applied guidance, they

---

84   See Hailbronner *op. cit.* at pp. 1024 *et seq* where Article 4 PD is considered and analysed – para 19 at pp. 1028-1030 in particular.

form the basis of what is likely in practice to be taken into account and reflected in making the assessment of the claimant's personal credibility.

Whichever provision of Article 4.1 applies, however, the application of Articles 4.3 and 4.4 in the course of the assessment both of the claimant's profile and future risk will need to be observed and applied by persons who meet the requisite skill levels and act '*individually. objectively and impartially*'.[85]

The provisions of the APD are, of course, primarily aimed at regulating the duties and requirements imposed on MS decision-makers at first instance level but, to the extent that their application is mandatory, raise issues where the judge will be required to consider the lawfulness of the first instance decision.

They are moreover not limited to issues of the applicable burden of proof in asylum decisions. They extend also to guidance as to the range of issues required to be covered in the assessment and the normative level of state protection against which to judge the situation in the claimant's country of origin.

Article 4.2 QD contains, as already noted, a prescriptive list of what is comprised in the 'elements' referred to in Article 4.1.

Article 4.3 QD imposes the mandatory requirement that the claim is to be considered 'individually' thus recognising that the situation of each claimant may be unique and that risk must be assessed in relation to his or her individual position. Thus, it may be commonly accepted that members of particular ethnic groups are subject to discrimination in their country of origin but that in general it does not reach the level required to become persecutory. That does not mean, however, that the individual claimant member of that ethnic group cannot succeed on the basis of his personal profile where, for example, a level of political activity in promoting his group's cause leads to specific and adverse interest on the part of the authorities in the claimant.

Sub-articles (a) to (e) of Article 4.3 QD set out a non-prescriptive list of issues in relation to the claim which are to be taken into account in the assessment of the facts. As we have already pointed out, these issues include areas which require that element of co-operation in assessing the facts on the basis of the principle of equality of arms (sub-articles (a), (c), (d) and (e)).

---

85   The relevant provisions are contained in Articles 8.2 and 13.3(a) PD. Article 8.2 PD provides:
Member States shall ensure that decisions by the determining authority on applications for asylum are taken after an appropriate examination. To that end, Member States shall ensure that:
(a) applications are examined and decisions are taken individually, objectively and impartially;
(b) precise and up-to-date information is obtained from various sources, such as the United Nations High Commissioner for Refugees (UNHCR), as to the general situation prevailing in the countries of origin of applicants for asylum and, where necessary, in countries through which they have transited, and that such information is made available to the personnel responsible for examining applications and taking decisions;
(c) the personnel examining applications and taking decisions have the knowledge with respect to relevant standards applicable in the field of asylum and refugee law.
Article 13.3(a) is concerned with the requirements for a personal interview and requires the MS to:
Ensure that the person who conducts the interview is sufficiently competent to take account of the personal or general circumstances surrounding the application, including the applicant's cultural origin or vulnerability, insofar as it is proper to do so.

Article 4.4 concerning accepted past persecution or serious harm as part of the claimant's profile is, however, directly concerned with the application of the burden of proof as it raises a rebuttable presumption of similar future risk.

The remainder of Chapter II QD contains guidance as to elements which are relevant to specific situations: *sur place* claims (Article 5); who may be actors of persecution or serious harm (non-prescriptive) (Article 6); who are actors of protection (prescriptive) (Article 7); and the effect of the ability to access internal protection in the country of origin (Article 8).[86]

Article 7.2 2004 QD sets out non-exhaustively the elements which will usually be required to demonstrate the existence of protection in the country of origin as follows:

> Protection is generally provided when the actors mentioned in paragraph 1 take reasonable steps to prevent the persecution or suffering of serious harm, inter alia, by operating an effective legal system for the detection, prosecution and punishment of acts constituting persecution or serious harm, and the applicant has access to such protection.

The 2011 QD inserts a new first sentence to Article 7.2 (effective from 22 December 2013) in mandatory terms:

> Protection against persecution or serious harm must be effective and of a non-temporary nature.

Compliance with these requirements would render the country of origin generally safe, creating a presumption that its nationals would not qualify for refugee or subsidiary status recognition although such a presumption is capable of rebuttal in the case of the individual claimant differentiating his or her situation from the norm.

We would suggest, however, that the EU legislation making up the CEAS must be looked at as a whole and that provisions in other directives or regulations may inform the interpretation of similar concepts contained elsewhere. In this connection, the concept of safe country of origin is also relevant to the PD because it may affect the nature of the processing of the claim by accelerating certain elements of the process. Articles 29 and 30 PD contain detailed provisions as to the designation of third countries as safe countries of origin for this purpose and the specific requirements for such designation are set out at Annex II.[87] We suggest

---

86 In the case of Article 8 QD there are important differences between the 2004 and 2011 QDs but the change in provisions will not take effect in law until 13 December 2013. Nevertheless, the changes introduced in the later Article 8 are arguably no more than declaratory of the situation which already applies on international IP law principles. Internal protection issues can arise only when it has been accepted that the claimant will be at risk in part of his country of origin (usually either his or her home area or at point of entry and/or during the journey to the home area). In such cases it will be for the State party to rebut the presumption of entitlement of recognition of IP status. The recast Article 8 introduces a mandatory requirement for up-to-date information to be obtained from relevant sources, of which UNHCR and EASO are specifically mentioned, thus once more emphasising the cooperative nature of the assessment process.

87 The provisions of Annex II PD are as follows:

→

that these requirements need at least to be reflected in the reasoning assessing whether the claimant's country of origin is to be regarded generally as a safe country for IP purposes.

The provisions of the PD previously referred to also prescribe requirements which go beyond issues of burden of proof and relate specifically both to qualification of decisions makers at first instance and the methodology to be employed in the assessment of the claimant's case. Thus, recital (10) provides:

> It is essential that decisions on all applications for asylum be taken on the basis of the facts and, in the first instance, by authorities whose personnel has the appropriate knowledge or receives the necessary training in the field of asylum and refugee matters.

Articles 4.3, 8 and 13.3(a) PD (referred to above) are all relevant to the observance of that principle.

Articles 8.2(a) to (c) are particularly important in these respects. They contain the mandatory requirement that the assessment process is throughout to be '*taken individually, objectively and impartially*' by appropriately trained personnel with knowledge of '*relevant standards applicable in the field of asylum and refugee law*' who have access to '*precise and up-to-date information ... from various sources such as the ... (UNHCR), as to the general situation prevailing in the countries of origin of the applicants ...*'.

It follows, therefore, that in addition to specific guidance and requirements which we have examined above, MS are obliged under the provisions of the QD and PD to ensure that decisions relating to the recognition of refugee status (and as a matter of practice in subsidiary protection recognition status also) are taken by properly trained decision-makers following appropriate examination of the claims put forward to establish the claimant's past profile, taking into account relevant COI evidence, on an individual, objective and impartial basis. We would suggest that compliance with the requirements going to methodology of decision-making will be substantially assisted by the application of the Judicial Standards set out in Part III of this paper.

A country is considered as a safe country of origin where, on the basis of the legal situation, the application of the law within a democratic system and the general political circumstances, it can be shown that there is generally and consistently no persecution as defined in Article 9 of Directive 2004/83/EC, no torture or inhuman or degrading treatment or punishment and no threat by reason of indiscriminate violence in situations of international or internal armed conflict.
In making this assessment, account shall be taken, inter alia, of the extent to which protection is provided against persecution or mistreatment by:
(a) the relevant laws and regulations of the country and the manner in which they are applied;
(b) observance of the rights and freedoms laid down in the European Convention for the Protection of Human Rights and Fundamental Freedoms and/or the International Covenant for Civil and Political Rights and/or the Convention against Torture, in particular the rights from which derogation cannot be made under Article 15(2) of the said European Convention;
(c) respect of the non-refoulement principle according to the Geneva Convention;
(d) provision for a system of effective remedies against violations of these rights and freedoms.

Further, we would consider that it necessarily follows that, in order to discharge those weighty duties, decision-makers must be independent of government direction in carrying out that function whether at first instance or judicial level.

6.4. The standard of proof

The CEAS has as its ultimate goal the harmonisation of the application of IP law throughout the EU but the PD seeks to impose only minimum standards of procedure and, save for those elements which are mandatory, MS are free to apply their national laws of legal procedure in considering IP claims. Article 39 PD obliges each MS to provide refused claimants with '*an effective remedy before a court or tribunal*' against decisions concerning such claims but is otherwise silent as to the process.[88] The EU Charter now provides the right to an effective remedy and to a fair trial under Article 47 which arguably clarifies the scope of the effective remedy required by Article 39 PD, and the national laws of each MS may also contain relevant principles as to the right of access to justice and to an effective remedy independently of the provisions under the EU.

The basis on which national judges make their findings of fact remains, however, the subject of differences in approach, founded in the legal theories in Common or Civil law, as to the process by which facts may be lawfully found.[89]

---

88   The recast APD which is currently before the European Parliament (and is intended to be passed during 2012 according to the current timetable) contains an important addition to the proposed Article 46 as follows:
'*3. Member States shall ensure that the effective remedy referred to in paragraph 1 provides for a full examination of both facts and law, including an ex nunc examination of the international protection needs pursuant to [the 2011 QD], at least in appeal procedures before a court or tribunal of first instance.*'
The proposed new clause may arguably merely be declaratory of the position which already applies under EU primary legislation since the CJEU held in *Samba Diouf v Luxembourg* [CJEU 2011 C-69/10] that the mandatory content of the right recognised by Article 47 EU Charter (with which Article 39 PD was wholly consistent) '*expressly guarantees that 'applicants for asylum have the right to an effective remedy before a court or tribunal' against administrative decisions rejecting an application in any of the cases provided for in paragraph 1 of that article, that is to say on grounds of substance, form or procedure*'.
If this provision is enacted it will clearly have substantial impact on the current procedures of those MS who, like the Netherlands, do not permit the initial decision-maker's factual findings to be reopened but confine review to points of law.

89   These differences of approach and their effect are the subject of a paper by Christopher Engel published in August 2008 entitled 'Preponderance of the Evidence versus *Intime Conviction* – A Behavioural Perspective on a Conflict between American and Continental European Law (accessible at http://ssrn.com/abstract+1283503). He deals with the European (Civil law) approach as follows:
'By contrast, the standard of proof in civil law countries is predominantly interpreted as not being probabilistic (Clermont and Sherwin 2002:265). The classic formulation is in art. 353 of the French Code of Criminal Procedure:
"The law does not ask judges for an explanation of the means by which they are convinced, it does not set any particular rules by which they must assess the fullness and adequacy of the evidence; it stipulates that they must search their conscience in good faith and silently and thoughtfully ask themselves what impression the evidence given against the accused and the defence's

$\rightarrow$

We do not suggest that certain elements of factual evidence will not under both systems be given objective weight – for example, medical evidence as to a clearly diagnosed condition or the effect of, say, DNA test results clearly require objective consideration – but it is clear that under the Civilian system a final element of judicial subjectivity is introduced as the decisive factor in reaching findings of fact.

There is no doubt that there are substantial differences in the rate of recognition of claimants from similar backgrounds in different MS.[90] The ASQAEM Report records that, in the case of Iraqi claimants applying in six of the eight countries considered, overall recognition rates varied between 65% and 97% of claimants and recognition of entitlement to refugee status (as opposed to subsidiary status) varied even more markedly (between 0% and 63% of claimants). These figures would seem to underscore the concerns of the European Commission that the standards applied in decision-making vary substantially between MS thus undermining the secondary goal of the CEAS to prevent 'asylum-shopping' on the part of claimants. This Report includes a suggested check-list for judges including the following primary issue under the item 'Credibility Analysis':

Has the decision-maker identified and applied the correct standard of proof (balance of probability/preponderance of the evidence/more likely than not) including the application of the benefit of the doubt for establishing the facts of the applicant's story?

This appears to be derived from the UNHCR Note on Burden and Standard of Proof in Refugee Claims published in 1998 but, whilst this may reflect the posi-

---

arguments have made upon them. The law asks them only one question which sums up all of their duties 'Are you personally convinced'?"

This standard is also applied in civil law disputes (Bredin 1996:23), although there is no explicit provision to the effect in French law (Taruffo 2003:667).

In German law, the situation is even clearer. According to § 286 I 1 Code of Civil Procedure

"Paying due regard to the entirety of the proceedings, including the evidence presented, if any, it is for the court to decide, based on its personal conviction, whether a factual claim is indeed true or not".

In the leading case, the German Supreme Court has made it clear that the judge may not content herself with a mere assessment of probabilities. Even a very high probability would not be enough. Initial doubt is acceptable. But the judge must have overcome this doubt (Bundesgerichtshof BGHZ 53, 245, 255 f. – Anastasia). This is not meant to defer to judicial discretion, but to judicial intuition (MUSIELAK-FOERSTE § 286 ZPO, R 17). The standard is an empirical one (Schulz 1992:42). The crucial feature is "the psychic state of taking a fact for true" (Schulz 1992:43). The test is built on "ethos, experience and intuition" (Schulz 1992:168).'

IP decisions come before the Administrative Courts in Germany and s.108 Code of Administrative Court Procedure provides:

'(1) The court shall rule in accordance with its free conviction gained from the overall outcome of the proceedings. The judgment shall state the grounds which were decisive for the judicial conviction.

(2) The judgment may only be based on facts and results of evidence on which those concerned have been able to make a statement.'

90   See the UNHCR ASQAEM (Asylum Systems Quality Assurance and Evaluation Mechanism Project in the Central and Eastern Europe sub-region) Final Regional Report published by UNHCR in February 2010 which investigated the position in eight countries (Austria, Bulgaria, Germany, Hungary, Poland, Romania, Slovakia and Slovenia).

tion of the UNHCR in the ASQAEM (although perhaps not now universally an 'official' UNHCR position), it does not accord with the reality of the competing systems of judicial assessment which exist in the MS, some of which we have highlighted above.

6.5. Stage 2 risk assessments – is there a distinction between refugee and subsidiary protection status?

We noted in Part I of this Paper that a failure to distinguish between the various stages of assessment in asylum claims has led to practical difficulties in determining the basis on which judges have reached their decisions and we must now turn to the second stage to deal with one particular matter which must be addressed.

We have already noted that neither the QD nor the PD impose any standard of proof to be applied in IP claims[91] although, as Hailbronner records (p. 1026), in the original drafting process the Commission's proposal was that:

> The criterion of well-founded fear [should be applied] to refugee protection as well as to subsidiary protections the Commission understood 'persecution' as being a type of serious unjustified harm. The draft art. 7 lit (b) introduced 'reasonable possibility' as a standard of evidence. ...
>
> The risk assessment based on 'reasonable possibility' has, however, been deleted during the negotiation process. The amendment thus may indicate a different standard for refugee protection since the 'real risk' test has been introduced with regard to subsidiary protection. Member States did not agree on the standard of evidence. Germany, Ireland and Austria wanted to replace 'reasonable possibility' with 'reasonable likelihood'. In the progress of negotiations, Germany proposed to use the term 'considerable probability'. France objected that this term would not establish an assessment criterion, but consisted of a description of the assessment procedure and should therefore be deleted. The Directive hence neither elaborates on the term 'well-founded fear' nor on the criterion of 'real risk' and nor does not provide for any evidentiary standard.

This passage reinforces that the question of applicable standards and shows this is very much a live issue for two reasons. Firstly, that there are real differences, between MS, which have prevented agreement on a common standard of proof. Secondly, it raises the question of whether there is a difference in the tests of refugee and subsidiary protection status.

The first point we accept to be well made in part and we will deal with it in more detail later in this Discussion paper when we consider whether there are arguably differences in the approach to the initial establishment of the claimant's profile and the subsequent task of evaluating prospective risk having regard to applicable European jurisprudence.

---

91   The recast PD is equally silent on the issue.

As to the second issue it is our position that there is no distinction between the test for recognition of refugee and subsidiary protection status for the reasons which we now set out.

It is generally accepted in international jurisprudence that in order to be well founded the refugee's subjective fear of persecution must be objectively sustainable.[92] The provisions of Chapter II of the QD reflect such an approach in the mandatory terms of Article 4.3(a) requiring MS to investigate the objective situation in the country of origin. In the definition of *'person eligible for subsidiary protection'* at Article 2(e), however, the definition requires that *'substantial grounds for believing that the person concerned ... would face a real risk of suffering serious harm'* as defined in Article 15 are to be demonstrated.

We note that the question has been raised by various academic commentators as to whether the 'real risk' test differs from the Geneva Convention test of 'well-founded fear'.[93] Whilst we accept that there may be some differences of academic opinion on the issue, the practical case for construing the standard of proof – or where that is a concept which has no strict application in a MS's procedural law, the nature of the issue to be proved by the claimant – as being the same in the case of either status is highly compelling and has much to commend it. The recognition of each status requires a finding as to whether a claimant is entitled to international protection.[94]

For the purposes of the QD such a need arises only where there may be persecution for a GC reason or serious harm which may, but for the absence of the nexus of the appropriate GC reason, befall the claimant. The only arguable exceptions in the serious harm concept to this direct correlation with the concept of persecution are execution which is lawful under the national law of the country of

---

92   See also generally paras 37 to 50 of the UNHCR Handbook op cit.

93   H Battjes op cit states at Chapter 5.3.1: *'As to subsidiary protection, article 2(e) QD requires that the 'risk' be 'real'. This criterion occurs in the case law of the [ECtHR]... It can be argued that the real risk criterion sets a stricter standard than well-founded fear. The [QD] does not elaborate on this standard. But it appears that the distinction in risk assessment between qualification for refugee and for subsidiary protection status is intentional, as the real risk criterion also replaces the well-founded fear test that applied to subsidiary protection in the Commission's Proposal for the [QD].'* Gregor Noll in 'Evidentiary assessment and the EU qualification directive' *op. cit.*, however, argues the opposite case, namely that well-founded fear under the Geneva Convention imposes a higher standard of proof than the Article 2(e) QD standard of *'substantial grounds for believing ...[that] a real risk'* exists (see footnote 5 of his paper).

94   In its Explanatory Statement to the QD (2001/0207(CNS) of 12.09.2001), the Commission would appear to suggest that the distinctions mentioned in the preceding footnote were not intended to be drawn from the wording of the definition section of the PD as originally proposed. Despite the changes in wording to which H Battjes draws attention, it should be remembered that Recital (6) as enacted clearly identifies one of the main objects of the Directive as being *'to ensure that Member States apply common criteria for the identification of persons genuinely in need of international protection'*: but, the original proposal referred simply to the ensuring of a minimum level of protection. It is equally arguable that the final form referring to 'real risk' rather than 'well-founded fear' was selected simply because the concept of serious harm was more clearly grounded in claims in respect of which the ECtHR had jurisdiction, so that there was already a body of European jurisprudence relevant to that concept: the change to Recital (6) sufficed to clarify that the criteria for recognition for international protection were common to both forms of protection status.

origin or serious harm as defined in Article 15(c) QD. But even in those two cases, the test to be applied remains that of real risk.

It is suggested that it would not only be impracticable, but wrong in principle, to impose a difference in the standard of proof for persecution and serious harm.[95] There is also international jurisprudence on the standard of proof of well-founded fear of persecution which supports the argument that the standard applicable is one of real risk.[96]

The difficulty of applying differential standards in the recognition of claims to international protection status will, of course, be particularly apparent in the majority of MS who elect to apply the PD both to asylum and subsidiary protection status claims. It is suggested that the ECtHR concept of real risk applies equally to the proving of Article 3 ECHR asylum, refugee status, as well as subsidiary protection claims. There is support for this view also from the terms of the CJEU judgment in *Germany v Y and Z* (op cit) which refers in terms to real risk of persecution.[97]

---

95 The Immigration Appeal Tribunal of the United Kingdom was required to consider precisely this issue when the Human Rights Act 1998 (largely incorporating the ECHR into national law) came into force in October 2000. In *Kacaj* [2000] UKIAT 23044 it was held that there was no difference in the tests for asylum and Article 3 infringements, which was the existence of a 'real risk'. The President, Collins J, said at para 12: *'Various expressions have been used to identify the correct standard of proof required for asylum claims. These stem from language used by Lord Diplock in R v Governor of Pentonville Prison ex p. Fernandez [1971] 2 All ER 691 at p. 697, cited by Lord Keith in Sivakumaran at [1988] 1 All ER 198. Lord Diplock said that the expressions 'a reasonable chance', 'substantial grounds for thinking' and 'a serious possibility' all conveyed the same meaning. There must be a real or substantial risk of persecution. The test formulated by the European Court requires the decision maker and appellate body to ask themselves whether there are substantial grounds for believing that the applicant faces a real risk of relevant ill-treatment. That is no different from the test applied to asylum claims. The decision maker and the appellate body will consider the material before them and will decide whether the existence of a real risk is made out. The words 'substantial grounds for believing' do not and are not intended to qualify the ultimate question which is whether a real risk of relevant ill-treatment has been established. They merely indicate the standard which must be applied to answer that question and demonstrate that it is not that of proof beyond a reasonable doubt. ... In our view, now that the European Court has fixed on a particular expression and it is one which is entirely appropriate for both asylum and human rights claims, it should be adopted in preference to any other...'*
The ECtHR jurisprudence referred to is *Soering v UK* [1989] 11 EHRR 439 as confirmed in *Cruz Varas v Sweden* [1999] 14 EHRR 1.
96 See, e.g., *Chan v Minister for Immigration and Ethnic Affairs* [1989] 169 CLR 379 in which the High Court of Australia approved the formulation of the standard as 'a real chance of persecution' – such an expression was to be used 'because it clearly conveys the notion of a substantial, as distinct from a remote chance, of persecution occurring' per Mason CJ *ibid*. Similar formulations have been applied in New Zealand (Refugee Appeal No 523/92 *Re RS*, 17 March 1995).
97 It would appear that the terms 'real risk' and 'genuine risk' are used interchangeably in the judgment but see, in particular, paragraph 2 of the Ruling of the Grand Chamber which reads *'Article 2(c) of Directive 2004/83 [the QD] must be interpreted as meaning that the applicant's fear of being persecuted is well founded if, in the light of the applicant's personal circumstances, the competent authorities consider that it may reasonably be thought that, upon his return to his country of origin, he will engage in religious practices which will expose him to a real risk of persecution. ...'*

6.6.   Do Stage 1 and 2 assessments differ?

We turn now to the question of whether there may arguably be differences in the approach to assessment of the claimant's profile and the assessment of future or prospective risk on return.[98]

It has been a fundamental precept of this Paper that the assessment of credibility in relation to asylum claims is concerned with two issues, one establishing and accepting what *has* happened in the past, and presently prevails, while the other prognosticating what *may* happen in the future. This twofold process requires first that the claimant's 'profile' be established on the basis of the claimant's account of his past and present account. The establishment of past facts is an exercise with which all judges are familiar even though special considerations must be applied to its exercise in the case of asylum claims. The second part of the assessment, however, is predictive and requires that the judge consider what may happen in the future on the assumed return of the claimant to his own country. This future prognostication is an exercise unique to asylum claims and necessarily and logically is much more speculative than the determination of the first issue.

Paragraphs 195 to 205 of the UNHCR Handbook, to which we have referred earlier, are headed 'Establishing the facts' and paragraph 205 summarises the examiner's duty as first assessing the claimant's credibility and evaluating the evidence *'in order to establish the objective and the subjective elements of the case'* before proceeding to *'relate these elements to the relevant criteria of the [GC], in order to arrive at a correct conclusion as to the applicant's refugee status'.*

In the ASQAEM it appears the UNHCR takes the view that establishment of the facts relied on for establishing the accepted personal profile of a claimant should be based on the common law concept of the balance of probabilities – that is the usual standard applicable in civil litigation under that system.[99]

This does not, however, accord with the approach in the United Kingdom, Ireland and many other common law jurisdictions like Australia and New Zealand which apply the "lower standard" of 'reasonable likelihood' (or alternatively termed, 'real chance', 'reasonable chance', considerable probability' or 'real *risk*') at both stages of the asylum assessment.[100] (We have also noted in Part I that the

---

98   We are indebted to Judge Dana Baldinger of the Court of Amsterdam and the Court of 's-Hertogenbosch of the Netherlands and Researcher at the Centre for Migration Law of the Radboud Universiteit of Nijmegen for access to some of the research materials for her dissertation on 'Evidence, proving and judicial scrutiny in international asylum law, implications for national asylum courts' and to permission to quote there from. We are also indebted to those judges of MS who have provided information on this aspect in response to the questionnaire circulated in the course of preparation of this Paper.

99   See the ASQAEM Report *op cit* and the UNHCR Note on Burden and Standard of Proof in Refugee Claims (1998) there referred to – particularly paragraphs 3, 8 and 11 of the Note which, while noting the difference between the Common Law and Continental approaches to establishment of facts, nevertheless concludes: *Credibility is established where the applicant has presented a claim which is coherent and plausible, not contradicting generally known facts, and therefore is, on balance, capable of being believed.*

100   See Kaja v SSHD [1995] Imm AR 1 where the Tribunal said: Asylum cases differ from most other cases in the seriousness of the consequences of an erroneous decision in the focus of the decision on the future and the inherent difficulties of obtaining objective evidence. Given that in

→

contextual use of the word '*risk*' as often used in the UK, and ECtHR decisions, for the assessment of past facts, as well as future assessment, whilst not effectually incorrect, are unfortunate, in English, as *risk* is a word far more appropriately used for future or predicative assessment.)

We have already noted the provisions of French and German law relative to assessment of facts.

The German courts have full power to review and adjudicate upon issues both of fact and law at first instance and on appeal to the Higher Administrative Court; it is only the German Federal Appeal Court which is restricted to considering questions of law.

The German Federal Appeal Court Judgment of 16 April 1985 – 9 C 109.84 (paragraph 16) is authority for the propositions that asylum cases require full judicial conviction of the truth, not only of a probability but that the court must be content with a reasonable grade of certainty, taking appropriate account of the hardship of presenting proof and laying stronger emphasis on the claimant's own evidence than is normally the case: the relevance of the claimant's assertions should be considered with goodwill: an appeal must not be dismissed on the basis that there is no further proof beyond the credible assertions of the claimant: the judge is generally entitled to consider a party's claim true without taking other evidence and this is all the more the case with asylum procedures given the typical difficulty of providing evidence beyond the claimant's own testimony.

In a recent decision of the Federal Court of Appeal of 17 November 2011 (BVerwG 10 C 13.10) dealing with the level of risk in a situation analogous to one under Article 15(c) QD where the claimant relied on the general situation to support the claim that his life would be in danger if he were returned to his country of origin, the Court observed at paragraph 20:

'At any event, for the presumption of a substantial individual danger, Section 60 (7) Sentence 2 of the Residence Act requires that there must be a *considerable probability* that the person concerned will be threatened with harm to the legally protected interests of life or limb. This proceeds from the characterising element '... face a real risk ...' in Article 2 (e) of Directive 2004/83/EC. The standard of probability contained therein is oriented to the case law of the European Court of Human Rights. In reviewing Article 3 of the ECHR, that court focused on the *real danger* ('real risk'; see, for example, ECtHR (Grand Chamber), judgment of 28 February 2008 – No. 37201/06, Saadi/Italy – NVwZ 2008, 1330 <at 125 et seq.>); *this is equivalent to the standard of considerable probability* (judgment of 27 April 2010, op. cit., at 22 on Section 60 (2) of the Residence Act and Article 15 (b) of Directive 2004/83/EC).' (Emphasis added)

---

the light of these factors a well-founded fear is shown by establishing a serious possibility that persecution may occur, it seems contrary to that focus and impractical to apply a different standard of proof to the establishment of facts on which the assessment is based.

The reference to '*reasonable likelihood*' is derived from the House of Lords decision in *R v SSHD ex parte Sivakumaran* [1991] Imm AR 80.

In Croatia the courts apply the standards of assessment derived from the practice of the ECtHR, international treaties and, particularly, from the QD and PD in establishing the claimant's profile as well as having regard to the criteria in the UN-HCR Handbook to which specific reference was made in the judgment of 10 January 2010 by the Croatian Administrative Court in Case No. Us-9432/ 2007. Specific reference was made to application of the standards of consistency in presentation of facts (Usl-1287/12 of 15 June 2012), application of the principle of *res judicata* (Usl-1530/12 of 12 June 2012), and the requirement of the consideration of COI evidence is commonplace.

In Finland the courts have full power to review both issues of fact and law but in practice leave to appeal is only rarely granted where the issue is based simply on the sustainability of factual credibility assessment. The Supreme Administrative Court has, however, granted leave to appeal turning on the ruling of the CJEU in *Elgafaji v Staatssecretaris Van Justice* C.465/67, in the weight to be given to language tests as to the nationality of the claimant, and in cases where it appeared that a higher standard of proof had been applied to determining refugee status than to subsidiary protection status. All these may, however, be regarded as raising issues of law rather than fact so that it would appear that in Finland deference is generally paid by the courts to fact-finding by the first instance decision-maker.

The ASQAEM Report concludes from its investigations that, in order of difficulty of proof, the standards of proof applied in the countries researched varied from 'Beyond any doubt' through 'Beyond a reasonable doubt', *Intime Conviction*, and 'Balance of Probabilities' to 'a Real Chance' and that:

> 'we have even encountered different standards being used by different decision-makers within a country and even different standards employed within a single decision.'

This not only highlights judicial failure to distinguish clearly between the two stages of assessment but suggests that there is a marked disparity of practice and basic evidentiary procedural requirements between MS, in first instance decision-making. The CEAS does not currently directly address this issue and it highlights the urgent need for judicial discussion on how possible harmonisation across MS might take place so there can be clear harmonised guidance to first instance decision makers.

6.7. Member States legislative practice in imposing guidance on credibility assessment

There is a further aspect relevant to factual findings which must be mentioned in connection with the disparity between MS' practices. There is a growing tendency on the part of some MS to legislate as to the weight to be given to some issues both by decision-makers at first instance and judges on appeal or review where the courts have the full power of review on both facts and law. Two examples will suffice.

In the Netherlands, s.31(2) of The Aliens Act 2000 provides:

In the examination of the [asylum] request, circumstances including the following shall be taken into account [as appropriate]: ...

f. the alien cannot corroborate his request with travel or identity documents or other documents that are needed to consider his request, unless the alien can make out a credible case that the absence of these documents is not imputable to him.

In *Mir Isfahani v The Netherlands* [ECtHR Application no 31252/03], where the application of this provision was in issue, the Government submitted that an absence of documents concerning an asylum seeker's identity, nationality and travel route did not by itself constitute sufficient grounds to reject an application for asylum. However, where such an absence could be attributed to the asylum seeker, it undermined the credibility of his or her account to the extent that he or she bore a heavier burden of proof in establishing the validity of the application; the account should then not contain any gaps, vague statements, absurd turn of events or contradictions concerning relevant details.

In the United Kingdom, s. 8 of the Asylum and Immigration (Treatment of Claimants etc.) Act 2004 headed '*Claimant's credibility*' provides:

In determining whether to believe a statement made by or on behalf of a person who makes an asylum claim or a human rights claim, a deciding authority shall take account, *as damaging the claimant's credibility*, of any behaviour to which this section applies. (emphasis added)

The section then goes on to provide that it applies to any behaviour designed or likely to conceal information, mislead or obstruct, or to delay the asylum process and determination of the claim. Subsection (3) goes on to specify that specific kinds of behaviour are in any event to be treated 'as designed or likely to conceal information or to mislead', namely:

a) failure without reasonable explanation to produce a passport on request to the immigration officer or to the Secretary of State;
b) the production of a document which is not a valid passport as if it were;
c) the destruction, alteration or disposal, in each case without reasonable explanation, of a passport;
d) the destruction, alteration or disposal, in each case without reasonable explanation, of a ticket or other document connected with travel, and
e) failure without reasonable explanation to answer a question asked by a deciding authority.

'*Deciding authority*' is defined as including an immigration officer, the Secretary of State and the Asylum and Immigration Tribunal.

It is difficult to see how these actions, which may in some cases be intended to conceal or obfuscate the claimant's true nationality, can properly be categorised on a blanket basis as either imposing a higher standard of proof or being required to be taken into account as damaging general credibility when they are not directly concerned with the core facts of the claimant's past history and have no relevance whatsoever to the issue of prospective future risk.[101] We suggest that provisions of this nature place an undue emphasis on credibility as an end in itself and are inconsistent with the approach in the UNHCR Handbook as to the approach to ascertainment of the personal profile and to the general requirement that the totality of the evidence should be objectively assessed 'in the round'.

6.8. The approach in European and international fora

The approach of both the CJEU and the ECtHR has a direct relevance to the standards applicable to risk assessment under the CEAS as, to a more limited extent, do the bases upon which other international bodies concerned with IP issues operate – notably the Human Rights Committee (HRC) created under the ICCPR and the Committee against Torture (ComAT) created under CAT. We turn now to consider whether the ECtHR and these Committees impose any internationally applied standard concerning the assessment of the personal profile of the claimant as well as the assessment of future risk.[102] These three bodies each have competence to reinvestigate the factual findings going to the personal profile of claimants before them. However their decisions appear to show that it is a power which is by no means consistently employed and that they will normally accord deference to the facts as found by the respondent State, unless it appears that in making that assessment irrelevant or unwarranted considerations have been taken into account so as to taint the basis of assessment employed.

The three cases before HRC where credibility was reconsidered appear to have turned on the point that elements of the claims which were accepted at State level were sufficient of themselves to hold that the claimants should have been recognised as in need of international protection and that adverse findings of credibility relating to peripheral aspects did not justify rejection of the whole claim.

The ComAT accords considerable deference to the factual findings made by the State party although it will make its own findings of fact in cases where '*the manner in which the evidence was evaluated was clearly arbitrary or amounted to a denial of justice, and that domestic courts clearly violated their obligations of impartiality*'[103] although it does not further elaborate what amounts to those irregularities of approach. The Committee has relied on, for example, an adverse decision in which the State had sought to balance their decision on national security

---

101 See the commentary at paragraph 12.167 in MacDonald's Immigration Law and Practice, 6th Edition, where after describing the UK provision as '*extraordinarily draconian*' the text comments:

'*It is often unfair to make adverse credibility findings on the basis of the use of lies or evasion as to the means of escape, false documents or the destruction of documents, or failure to claim promptly. Such actions have nothing to do with the merit of the asylum claim, and should not be used to diminish credibility – at least, not indiscriminately or without a careful assessment in relation to the facts of individual cases and the applicant's explanation*'. It might be added that such legislative injunctions look suspiciously like attempts to interfere with judicial independence and are, in principle, to be deprecated.

102 We have adopted much of the analysis of Judge Dana Baldinger (*op. cit.*).

103 *J.A.M.O et al v Canada* (2008).

conditions weighed against the assumption of past torture,[104] and where there had been a failure to take into consideration important facts or evidence.[105] Where it does make its own factual assessment it requires 'general veracity': the claim must be sufficiently detailed; it must be accurate and consistent in relation to core elements which should be plausible. Contradictions and inconsistencies may be explained by evidence of post-traumatic stress disorder (PTSD) resulting from past torture but the Committee decides on a case by case basis when contradictions and inconsistencies undermine 'general veracity'. Other explanations accepted include gaps or vague points following past torture, and difficulties in translation, but the Committee generally requires evidence corroborative of the core elements and where this is available even past misleading statements may be acceptably explained.[106] Generally, however, failure to put the case fully at the first available opportunity may adversely affect credibility. Consistency with COI evidence must also be demonstrated.

It would seem clear, therefore, that in those cases where the Committee does undertake its own assessment of facts, it follows the approach of objective consideration of the totality of the evidence in making its findings as to the claimant's past history, fully reflecting the difficulties which may be experienced by claimants and applying the principle of the benefit of the doubt in credibility assessment.

The ECtHR similarly accords deference to the credibility assessments of the contracting states. In *R.C v Sweden* [ECtHR 2010 App. No. 41827/07] the Court accepted that:

> ... as a general principle, the national authorities are best placed to assess not just the facts but, more particularly, the credibility of witnesses since it is they who have had the opportunity to see, hear and assess the demeanour of the individual concerned.

Nevertheless, the Court also acknowledges that, owing to the absolute nature and fundamental value of Article 3, it must make a thorough or rigorous examination of the existence of a real risk in appropriate cases. The circumstances which will give rise to the Court making an independent assessment of the claimant's credibility appear to be in the following situations.

1) Insufficient national proceedings as, for example: *Jabari v Turkey* [ECtHR 2000 App. No. 40035/98] where no material assessment at all was made, *R.C. v Sweden (op cit)*;and *Salah Sheekh v The Netherlands* [ECtHR 2007 App. No. 1948/04], where the national authorities relied on COI from only one source;

2) New facts and developments, including new evidence not assessed by the national authorities as, for example: *Hilal v UK* [ECtHR 2001 App. No. 45276/99], where the claimant had produced further evidence not before the national court; *N v Finland* [ECtHR 2005 App. No. 38885/02], where

---

104   *Dadar v Canada*, 4 December 2005, No. 258/2004 at paragraph 8.8.
105   *C.T. and K.M. v Sweden* (2007).
106   *Ayas v Sweden*, 12 November 1998, No. 097/1997.

there was a new witness; or where there has been a change in the situation in the country of origin as in *Salah Sheek (op cit),* where the Court was of the opinion that '*a full and ex nunc assessment is called for as the situation in a country of destination may change in the course of time.*'

3) A technically incorrect application of the standard of proof by taking into account impermissible considerations such as national security as in *Chahal v UK* [ECtHR 1996 App. No. 22414/93].

The ECtHR is also clear that, in assessing the second stage prospective risk of breach of Article 3 rights on return to the country of origin, the appropriate standard of proof to be applied is that of real risk irrespective of whether the Court has made its own fresh assessment of the claimant's past history.

Situations where the Strasbourg Court will make its own fresh assessment of that past history is, however, less clear. There is no apparent statement that the Court applies a particular standard of proof to a such fresh assessment but it appears that it proceeds rather on a case by case basis to consider whether the national court's factual 'profile' findings are sustainable, either on the basis of errors in their making or by reason of fresh evidence which the Court considers it appropriate to take into account having regard to the anxious consideration which is called for in cases where the absolute non derogable rights conferred by Article 3 are in issue. The Court may examine further evidence in reaching its assessment where it considers this necessary.

The Court's general approach to personal credibility issues is helpfully summarised in *R.C. v Sweden* as follows:

> '50. The Court acknowledges that, owing to the special situation in which asylum seekers often find themselves, it is frequently necessary to give them the benefit of the doubt when it comes to assessing the credibility of their statements and the documents submitted in support thereof. However, when information is presented which gives strong reasons to question the veracity of an asylum seeker's submissions; the individual must provide a satisfactory explanation for the alleged discrepancies (see, among other authorities, *Collins and Akasiebie v. Sweden* (dec.), no. 23944/05, 8 March 2007, and *Matsiukhina and Matsiukhin v. Sweden* (dec.), no. 31260/04, 21 June 2005). In principle, the applicant has to adduce evidence capable of proving that there are substantial grounds for believing that, if the measure complained of were to be implemented, he would be exposed to a real risk of being subjected to treatment contrary to Article 3 (see *N. v. Finland*, no. 38885/02, § 167, 26 July 2005 and *NA. v. the United Kingdom*, no. 25904/07, § 111, 17 July 2008). Where such evidence is adduced, it is for the Government to dispel any doubts about it.'

We draw attention to the use of the phrase '*the applicant has to adduce evidence capable of proving ...*' which appears to reinforce the point previously made that the essential standard is adducing evidence capable of being believed ('accepted') as opposed to evidence that is believed. It is the former test which is applicable and lends emphasis to the issues of shifting the burden of proof and burden-sharing and to application of the benefit of the doubt where particular elements of the account depend on the claimant's statements alone.

The Court's view that the burden of proof may shift to the State party is of particular importance and is wholly in line with the concept of cooperation, 'shared burden', between the claimant and the decision-maker advocated by the UNHCR Handbook at [196]. In *R.C. v Sweden* it was to prove decisive as appears from paragraph 53 of the Court's judgment:

'... the Court notes that the applicant initially produced a medical certificate before the Migration Board as evidence of his having been tortured (see paragraph 11). Although the certificate was not written by an expert specialising in the assessment of torture injuries, the Court considers that it, nevertheless, gave a rather strong indication to the authorities that the applicant's scars and injuries may have been caused by ill-treatment or torture. In such circumstances, it was for the Migration Board to dispel any doubts that might have persisted as to the cause of such scarring (see the last sentence of paragraph 50). In the Court's view, the Migration Board ought to have directed that an expert opinion be obtained as to the probable cause of the applicant's scars in circumstances where he had made out a *prima facie* case as to their origin. It did not do so and neither did the appellate courts. While the burden of proof, in principle, rests on the applicant, the Court disagrees with the Government's view that it was incumbent upon him to produce such expert opinion. In cases such as the present one, the State has a duty to ascertain all relevant facts, particularly in circumstances where there is a strong indication that an applicant's injuries may have been caused by torture.

A further principle frequently used is that of affording the claimant the benefit of the doubt, which the Court has expressed in the following terms:

'owing to the special situation in which asylum seekers often find themselves, it is frequently necessary to give them the benefit of the doubt when it comes to assessing the credibility of their statements'.[107]

The ECtHR requires the claimant's evidence to have '*general credibility*' but this does not imply the need for complete accuracy and consistency because:

'The Court acknowledges that complete accuracy as to dates and events cannot be expected in all circumstances from a person seeking asylum.'[108]

Nevertheless, major inconsistencies may undermine credibility (*Bello v Sweden* op cit). It is the core aspects of the claimant's basic story that must be credible: they must be consistent with COI (*R.C. v Sweden* op cit.); that basic story should re-

---

107 See for example, admissibility decisions ECtHR, *Matsiukhina and Matsiukhin v. Sweden* , 21 June 2005, Appl. No. 31260/04; ECtHR, *Mahin Ayegh v. Sweden* , 7 November 2006, Appl. No. 4701/05; ECtHR, *Collins and Akasiebie v. Sweden* 8 March 2007, Appl. No. 23944/05; ECtHR, *Achmadov and Bagurova v. Sweden* , 10 July 2007, Appl. No. 34081/05; ECtHR, *M. v. Sweden* 6 September 2007, Appl. No. 22556/05; ECtHR, *Elezaj and others v. Sweden* , 20 September 2007, Appl. No. 17654/095; ECtHR, *Limoni and others v. Sweden*, 4 October 2007, Appl. No. 6576/05, and the judgments ECtHR, *F.H. v. Sweden*, 20 January 2009, Appl. No. 32621/06/06, para. 95, ECtHR, *R.C. v. Sweden* , 9 March 2010, Appl. No. 41827/07, para. 50.

108 *Bello v Sweden* [ECtHR 2006 App. No. 32213/04].

main consistent throughout the proceedings.[109] But, remaining uncertainties, that do not go to the core aspects, may still leave the essence of a claim intact even if these had been regarded as major inconsistencies by the national court. In this respect it seems that the ECtHR approach, to the effect of inconsistencies by looking upon them as fatally undermining credibility where they go to the essence of the claimant's case, can even extend to categorising, even quite central parts of the account, as merely peripheral where the core aspects remain intact. For example, in *N v Finland (op cit.)* the Court said:

> 'the Court has certain reservations about the applicant's own testimony before the Delegates which it considers to have been evasive on many points and is not prepared to accept every statement of his as fact. In particular, his account of the journey to Finland is not credible. In light of the overall evidence now before it the Court finds however that the applicant's account of his background in the DRC must, on the whole, be considered sufficiently consistent and credible.'

Again, in *Said v. the Netherlands* [ECtHR 2005 App. No. 2345/02] the Court doubted the credibility of the applicant's statements regarding his claimed escape from armed guards, and in *R.C. v. Sweden* (op cit) a claimed escape from a revolutionary court, however both these uncertainties were found not to undermine the overall credibility of the basic story.

Whilst, therefore, the ECtHR stops short of prescribing any standard of proof which it applies in the assessment of personal credibility in Article 3 removal cases,[110] it does appear that its general approach to the burden of proof and the requirements both of co-operation between the parties in order to ascertain the truth of the claim, as well as its application of the principle of the benefit of the doubt in favour of the claimant is broadly (but not wholly) in line with the approach advocated in the UNHCR Handbook.

It would therefore appear that, whilst the jurisprudence of the international tribunals and the European Courts significantly guides and assists in relation to clarifying that the standard to be applied in assessing the future risk in asylum cases is that of 'real risk', however there is little apparent guidance that applies to the establishment of the claimant's accepted past and present facts or 'accepted personal profile'.

109　Late submission of statements going to core issues may undermine credibility absent a credible explanation for the delay in raising them. In *Tekdemir v. the Netherlands*, [ECtHR 2002, Appl. No. 49823/99], the Court rejected admissibility, noting that it was only in the course of national proceedings following a second asylum application that the applicant raised and relied on his kinship with the brothers A.X. and B.X., one of whom had obtained a residence permit and the other a favourable ruling in the proceedings on his asylum request. Only in the course of third national proceedings the applicant based himself on a claim that he had been tortured in Turkey, a fact which he had not raised in his previous asylum requests.

110　Its formulation of the standard of proof in inter-State litigation concerning claimed Articles 2 and 3 violations is classically that of 'beyond reasonable doubt' (see *Ireland v UK* [1978 2 EHRR 25] but this does not appear to be expressed as the appropriate standard in cases where the issue is whether removal would be in breach of Article 3 rights. For the purposes of the ECtHR, however, that formulation does not carry as stringent a requirement as it would normally impose upon the prosecution in criminal trials under the Common Law system.

6.9.   The current position in EU asylum law

As we have already seen it is clear that practice between the different MS' national courts contains considerable elements of variance as to how the 'profile' assessment is to be made.

The CJEU has not to date made any ruling on the issues of burden and standard of proof in refugee and /or subsidiary protection cases, although, as already noted, *Samba Diouf (op cit.)* is authority for the proposition that the scope of judicial review under Article 39 PD is equivalent to that provided for under Article 47 of the EU Treaty and therefore extends potentially to a full review of both facts and law on an *ex nunc* basis.

This principle is of the utmost importance and it was expressed by the Court in that case in the following terms:

> 42. In short, the content of the right to judicial protection recognised by Article 47 of the CFREU must be defined by reference to the meaning and scope conferred on that right by the ECHR (Article 52(3) of the CFREU), but, once defined, its scope must be that described by the CFREU, (7) that is to say, in the words of the Charter itself, the scope enjoyed by the 'rights and freedoms guaranteed by the law of the Union'. Consequently, for the purposes of this case, there is no doubt that that right is applicable to 'decisions taken on an application for asylum' given that the fact that such decisions are made subject 'to an effective remedy before a court or tribunal' is, according to recital 27 in the preamble to Directive 2005/85/ EC, simply the reflection of 'a basic principle of Community law', ultimately established as primary law by the Charter of Fundamental Rights of the European Union.

> 43. If we examine the right to effective judicial protection solely from the point of view of access to the courts, the European Union guarantees everyone the right to request protection from a court against any acts harmful to the rights and freedoms recognised by the European Union, it being of paramount importance that recourse to the courts should be effective, both in the sense that it must be legally capable of securing reparation, where appropriate, for the loss complained of, and in the sense that it must be a practical remedy, that is to say, that its pursuit must not be subject to conditions that make it impossible or extremely difficult to exercise.

> 44. That mandatory content of the right recognised by Article 47 of the CFREU is drawn from the ECHR as interpreted by the European Court of Human Rights, (8) with which Article 39 of Directive 2005/85/EC is quite naturally consistent, in that it expressly guarantees that 'applicants for asylum have the right to an effective remedy before a court or tribunal' against administrative decisions rejecting an application in any of the cases provided for in paragraph 1 of that article, that is to say on grounds of substance, form or procedure.

There can, accordingly, be no doubt that, whether as a matter of tradition or of national legal requirement, to the extent that the national courts have been accustomed to paying deference to the factual findings upon which the State has based decisions which come before the national courts on review or appeal, those courts are now required under EU law to have the power to reconsider those decisions on issues both of fact and law. If and when the recast PD is enacted and formally replaces the 2005 PD, the new Article 46, replacing Article 39, will by sub-article 3 make this requirement explicit but we would suggest that it is already implicit in the provisions of Article 47 of the EU Charter. Article 47 derives its inspiration from Articles 6 and 13 ECHR, hence the reference in paragraph 42 of the judgment in *Samba Diouf.*

We would therefore suggest that the jurisprudence of the ECtHR, which explains the basis on which the Court will carry out its investigations when reassessing the factual basis of an Article 3 ECHR claim and the principles which it will apply in so doing, is of direct relevance to the duties of MS's courts when themselves carrying out such a reassessment.

The principles as to the judge's duty in assessing the credibility of the claimant, which are to be derived from the ECtHR jurisprudence, we have rehearsed above, are in essence that the claimant's account should be generally accepted as credible and that the claimant has discharged the burden of proof in this respect when:

- The claimant's account is sufficiently detailed
- It is internally consistent in its core aspects throughout the assessment process in two senses:
  first, that it is brought forward in a timely manner and that any later additions or variations to the account are the subject of credible explanation;
  second, that major inconsistencies and alterations in the core story may render it incredible
- So far as possible corroborative evidence is produced to substantiate those elements which ought on the claimant's account to be capable of corroboration by the claimant
- The account is consistent with COI.

If, taking into account all relevant evidence those basic requirements are met, then the fact that there are discrepancies or inconsistencies in relation to peripheral matters is largely irrelevant[111] and, where prima facie evidence of a relevant issue – e.g. past persecution – is raised on the claimant's evidence, the role of the State party is not reactive but proactive.

All these propositions are derived from the case-law to which we have referred above, but, as we have seen, the ECtHR approaches the issue of credibility assessment on a case by case basis so that it would be unrealistic to confine those issues, which are relevant to credibility assessment, simply to the issues which arose in decided cases in the absence of a general statement of the principles which the ECtHR applies in such assessments.

---

111 The question of relying on discrepancies and inconsistencies as indicative of false testimony raises some difficult and controversial issues. These issues are cogently discussed in a paper by James P Eyster published in the Boston University International Law Journal, Vol 30 on 2 April 2012. The author cites a number of psychiatric papers in support of his basic proposition that consistent human recall of past events is the exception rather than the rule.

6.10. Conclusion

The above propositions we consider currently reflect broader principles that are generally applicable in EU asylum law. We suggest that there are two such principles which must be reflected in assessing the credibility of the claimant's past history: firstly, that the responsibility for making that assessment is shared between the claimant and the State party; secondly, that having regard to the innate difficulties which many claimants face in substantiating their claims, the claimant should be regarded, where appropriate, as being entitled to have any residual doubt resolved in his favour.

Unless and until a general requirement is introduced as part of the CEAS introducing '*common procedures for the granting and withdrawing of uniform asylum or subsidiary protection status*',[112] we consider that application of the basic criteria and judicial standards contained in Part III of this Paper will go far to ensuring uniformity of approach in the assessment of the claimant's accepted past and present facts (or 'personal profile'). This will include taking due account of the specific difficulties which claimants face in presenting their evidence and the shared nature of the assessment process, required by Article 4.1 QD and advocated by UNHCR.

We also suggest that application of the Part III criteria and standards will significantly assist judges to maintain a principled and objective approach. It is a unique and challenging area of the law where judges are constantly called upon to reach findings on not only what has happened, but also, using those findings, and other relevant evidence, is there a real chance of events happening in the future. And all this be done in relation to countries with which they are often very unfamiliar and whose culture, language, traditions and circumstances are likely to be different from their own experience.[113] Finally it must always be recalled that flawed or poor decisions can have the potential of resulting in the direst of consequences.

---

112 As provided by Article 78(d) TFEU.
113 The words of the distinguished American judge and jurist, Benjamin N Cardozo, remain as pertinent today as they were in 1921 when he observed: "*The great tides and currents which engulfed the rest of men do not turn aside in their course and pass the judges by. ... The spirit of the age, as it is revealed to each of us, is too often only the spirit of the group in which the accidents of both our education or occupation or fellowship have given us a place. No effort or revolution of the mind will overthrow utterly and at all times the empire of these subconscious loyalties. ... Deep below consciousness are the forces, the likes and dislikes, the predilections and the prejudices, the complex of instincts and emotions and habits and convictions, which make the man, whether he be litigant or judge.*"

Appendix: UNHCR General Guidance

In the text, (e.g., § 6.2) reference has been made to the General Guidance in the UNHCR Handbook. The complete text is as follows:

(1) Principles and methods

195. The relevant facts of the individual case will have to be furnished in the first place by the applicant himself. It will then be up to the person charged with determining his status (the examiner) to assess the validity of any evidence and the credibility of the applicant's statements.

196. It is a general legal principle that the burden of proof lies on the person submitting a claim. Often, however, an applicant may not be able to support his statements by documentary or other proof, and cases in which an applicant can provide evidence of all his statements will be the exception rather than the rule. In most cases a person fleeing from persecution will have arrived with the barest necessities and very frequently even without personal documents. Thus, while the burden of proof in principle rests on the applicant, the duty to ascertain and evaluate all the relevant facts is shared between the applicant and the examiner. Indeed, in some cases, it may be for the examiner to use all the means at his disposal to produce the necessary evidence in support of the application. Even such independent research may not, however, always be successful and there may also be statements that are not susceptible of proof. In such cases, if the applicant's account appears credible, he should, unless there are good reasons to the contrary, be given the benefit of the doubt.

197. The requirement of evidence should thus not be too strictly applied in view of the difficulty of proof inherent in the special situation in which an applicant for refugee status finds himself. Allowance for such possible lack of evidence does not, however, mean that unsupported statements must necessarily be accepted as true if they are inconsistent with the general account put forward by the applicant.

198. A person who, because of his experiences, was in fear of the authorities in his own country may still feel apprehensive vis-à-vis any authority. He may therefore be afraid to speak freely and give a full and accurate account of his case.

199. While an initial interview should normally suffice to bring an applicant's story to light, it may be necessary for the examiner to clarify any apparent inconsistencies and to resolve any contradictions in a further interview, and to find an explanation for any misrepresentation or concealment of material facts. Untrue statements by themselves are not a reason for refusal of refugee status and it is the examiner's responsibility to evaluate such statements in the light of all the circumstances of the case.

200.   An examination in depth of the different methods of fact-finding is outside the scope of the present Handbook. It may be mentioned, however, that basic information is frequently given, in the first instance, by completing a standard questionnaire. Such basic information will normally not be sufficient to enable the examiner to reach a decision, and one or more personal interviews will be required. It will be necessary for the examiner to gain the confidence of the applicant in order to assist the latter in putting forward his case and in fully explaining his opinions and feelings. In creating such a climate of confidence it is, of course, of the utmost importance that the applicant's statements will be treated as confidential and that he be so informed.

201.   Very frequently the fact-finding process will not be complete until a wide range of circumstances has been ascertained. Taking isolated incidents out of context may be misleading. The cumulative effect of the applicant's experience must be taken into account. Where no single incident stands out above the others, sometimes a small incident may be "the last straw"; and although no single incident may be sufficient, all the incidents related by the applicant taken together, could make his fear "well-founded" (see paragraph 53 above).

202.   Since the examiner's conclusion on the facts of the case and his personal impression of the applicant will lead to a decision that affects human lives, he must apply the criteria in a spirit of justice and understanding and his judgement should not, of course, be influenced by the personal consideration that the applicant may be an "undeserving case".

(2) Benefit of the doubt

203.   After the applicant has made a genuine effort to substantiate his story there may still be a lack of evidence for some of his statements. As explained above (paragraph 196), it is hardly possible for a refugee to "prove" every part of his case and, indeed, if this were a requirement the majority of refugees would not be recognized. It is therefore frequently necessary to give the applicant the benefit of the doubt.

204.   The benefit of the doubt should, however, only be given when all available evidence has been obtained and checked and when the examiner is satisfied as to the applicant's general credibility. The applicant's statements must be coherent and plausible, and must not run counter to generally known facts.

(3) Summary

205.   The process of ascertaining and evaluating the facts can therefore be summarized as follows:

(a)   The applicant should:

    (i)   Tell the truth and assist the examiner to the full in establishing the facts of his case.

   (ii)   Make an effort to support his statements by any available evidence and give a satisfactory explanation for any lack of evidence. If necessary he must make an effort to procure additional evidence.

  (iii)   Supply all pertinent information concerning himself and his past experience in as much detail as is necessary to enable the examiner to establish the relevant facts. He should be asked to give a coherent explanation of all the reasons invoked in support of his application for refugee status and he should answer any questions put to him.

(b)   The examiner should:

    (i)   Ensure that the applicant presents his case as fully as possible and with all available evidence.

   (ii)   Assess the applicant's credibility and evaluate the evidence (if necessary giving the applicant the benefit of the doubt), in order to establish the objective and the subjective elements of the case.

  (iii)   Relate these elements to the relevant criteria of the 1951 Convention, in order to arrive at a correct conclusion as to the applicant's refugee status

13W70505/ T2/ 9789462400610